The New Deal

The New Deal

Edited with an Introduction by

Carl N. Degler

 a New York Times Book

Quadrangle Books

CHICAGO

Library of Congress Catalog Card Number: 73-78319

The publishers are grateful to the contributors herein
for permission to reprint their articles.

Contents

Introduction: What Was the New Deal?   3

1. The Social and Intellectual Context of the New Deal

The New Ordeal of Democracy   32
  by Anne O'Hare McCormick
John Dewey Surveys the Nation's Ills   41
  by S. J. Woolf
Thomas Depicts the Socialist Utopia   48
  by S. J. Woolf
Roosevelt's View of the Big Job   55
  by Anne O'Hare McCormick
Three "Pied Pipers" of the Depression   64
  by Francis Brown

2. The New Deal as Reform

Roosevelt Surveys His Course   76
  by Anne O'Hare McCormick

Roosevelt Recharts His Course   *85*
    by Delbert Clark

A New Pattern of Life for the Indian   *94*
    by Frank Ernest Hill

A Dream Takes Form in TVA's Domain   *103*
    by R. L. Duffus

A Crisis for Our Youth: A Task for the Nation   *112*
    by Aubrey Williams

The CCC Marches Toward a New Destiny   *120*
    by Frank Ernest Hill

The Nation Weighs a Vast Housing Program   *128*
    by Albert Mayer

The Big World At Last Reaches Gee's Bend   *136*
    by John Temple Graves II

3. The Central Task

Beyond Relief: The Larger Task   *149*
    by Harry Hopkins

Work Relief: The Program Broadens   *156*
    by Jacob Baker

Unemployment: Must It Be Permanent?   *164*
    by R. L. Duffus

Behind the Farm Problem: Rural Poverty   *171*
    by Rexford G. Tugwell

The Storm Center of the Banking Bill   *180*
    by Francis Brown

4. The Question of Revolution

1933–1934: Two Momentous Years   *190*
   by Allan Nevins

Five Years, and the New Deal Ponders   *200*
   by Delbert Clark

Where Is the Nation Heading?   *207*
   by Harold L. Ickes

The New Deal's "Revolution" Defended   *220*
   by Donald R. Richberg

Suggested Reading   *235*

Index   *239*

The New Deal

Introduction

What Was the New Deal?

ASK ANYONE who has lived through the 1930's what the New Deal was and you will receive a variety of answers. Most will undoubtedly praise it as a great program of domestic reform; some will see it as the gift of Franklin Roosevelt; a few will damn it as a violation of American tradition. But virtually all will agree that it showed the importance if not the necessity of economic depression for bringing about reform. Certainly a number of the reforms introduced by the Roosevelt administration began as responses to the problem of unemployment or as means to stimulate the depressed economy. No one can read the articles in this book without being impressed by the way in which the Depression dominated the thoughts and shaped the efforts of the New Dealers. It is not surprising, therefore, that on the basis of the New Deal of the depression-ridden 1930's most Americans see reform in general as a child of economic adversity.

Yet that general conclusion is but another measure of the continuing impact of the New Deal upon the American mind. The fact is that the New Deal's origin in the midst of depression is unique in the history of American political reform. No other depression gave birth to a major reform movement, and no other reform movement of national proportions achieved success during a depression. So long as the United States has been an industrial nation—that is, since the Civil War—reform on the national level has been an accompaniment of prosperity, not depression. The first great industrial decline, that of 1873, for example, spawned no reform movement at all, and in the end it killed off the budding labor movement of the time. It might be asserted that the depression of 1893 encouraged Populism and the William Jennings Bryan wing of the Democratic party, but neither of these reform impulses won national acceptance. In fact, out of that depression issued the triumph of conservative William McKinley and Mark Hanna. Nor should it be forgotten that four years of depression from 1929 to 1933 produced only a modicum of reform under Herbert Hoover.

On the other hand, during the prosperous years of the first decade and a half of the twentieth century the Progressive movement came into full flower, and in the course of the prolonged prosperity of the 1960's the reform legislation of the Kennedy and Johnson years was enacted. In short, the New Deal was much more than simply a natural or expected response to economic collapse; the downswing in the business cycle was the occasion for the New Deal, not its cause. What the New Deal was and what it tried to do were very much the consequence of the particular men and women who called themselves New Dealers. The most important of them was the man who first bestowed the name and guided the enterprise.

I

Although Franklin Delano Roosevelt was called everything from a fascist to a communist in his lifetime, and the reforms over which he presided brought about sweeping changes in American life, he was no radical and never had been. From the beginnings of his presidency he had emphasized his essentially conservative approach to the problems of society. "Our task of reconstruction," he told Congress in July 1934, "does not require the creation of new and strange values. It is rather the finding of the way once more to known, but to some degree forgotten, ideals and values. If the means and details," he cautiously suggested, "are in some instances new, the objectives are as permanent as human nature." In his second fireside chat in September of the same year, Roosevelt again emphasized the continuity with the past. "In our effort for recovery we have avoided, on the one hand, the theory that business should and must be taken over into an all-embracing government. We have avoided on the other hand, the equally untenable theory that it is an interference with liberty to offer reasonable help when private enterprise is in need of help. . . ." As these statements imply, he was not only conservative in his own outlook but also sensitive to the danger of being a leader without followers. He recognized that the nation might not, even in the depths of its most severe economic crisis, follow his lead. Anne O'Hare McCormick, a reporter for the *New York Times,* wrote in November 1934 after an interview with the President, that he was certainly interested in social innovations, like the Tennessee Valley Authority and the long-range decentralization of industry. But he was also fearful, she went on, of sponsoring reforms that might be too far in advance of the country. At White House conferences with his aides, she reported, a statement often to be heard was, "The people aren't ready."

Roosevelt's conservatism was intrinsic as well as politic; innovations had to fall within the confines of his general philosophy. Not every new idea was entertained with a view to adoption. Abstractly, as well as practically, Roosevelt was a supporter of the American social system; indeed, he never really questioned it, for he was at once a product of it and a beneficiary. When not holding public office, he and his family lived quite comfortably on the income from his and his wife's inherited wealth. Once a young reporter quizzed him about his social philosophy, asking if he were a communist, a fascist, or a capitalist, to which the President responded with firm negatives but with mounting puzzlement as to what the young man was getting at. Finally, the reporter, equally baffled by his inability to fit the President into ideological categories, demanded to know what the President's political or social philosophy was. The best he got for an answer was, "I am a Christian and a Democrat." If the going economic system is understood to be subsumed under "Democrat," then these two words summarize well both the limitations and the sources of the humanitarian impulses that animated the reform ideas of Franklin Roosevelt. Far from opposing the system, he proudly named himself its savior. During the campaign of 1936, when he was under attack for allegedly subverting the traditional American economy, he told his audience, "It was this administration which saved the system of profit and free enterprise after it had been dragged to the brink of ruin by these same leaders who now try to scare you."

What prevented Roosevelt from being simply another defender of the status quo was his genuine concrete concern for human beings coupled with a distrust of abstractions. Andrew Mellon, Secretary of the Treasury under Calvin Coolidge, envisaged some good emanating from a depression. "It will purge the rottenness out of the system," he once told Herbert Hoover. "High costs of living and high living will come down. People will work harder, live a more moral life. Values will be adjusted, and enterprising people will pick up the wrecks from less competent people." But when an economist similarly suggested to FDR that a depression might serve a salutary purpose, his humane concern and distrust of theory revolted. Frances Perkins, who was present at the interview, reported that she never forgot "the gray look of horror" that came over the President's face when he heard the argument. "People aren't cattle, you know!" he exploded.

Undoubtedly one of the bases for Roosevelt's popularity was that he thought and talked in the concrete. Like the ordinary citizen, the President always demanded to know how a particular policy would affect the flesh-and-blood farmer, the worker in the factory, the housewife in the kitchen. Nothing infuriated him more than to be accused of being an abstract theorist by men who themselves measured his policies against an abstract theory. Again and again, for example, businessmen would ask him when the government's budget was going to be balanced, but, as FDR tartly remarked, "A balanced budget isn't putting people to work. I will balance the budget as soon as I take care of the unemployed."

One of the consequences of his rejection of theory was that his mind could easily hold contradictory ideas at the same time; the New Deal never had a guiding principle or philosophy because Franklin Roosevelt never had one. There was nothing he liked more than to be able to bring together divergent ideas and have them apparently complement one another. In 1936, for instance, he enthusiastically lectured newspaper reporters on the Swedish middle way, about which he had recently been reading. In the course of his remarks he clearly revealed his own distrust of dogma and his preference for ideological diversity. "In Sweden, for example," he told the reporters, "you have a royal family and a Socialist Government and a Capitalist system, all working happily side by side. . . . They have these cooperative movements existing happily and successfully alongside of private industry and distribution of various kinds, both of them making money." It was this same interest in contradiction and ideological diversity that permitted Rexford Tugwell, a former professor with radical views, and Jesse Jones, a conservative Texas banker, to serve as his advisers simultaneously.

Finally, in assessing the effect of FDR's character on the making of the New Deal, one further trait deserves mention. Certainly there is much in the New Deal that bespeaks the urban society in which it operated: the Social Security program, the support of organized labor, the war upon unemployment, to name a few. Yet there is also a strong preference for country life running through the activities and interests of the New Deal. As William Leuchtenburg has pointed out, the ideal in the minds of the typical New Dealer was not the refurbished or renewed great metropolis but the small greenbelt town, the neat homestead village, the TVA community. Something of this reaching for the future in the past is evident in Harry Hopkins' article in Part 3.

One of the sources of this preference for the rural life is undoubtedly Franklin Roosevelt himself. His tastes were oriented toward the country even though most New Dealers were as urban as the distribution of population in the nation. He was almost romantic in his belief in the regenerative properties of rural life. When the census of 1920, for example, revealed that for the first time in American history most of the people lived in cities, Roosevelt lamented the passing of a golden age. As Governor of New York his concern for and interest in the problems of farmers was both genuine and a source of pride. It was only half jokingly that he described his permanent occupation while President as a farmer, for that is what he fancied himself in Dutchess County. It is not surprising, given Roosevelt's strong interest in the land, that most of the imaginative and truly experimental programs of the New Deal, like the greenbelt communities, farm resettlement, the AAA, and the TVA, were primarily or entirely concerned with the land and its improvement. On the other hand, New Deal legislation primarily concerned with urban issues, like the National Labor Relations Act or the Federal Housing Administration, simply did not engage the President's interest to the same degree. Generally such programs received their initial impetus outside the White House. In his persistent attachment to the land one can also discern yet another measure of Roosevelt's conservatism.

Because Franklin Roosevelt dominated Washington and the politics of the nation during his years in the White House, it is easy to assume that he was in fact the New Deal. This assumption, however, is wrong on several counts. For one thing, not all legislation that has passed into history as part of the New Deal originated in the White House or the executive offices. Sometimes important New Deal measures were spurred on by public demands, as was certainly true with Social Security. Roosevelt told his Secretary of Labor, Frances Perkins, that her committee must come up with a system of social insurance, for "the Congress can't stand the pressure of the Townsend Plan unless we have a real old-age insurance system, nor can I face the people without having . . . a solid plan which will give some assurance to people of systematic assistance upon retirement."

Furthermore, the prevalent belief that Congress for most of the New Deal years was no more than an approving body, waiting patiently to hear from the chief at the other end of Pennsylvania Avenue, has no basis in fact. A number of important New Deal laws as well as significant modifications in presidentially sponsored reforms originated in Congress. Thus the National Labor Relations Bill passed the Senate and was already being considered by the House of Representatives before any support came from the White House. Even during the famous Hundred Days at the beginning of his first term, not all important legislation emanated from the President. The Federal Deposit Insurance Corporation, certainly considered today to be one of the major contributions of the New Deal, became a law without either Roosevelt's initiative or support. He signed it as part of a broader banking bill. And as a final example it can be added that in 1936 Senator Robert Wagner of New York received only token support from FDR for his low-cost housing bill. Yet in 1937 when the bill was enacted, it too passed into history as one of the major innovations of the New Deal.

II

To emphasize Roosevelt's conservatism, as has been done here, is to raise the question of whether the New Deal was anything more than a continuation or fulfillment of the great reform impulse of Progressivism at the beginning of the twentieth century. Certainly there are connections between the two. FDR himself, for example, was a fervent and lifelong admirer of his distant relative Theodore Roosevelt, as well as having been Assistant Secretary of the Navy in the Wilson administration. In 1920, Franklin Roosevelt had campaigned on a Wilsonian Progressive platform as the vice-presidential candidate of the Democratic party. And a number of the leading members of the New Deal were themselves former Progressives.

Suggestive as these impressions may be in showing continuity between the two reform movements, a more systematic examination of Progressive leaders presents a contrary view. Otis Graham has demonstrated, for example, that most of the Progressives who lived into the 1930's in fact rejected the New Deal. Out of 105 Progressives who were still alive in the 1930's and left expressions of their attitudes, only forty supported the New Deal, Graham found, while sixty opposed it. (Five more went beyond the New Deal, finding it inadequate.) In short, if there was continuity of ideas between the Progressive period and the New Deal, most of those Progressives who lived to see FDR's efforts did not recognize it.

Helpful as Graham's study is, however, it does not settle the question. After all, almost 40 per cent of the Progressives did find the New Deal congenial. That in itself suggests there was some connection between the two great reform movements of the twentieth century. Indeed, one of the difficulties in discussing the degree of continuity between the New Deal and the Progressives is that no historical movement is without some connection with its predecessor. Even the most abrupt historical shift finds men from a different and earlier period living in the new, still influenced by their old ideas and habits. Social and intellectual change is only relative; each historical period is at once new and old. The operative question is which seems to predominate. For in assessing the past the historian must be concerned with discontinuity as well as the persistence of old ways. By marking those points in the flow of history at which the stream of history shifts or deepens, he provides guideposts so that men may understand where they have been and where they are tending. Only in this way do men obtain their intellectual bearings, locating themselves in the jumble of events which is life without history. In fact, the principal purpose of this book is to show that, despite the inevitable connections between earlier years and those of the New Deal era, the Age of Roosevelt marked a watershed in the history of the American people. Those Americans who lived after the 1930's lived in a different world from those who lived before. In effect, that is what the majority of Progressives analyzed by Otis Graham were concluding; they lived in both eras and, though one might have expected that, being reformers, they would have welcomed the New Deal, most of them did not.

III

Although those Progressives who rejected the New Deal suggest a break between the two reform movements, the most convincing evidence for discontinuity comes from an examination of the New Deal itself. Here, too, however, students have disagreed. It has been argued, for example, that a number of the so-called innovations of the New Deal, like the Tennessee Valley Authority, price supports for farmers, and government regulation of business, among others, were previously suggested, if not actually put into practice, by the Progressive movement a quarter of a century earlier. That argument, however, is no more than an example of the truism that no period of history is completely original in its ideas. To suggest that the New Deal is really a continuation of the Progressive era because in the Progressive Platform of 1912 some of the practices of the New Deal were advocated, is tantamount to saying that the French Revolution was not a significant change because it drew upon the ideas of the *philosophes* who wrote in an earlier period. There is a great difference between advocacy of change and the putting of such suggestions into practice. To a citizen of Tennessee there was a real difference, for instance, between the vague advocacy of hydroelectric power in the Progressive Platform of 1912 and the actual creation of the Tennessee Valley Authority, which brought cheap electrical power into his home, new recreational areas into his reach, and new industry into his region. (Something of what the TVA meant to the South can be gleaned from the article by R. L. Duffus, reprinted in Part 2.) Similarly, it is true that some of the old Progressives advocated the intervention of the federal government in the field of housing in order to establish standards of construction, but it remained for the New Deal to put the government into the business of building houses.

Actually, the New Deal went considerably beyond the reform ideas of the Progressives, if only because it was compelled to wrestle with a depression—a problem that did not plague the Progressives. Among the depression-born innovations of the New Deal were the Federal Writers' Project, the Federal Arts Projects, and the Federal Theater, all of which not only catapulted the federal government into primarily uncharted areas but introduced art to the mass of Americans. In the first year of the Federal Theater, for example, sixty million people in thirty states saw plays for less than a dollar a seat and at times for nothing at all. As one foreign visitor exclaimed: "Art in America is being given its chance; there has been nothing like it since before the Reformation. . . ." Not all of the art and writing produced under these programs was of high quality, but some of it was. More important, the projects provided work for artistic talents otherwise in danger of deterioration through disuse. Many skills saved from idleness at that time enriched the nation's aesthetic treasury in subsequent years.

Another innovation in American reform that was a response to the Depression was the unprecedented attention given to young people. Some suggestion of the novelty of this concern is provided by the two articles in this book on the Civilian Conservation Corps and the National Youth Administration, the two New Deal agencies devoted to the welfare of young men and women.

Unrelated to the Depression, but clearly a departure from the activities of the Progressives, who did not interest themselves in the subject at all, was the New Deal's policy toward the Indians. The dimensions of that overturn in governmental action in this field are set forth in an article by Frank Ernest Hill in Part 2, but a more recent judgment by an Australian student of comparative aboriginal affairs is well worth quoting here. "For good or for ill," writes A. Grenfell Price, "the American New Dealers effected a fundamental revolution in Indian policy. . . . They swung the Republic from an avowed attempt to absorb the Indians as quickly as possible to a policy of rehabilitating them as vigorous minority groups. . . . The New Dealers did not . . . act from blind philanthropy. They deliberately sought to continue and even to increase an unabsorbed minority because they believed, almost fanatically, that the Indian was a worthwhile factor in American life."

Indians and youth were only two of the social groups in which the New Deal took an interest, but which the Progressives had ignored. Negroes were another. In some respects, it is true, the New Deal's recognition of the Negro did not seem to be much greater than that of the Progressives. Nothing in the large body of New Deal legislation, for instance, can be singled out as specifically intended to improve the lot of black people in particular, and at no time prior to 1941 did Franklin Roosevelt make the kind of official statement in opposition to segregation and discrimination that Harry Truman included in his Fair Deal. Yet it would be misleading to leave the impression that the New Deal ignored the Negro as the Progressives certainly did. The principal reason such a conclusion would be misleading is that under the New Deal the political allegiance of blacks shifted dramatically from the Republicans to the Democrats. That this shift in the voting preference of Negroes was a response to the actions of the New Deal rather than simply to dissatisfaction with the traditional Republican allegiance is shown by the fact that even in the election of 1932—in the midst of the Depression— most Negroes still voted Republican. By the election of 1936, however, the black voter in the North had joined the Roosevelt political coalition.

If there was no specific New Deal legislation in behalf of the Negro, what then brought about the shift that has been so significant for the Negro and for the nation ever since? Part of it was that the New Deal gave new recognition to Negro hopes and aspirations. For example, Harold Ickes, Secretary of the Interior and once president of the Chicago NAACP, desegregated his department when he took office, and from time to time he brought prospective Negro appointees to the President's attention, such as William H. Hastie, who became the first Negro appointed to the federal judiciary. Ultimately, virtually every New Deal agency contained Negro officials or Negro advisers, for, as Leslie Fishel has written, "Never before had Negro leaders participated in government affairs as freely and as frequently."

Another part of the explanation is that Mrs. Roosevelt made public her strong opposition to racial discrimination, acting in the process as a lightning rod for the President, who believed that his dependence upon Southern votes in Congress prevented his speaking out in behalf of Negro equality. Then, too, as a matter of course the New Deal included the Negro in its various agencies of relief and rehabilitation, the effect of which was considerable since Negroes figured heavily among the poor and unemployed. (For a concrete example of the New Deal's impact upon the life of blacks, even in the rural South, see the article in Part 2 by John Temple Graves II.)

Generally, to be sure, the New Deal did not disturb patterns of segregation in the Armed Forces, in the Civilian Conservation Corps, or indeed wherever those patterns were locally supported.

But at least segregation in government offices in Washington, which had been introduced by the Progressives, was abandoned. The CCC enlisted about 8 per cent of its 2.5 million young men from the Negro community, a figure that was somewhat short of the 10 per cent that Negroes constituted in the general population. Since Negroes were disproportionately represented among the unemployed, however, that figure was even more inadequate than might at first appear. The principal work relief agency, the Works Progress Administration, unlike the CCC, did not have quotas on blacks, so that in January 1935 Negroes made up almost 30 per cent of WPA workers. Other New Deal agencies built schools, hospitals, and housing units for Negroes, as well as lending money to Negro colleges and universities. Southern Negroes under the New Deal also voted in elections held under the Agricultural Adjustment Act and the National Labor Relations Act, though generally they were disfranchised in political elections in the Southern states. In short, however inadequate by present standards may have been the New Deal's recognition of the legitimate rights of Negroes, it gave more tangible recognition to the hopes and aspirations of black men than any other administration since Lincoln's. And because of that recognition, Negroes supported the New Deal on election day.

The Roosevelt administration's efforts in behalf of the black man may have been indirect, but the New Deal made no secret of its commitment to the cause of organized labor. Here, too, is a significant difference between the Progressive movement and the New Deal. Although the Clayton Act of 1914 exempted labor unions from the prohibitions of anti-trust legislation, the Progressives were not really concerned with encouraging union organization. On the other hand, the New Deal's support of organized labor was among its most innovative measures. In Section 7A of the National Recovery Act of 1933, and then in the more comprehensive National Labor Relations Act of 1935, the New Deal threw the weight and legal authority of the federal government behind labor's right to organize and in support of the principle that management must bargain in good faith with union representatives. As recently as 1932 the Norris-LaGuardia anti-injunction act had given workers the freedom to organize without fear of court injunctions, but employers still retained the right to oppose unionization. As a federal Court of Appeals said in 1948, "prior to the National Labor Relations Act no federal law prevented *employers* from discharging employees for exercising" the right to organize or from refusing to recognize or bargain with labor organizations. In short, the court went on, "The NLRA created rights *against employers* which did not exist before." The immediate social consequence was the transformation of the American labor movement. Thanks to the protection that Section 7A of the NRA and later the National Labor Relations Act offered to union organizing, the great mass-production industries like steel, automobiles, rubber, airplanes, and textiles were organized for the first time in American history. Membership in labor unions shot up from 3.5 million in 1930 to nine million in 1940. Insofar as Americans today live in a society in which large-scale unions play a crucial role, that situation is attributable to the New Deal's interest in and support of organized labor.

The New Deal's concern for unorganized industrial workers was admittedly less spectacular. The principal measure was the Fair Labor Standards Act of 1938, which is usually described as the last piece of New Deal legislation. It set minimum wages and maximum hours for certain classes of industrial workers and prohibited labor by children under sixteen years of age. The coverage of the act was quite limited, but even so the new law helped to iron out differences in pay rates between the low-wage South and the more industrially advanced North. More important was the opening that the act provided for extending the floor under wages to greater numbers of workers in subsequent years. Since the 1930's the act has been amended several times in order to embrace more wage earners; the minimum wage has been raised by Congress from the original rate of 40 cents an hour to the present $1.30 for those occupations only newly covered, and to $1.60 an hour for those already included under the act.

IV

One reason why some historians have asserted that the New Deal was a continuation of Progressivism is the lack of any differentiating ideology in the New Deal. Certainly it is true, as we have seen, that Roosevelt himself had no sharply defined philosophy either before or after he entered the White House. He deliberately chose advisers with diverse outlooks since it was also consonant with his view of things that clashing minds produced fresh and useful ideas. Consequently, it is not surprising that there is no single document epitomizing the economic and social philosophy of the New Deal. Roosevelt's oft-cited address to the Commonwealth Club in San Francisco during the campaign of 1932 falls short of the requirement. The speech was actually written by Rexford Tugwell and Adolf Berle, Jr., and was barely seen by FDR before delivery. Tugwell and Berle were both knowing and articulate New Dealers, to be sure, but neither of them could speak with authority for their more conservative chief. And, more important, the ideas in that speech are much more pessimistic about the future than Roosevelt in fact was.

Unable to find a clear underlying or cohesive philosophy for the New Deal, historians have fallen back upon calling it pragmatic, eclectic, or improvising. Concretely what these terms signify is that the New Deal tried a variety of approaches in trying to meet what it considered a social or economic problem. If the solution seemed to meet the issue fairly well, it became a New Deal agency; if not, it was abandoned. Not surprisingly, the means the New Deal used to attack problems displayed no clear line of ideology. Government and business cooperation was the approach taken by the NRA, but in the TVA, government and business were in competition. If financial inducements instead of coercion were used in the AAA to help farmers raise prices, in the National Labor Relations Act the New Deal compelled management to accept trade unions and to bargain with them. The only factor that linked all these approaches was the federal government as an energizing force. Nor was there any goal toward which all the solutions were directed, nor even any ideological justification for the order in which problems were attacked, other than that depression-created problems seemed to rate priority. Even that generalization, however, does not always hold, for the TVA—hardly an answer to a problem created by the depression—was set up during the Hundred Days along with the NRA and the AAA.

In their search for some rhyme or reason behind the sprawling body of legislation enacted by the first two Roosevelt administrations, some historians have been attracted to the idea that there were in fact two New Deals. (This interpretation, incidentally, was set forth as early as the summer of 1935 by journalist Delbert Clark in an article reprinted in Part 2.) According to this view, during the First New Deal Roosevelt worked closely with business to raise prices and regularize economic activity, with the National Industrial Recovery Act being the key measure. The Second New Deal began in the summer of 1935 when FDR was disappointed with and chagrined at the lack of cooperation and even hostility shown by business toward his program. As a result, he then turned to measures to help the disadvantaged, abandoning his efforts at cooperation between government and business. The representative measures for the Second New Deal are Social Security and the National Labor Relations Act. More recently, some historians, notably Arthur Schlesinger, Jr., have argued that in shifting from the First to the Second New Deal, the philosophy changed from a concern with economic and social planning to one in which competition was the principal means for regulating the economy. Schlesinger summarized his view of the differences: "The First New Deal characteristically told business what it must do. The Second New Deal characteristically told business what it must *not* do."

This neat division, however, for all its usefulness in bringing some order into the mass of diverse and sometimes contradictory legislation of the New Deal, misleads more than it helps. Roosevelt himself, for example, did not see any shift in his outlook during 1935. When asked if he believed in Louis Brandeis' emphasis upon competition as the way to control business, he answered that Brandeis was "one thousand per cent right in principle"—but at times government had to step in to regulate, too! As always, he shied away from ideological consistency. "This country is big enough to experiment with several diverse systems and follow several lines," he once told Adolf Berle, Jr. "Why must we put our economic policy in a single systematic straitjacket?"

Since statesmen are not always the best guides to the nature of their policies, a more important reason for doubting the existence of two New Deals is that the actual legislation does not fit the pattern. Thus in the course of the first two years, there is not only the NRA, which was the chief measure providing for co-operation between business and government in the economy, but also the Tennessee Valley Authority, which was as reformist and "anti-business" as any piece of New Deal legislation. Similarly, in the Second New Deal, Social Security may be a good example of FDR's new interest in social groups other than businessmen. But how does one fit in the National Labor Relations Act, which was introduced by Senator Robert Wagner and which neither Roosevelt nor his Secretary of Labor Frances Perkins wanted to have anything to do with before its passage in the Senate? Or what is to be done with the fact that Raymond Moley, one of FDR's principal advisers during the First New Deal, resigned during the Second? Moley was clearly one of the more conservative members of the Brain Trust; yet his influence was greatest during the alleged more "radical" stage of New Deal social thinking. Then he left when that thinking became supposedly more traditional after 1935. In any event, the only piece of legislation after 1935 that qualifies as an unambiguous example of the supposedly new interest in a competitive economy is the Holding Company Act of 1935. It was an important piece of legislation, but, if one swallow does not make a summer, neither does one law make a Second New Deal. We now know, too, that as late as 1938 Roosevelt contemplated reviving some form of the NRA, though the approach it epitomized was supposedly abandoned along with the First New Deal. The fact is, in sum, that the New Deal was too amorphous, too devoid of a basic ideology or philosophy to produce such a neat pattern. The New Dealers as a group, as the chief himself was fond of advising, preferred to "play it by ear."

Yet it might be asked, was not the New Deal interested in

planning and did not this interest suggest a philosophy? It is true that if one looks at the writings of many New Dealers during the 1930's the word "planning" pops up repeatedly. For example, Secretary of the Interior Harold Ickes wrote an article for the *New York Times* in 1934 entitled "Ickes Hails National Planning." Later the same year Anne O'Hare McCormick of the *Times* interviewed the President and reported that "What attracts him most is social planning, especially when it can be projected in the form of model communities, which he likes to scatter over the country as samples of what the common life could be with a wider distribution of wealth and wider public ownership of natural resources."

If, however, one examines more closely what most New Dealers, including the President, meant by planning, it is clear that the meaning was far removed from the modern conception of a national plan, which even then someone like Rexford Tugwell recognized would entail strict control over wages and prices as well as profits. In short, it would have required an exercise of national power far beyond the wildest dreams of Roosevelt, or even Ickes. Ickes, for example, made clear in his *New York Times* article that what he had in mind when he spoke of "planning" was little more than foresight. His advice was that Americans ought to husband their resources against future needs. He called attention, among other things, to the growing demand for water. Such admonitions were certainly useful, but they hardly qualify as social planning, as economists even of that time understood the term.

Nor should agencies like the TVA or the AAA be viewed as more than gestures in the direction of planning. In both instances the degree of control was limited to an aspect of a region only, as with the TVA in the South, or to a part of an industry, as with AAA and farming. In the case of the TVA, the federal government competed with a private industry and thus affected prices in a direct and significant fashion; in the case of the AAA, the federal government controlled production, and thereby prices, by offering financial inducements to producers. In neither instance was the planning more than minimal.

Nor can the New Deal earn credit for introducing deficit spending as an effective means of fighting the Depression. Before Roosevelt entered the presidency, Herbert Hoover had deliberately broken with the time-honored tradition that proclaimed a balanced budget as government's primary contribution to recovery. Although Roosevelt certainly followed the path broken by Hoover, he never became an enthusiastic Keynesian. To Franklin Roosevelt an unbalanced budget remained a disgrace, acceptable only during a dire emergency. Not until the administration of John F. Kennedy did an American President fully recognize that an unbalanced budget was morally no worse than a balanced one, and that under certain circumstances it was undoubtedly wiser economically.

The New Deal's lack of any overall planning was more than the absence of a theory. Most New Dealers simply did not want an overall theory. In a profound sense, and in spite of the fact that most of the men and women who worked with and advised Roosevelt were highly educated, New Dealers were more interested in action than in ideas. To them the value of an idea lay not in itself but in what could be done with it in the real world. Despite the frequent newspaper cartoons that depicted Roosevelt's advisers as wearing caps and gowns, the typical New Dealer was a social engineer rather than an intellectual. As Harry Hopkins once said, "I am for experimenting . . . in various parts of the country, trying out schemes which are supported by reasonable people and see if they work. If they do not work, the world will not come to an end." The important thing, in short, was action, not theory. Even Tugwell, a Ph.D. and a former professor, wrote in his book *The Battle for Democracy,* published in 1935, "I speak in dispraise of dusty learning, and in disparagement of historical technique. Are our plans wrong? Who knows? Who can tell from reading history?"

Moreover, unlike the Progressives, the New Dealers exhibited few moral preconceptions about their reforms. As Edgar Kemler points out in his retrospective book on the New Deal, *The Deflation of American Ideals,* the intellectual difference between the New Dealers and the Progressives can be put quite succinctly. For the Progressives, in order to make society better it was necessary to make the people better; for the New Dealers, however, it was the institutions that required renovation, not the people. One was a moral approach to reform, the other amoral. No one voiced the new attitude better than Senator Robert Wagner in a defense of his housing bill in 1936. "It must be emphasized frankly and at once," he observed, "that the slum problem is not a problem of low individual standards of morals or of taste. It cannot be solved by education, nor by propaganda, nor by preachments about living." It could only be met by better housing and higher wages. (Wagner, incidentally, who grew up in the slums of New York City, embodied many of the social characteristics and concerns of the New Deal coalition as well. He was a New Yorker, an immigrant, a Catholic, and a friend of organized labor.)

As a result, under the New Deal, American reform lost that moralistic tinge or evangelical tone that is so characteristic of the Progressive movement. New Dealers, after all, worked quite happily with a city boss like Mayor Frank Hague of Jersey City, though municipal bosses had been one of the evils against which the Progressives had fought. Many Progressives had favored Prohibition, but some New Dealers like Tugwell and Hopkins puckishly linked drinking and reform. Hopkins, for example, said that he would like "to provide orchestras for beer gardens to encourage people to sit around drinking their beer and enjoying themselves. It would be a great employment relief measure."

V

In its time the principal criticism of the New Deal was that it sought to change, even to revolutionize American society. Because this charge was so common, many New Dealers, from FDR on down, stressed the conservative or traditional character of their program. Later, during the era of Senator Joseph McCarthy, the years of the New Deal were attacked for having been a narrow escape from socialism.

More recently, historians of a radical persuasion like Howard Zinn and Barton Bernstein have criticized the New Deal for what it failed to do. That it failed in a number of areas cannot be denied. Most glaring was its inability to eliminate unemployment, for that was the central task the New Deal had set itself. When Franklin Roosevelt came into office in March 1933, the number of unemployed throughout the nation was estimated at from twelve to fifteen million; in 1937, after almost five years of conscientious effort—the greatest ever made until then by a federal administration—the government still counted 10.5 million men and women without work. Nor was the radical redistribution of wealth, which some New Dealers had called for, achieved. An attack was made upon slums and poor housing in general by the New Deal, but it fell far below the needs of the country. The TVA, it is true, rehabilitated one region, but the "little TVA's" suggested for other regions did not get built or even planned. Some improvement in the lot of sharecroppers was accomplished through the Resettlement Administration, but that limited effort did not bring most of these marginal farmers into the mainstream of the economy. Some of the New Dealers then and later recognized that not everything promised had been attained. Tugwell, for example, in an article reprinted in Part 3, set forth quite candidly the long way still to go to eradicate or even ameliorate rural poverty. When the New Deal was over, Vice-President Henry Wallace, who had been Secretary of Agriculture during the thirties, frankly admitted that the job was not yet done. "We are the children of the transition," he wrote, "we have left Egypt but we have not yet arrived at the Promised Land."

The fundamental thrust of the criticism of the New Deal from radicals like Professors Zinn and Bernstein and from a former New Dealer like Rexford Tugwell, however, is not simply that the Roosevelt administration failed to achieve the goals it set itself. Their criticism is deeper than that. It is that, basically, the New Deal lacked the imagination to set more radical social goals for itself and the nation. Tugwell, for example, would have liked to see a fundamental reordering of the society through a comprehensive national plan. Zinn and Bernstein apparently would have liked more direct government participation in the economy, along the lines of the TVA, and they note that the New Deal made no direct attack upon, or even criticism of, the traditional patterns of racial discrimination in American society.

In suggesting what the New Deal might have been, such radical criticisms help define the New Deal; they compel us to acknowledge the ideological limitations within which it operated. Roosevelt himself, as we have seen, was certainly not prepared to overturn the status quo; he had come to save the system, not to destroy it. More important than even Roosevelt as a limitation on the experimentalism or radicalism of the New Deal was the society itself. It is revealing, for example, that virtually all of the truly experimental activities of the New Deal, from the Federal Theater to the greenbelt communities, were ultimately abandoned because of hostility from Congress—that is, from the immediate representatives of the people. In sum, even if the leaders of the New Deal had been prepared to change radically American social goals, the electorate would not have gone along. The fear that "the people are not ready" was not an excuse for timidity; it was a realistic evaluation of the American people's limited commitment to structural change. It is easy enough to suggest that more ought to have been done, but whether these alternatives were plausibly obtainable is a different but no less necessary question. In the end, one suspects it was the amazing sweep of the New Deal's achievements that is the real source of the modern radical criticism. If the New Deal managed to accomplish so much, such critics seem to be saying, why could it not have done more? In that lament there is more than a little praise of its achievement.

VI

What then, a generation after the death of Franklin Roosevelt, was the significance of the New Deal? What did it all add up to? One way of obtaining a sighting on this question is to look abroad. If some modern historians see the New Deal as a continuation of earlier reform movements, contemporary foreign observers were impressed by its novelty. Harold Laski, the English Socialist intellectual, for example, made just this point. Writing in the *Atlantic Monthly* in 1934, Laski described Roosevelt as the first statesman "to use the power of the state to subordinate the primary assumptions of that society to certain vital social purposes. . . . The first to attack not the secondary but the primary manifestations of the doctrine of *laissez-faire*. He is the first statesman who . . . without coercion . . . has placed in the hands of organized labor a weapon which, if it be used successfully, is bound to result in a vital readjustment of the relative bargaining power of Capital and Labor." John Maynard Keynes, the English economist whose writings later influenced New Deal policies, wrote FDR in 1933: "You have made yourself the trustee of those in every country who seek to mend the evils of our condition by reasoned experiment within the framework of the existing social system. If you fail, rational change will be gravely prejudiced throughout the world, leaving orthodoxy and revolution to fight it out."

Throughout the world the New Deal became synonymous with imaginative reform. Léon Blum's Popular Front in France was called "The French New Deal," and Paul Van Zeeland's government of national unity in Belgium in 1935 was attacked as "a slavish copy of the American New Deal." (Van Zeeland had studied at Princeton.) Opponents of the program of the Conservative party in Canada denounced it as "Burnett's New Deal." Students of social and economic reform from all over the world, including some from the Soviet Union, came to study the experimental projects of the New Deal, particularly the TVA. Some of the expectations aroused by the New Deal abroad seem extravagant today, but that excessive attitude itself offers a measure of the impact of the New Deal. If the New Deal succeeded, a British newspaper asserted, "it will spread to every civilized country and there will in reality be a new earth. If it fails, then not only America, but the world will have to begin all over again."

Striking as the impact of the New Deal abroad may have been, its greatest significance derives from what it did at home. Perhaps the best short summary of what the New Deal meant was offered by an envious Canadian: "In Canada we had no New Deal, no A.A.A. or other measures designed to give agriculture a 'parity' with urban industry, no Wagner Act for the trade unions, no great public housing schemes, no C.C.C. camps for unemployed youth, no T.V.A. to reconstruct a vast blighted area, no Federal Writers or Federal Artists Projects, no new parkways about our big cities and no new recreation camps among our lakes and forests; and—last but not least—no fireside chats." In that catalogue is measured in a few words the revolution in outlook that the New Deal brought to America.

For if there is a single change that sums up the nature of the New Deal revolution, it is the transformation in the attitudes of Americans toward government activity in the economy and society. Until the Depression and the New Deal, even politically and socially liberal Americans thought government's proper role in the economy was limited and peripheral. In 1935, for example, Roger Baldwin, a civil libertarian of impeccable credentials, could still oppose the Wagner labor bill because of the threat he thought such government involvement in labor relations posed to trade unions. In the depths of the Depression, in 1931, a group as concerned with the problems of the unemployed as the National Conference of Social Workers still refused to endorse the principle of federally supported relief for the unemployed. And it was not until 1932 that the American Federation of Labor came out for the first time in favor of government-sponsored unemployment insurance. Even after the New Deal was active, the American Civil Liberties Union was still worried by the threat of big government. "The enormous increase in the power of the federal government under the New Deal policies," the Union reported in 1934, "carries with it inevitable fears of inroads in the right of agitation. Alarms are widely expressed over alleged dictatorship by the President, the abrogation of states' rights and the vast economic powers of the federal government reaching out to every home and business in the land." If organizations and individuals of such liberal persuasion were convinced that government's role ought to be limited, it needs no extended argument to prove that more conservative citizens held similar ideas.

Another way of measuring the change in attitude brought about by the Depression and the New Deal is provided by the shift in the attitude toward labor unions. Today, after the New Deal, the right of labor to organize and to play a significant role in politics and the economy is taken for granted by most Americans, conservatives as well as liberals. But before the New Deal, the right to organize was still under attack, to such an extent that to one civil liberties advocate in 1938 it was the right most in need of being secured. "However important or significant may be the struggle for the political rights of fifteen million Negroes," Roger Baldwin declared in his Godkin Lectures of 1938, "however important or significant the defense of religious liberties; of academic freedom; of freedom from censorship of press, radio, or motion pictures, these are on the whole trifling in national effect with the fight for the rights of labor to organize."

Finally, in attempting to measure the reversal in public attitude toward the government's participation in reform and in the economy wrought by the New Deal, its effect upon socialism is certainly worthy of mention. Socialist ideology envisioned an active role for government in the economy, yet the advent of the New Deal almost obliterated the party's support. The explanation was given quite frankly by Norman Thomas, the party's presidential candidate in 1932 and 1936. "What cut the ground out pretty completely from us was this. It was Roosevelt in a word. You don't need anything more."

That the New Deal had an enduring influence on subsequent American society requires no proof. It is all around us today. It is evident in the Employment Act of 1946, which set up the President's Council of Economic Advisers to check on the health of the economy; it is evident in the actions of all subsequent administrations, Republican as well as Democratic, to fulfill the obligation to prevent a depression and avoid massive unemployment; it is evident in the fact that the whole body of New Deal legislation, once viewed as so radical and "indigestible," is still on the statute books. Of all the New Deal innovations, only the National Labor Relations Act has been seriously modified (by the Taft-Hartley Act of 1947), and even in that instance the fundamental principle that the federal government encourages and supports unionization has not been touched. Meanwhile, the Social Security Act and the minimum-wage and maximum-hour law have been extended to include ever larger numbers of citizens.

Indeed, the acceptance of the New Deal has been so complete that some historians have argued that that fact in itself proves that the New Deal was essentially conservative. Such an argument, however, fails to do justice to the extent of the revolution in attitude brought about by the New Deal in conjunction with the Depression. An analogy might be made with the abolition of slavery in the South after the Civil War. Like the New Deal, abolition was almost immediately accepted by white Southerners, though they had just fought a war to prevent precisely that result. Yet it is difficult to believe that the abolition of slavery was not a revolutionary event in the life of white Southerners who had lived with the institution. They accepted abolition, as later Americans accepted the New Deal, but in neither instance can one talk meaningfully about the persistence of old ways. Certainly there were connections with previous years in both periods; there always are. But if in some periods of history it is the continuity with the past that needs to be emphasized, in the case of the New Deal it is the novelty that is significant.

Conventionally the end of the New Deal is dated with the enactment of the Wages and Hours Act of 1938. But in a fundamental sense the New Deal did not end then at all. Americans still live in the era of the New Deal, for its achievements are now the base mark below which no conservative government may go and from which all new reform now starts. Not only did the Republican Eisenhower administration accept all the reform agencies and laws of the New Deal, but the reform efforts of the Democratic Truman, Kennedy, and Johnson administrations have been little more than fulfillments of the New Deal. The Democratic administrations' support of the Black Revolution since 1954, to be sure, has gone beyond the New Deal, and the laws on behalf of federal funds for education enacted under the Johnson administration were not precisely prefigured by the New Deal. But the use by Kennedy and Johnson of federal power and revenues for reshaping the economy and the society certainly had its beginning in the Roosevelt era. The principal difference between reform since 1945 and that of the 1930's is the absence of depression. The New Deal's long and unsuccessful struggle with unemployment and the reforms spawned by that concern are understandably not a part of modern reform. Hence superficially the New Deal seems more remote than it actually is. For the fact is that twenty-five years after the death of Roosevelt, his New Deal still sets the goals and defines the limits of reform in the United States. If this is a tribute to the New Deal it is also an indictment of contemporary American reformers.

Part 1

THE SOCIAL AND INTELLECTUAL CONTEXT OF THE NEW DEAL

THE NEW DEAL did not operate in a vacuum, nor were all its ideas the product of the minds and experiences of New Dealers alone. As we have seen already in the Introduction, the crisis of the Great Depression and widespread unemployment were the primary roots of the first Roosevelt administration. Anne O'Hare McCormick's first article in this section stresses the dangers to which the prolonged depression exposed democracy as Americans knew it. Under the impact of the Depression, she points out, the very nature of the American political system came under anxious and close scrutiny. A leaderless Congress was looking for guidance; a bewildered people hoped for some sense of direction. Although McCormick was writing several months before the great collapse of the banks in the winter of 1932–1933, it is evident that already the bankers had been blamed for the debacle. Against this background of distrust and indecision, the reader begins to understand why Franklin Roosevelt's warm manner and self-confident speeches during the campaign and in the course of his presidency buoyed up and electrified millions of Americans.

One expression of the dissatisfaction with the traditional political and social solutions to the Depression is provided by S. J. Woolf's interviews with John Dewey, the radical philosopher and educator, and Norman Thomas, the Socialist candidate for President. Both of these men started from a democratic socialist position and both found the current drift of events potentially revolutionary. Thomas' promise that if he were elected he would "mobilize the country for war on unemployment" anticipates in a striking way FDR's statement in his first Inaugural. "Our greatest primary task is to put people to work," the new President said. "It can be accomplished in part by direct recruiting by the government itself, treating the task as we would treat the emergency of a war. . . ." This was not to be the only time, as William Leuchtenburg has pointed out, that Roosevelt would fall back on the analogue of war when facing the problems of the Depression.

The interview with Roosevelt himself by Anne McCormick is included here because it took place before he was President, yet it sets forth the image of Franklin Roosevelt as he liked to be seen: a liberal in thought, who remained true to traditional principles while applying them to changing circumstances. As always, he conveniently locates himself ideologically between a radical and a conservative. Characteristically, he reveals his interest in and concern for the farmer, whom he erroneously, but revealingly, refers to as making up "half the population." (In 1930 farm families actually constituted no more than one-third of the population.)

The article on Coughlin, Long, and Townsend is reprinted here, although it was published in 1935, because these three popular alternatives to the New Deal influenced the programs of the Roosevelt administration. Townsend's effect, as has already been pointed out in the Introduction, was most noticeable in getting Social Security adopted; both Long and Coughlin, by demanding a better lot for the ordinary citizen, kept the stimulating fires of popular discontent lighted under the New Deal.

Huey Long was assassinated by an enemy in Louisiana less

than six months after this article appeared. His movement "Every Man a King," which was then gaining national strength, collapsed with his death. Townsend's appeal continued to grow even after the enactment of Social Security in the summer of 1935, principally because of the narrow coverage of the original act. But by 1936 the Townsend movement, too, was in decline. Father Coughlin's social conscience soured as time went on. He broke with Roosevelt in November 1935 and helped form a third party in 1936. By then his anti-Semitism and crankish monetary schemes had come to dominate his speeches, causing his popularity to fall off abruptly. During the Second World War Catholic Church officials barred him from the air.

The New Ordeal
of Democracy

by Anne O'Hare McCormick

THIS IS a story in two parts. The first is written in the Middle West, home address of America, and generalizes the talk to be heard almost anywhere in the United States during this highly controversial, politically heated and financially frigid campaign year of 1932. The second is written in Washington, the only place in the country whose business is in full production, and reports the outlook there in a time constantly spoken of but not yet recognized on Capitol Hill as an hour of national emergency. Thus it glances at the same picture from two angles, both pretty obtuse, one that of the representatives of the people, the other that of the people represented.

Together the two views form a commentary on the whole scheme of representative government, in principle so simple, in operation grown so complex that many begin to think it is unworkable in a crisis. At any rate the principle is now at test throughout the world. It is not too much to say that its vindication, not to say its survival, peculiarly depends on the decisions to be made in this country in the next few years, perhaps in the next few months.

From the *New York Times Magazine,* June 26, 1932, copyright © 1932, 1960 by The New York Times Company.

We are the oldest existing democracy. No nation has enjoyed universal manhood suffrage so long as ours. None has been so free to develop without outside interference, to shape its own environment, to create a system of government under the uniquely favoring circumstances of geographic security, economic independence and modern political ancestry. We have not been circumscribed by poverty of natural resources, by encroaching neighbors, by the fibroid traditions of old societies, by the compromises required of nations living in a crowd, like the nations of Europe. We have not been circumscribed at all. We voided the past by beginning late, with a century which gave birth to a new kind of civilization. We laid our own patterns in fresh soil. Industry is our contemporary and lent us speeds unknown before in exploiting the wealth of a rich continent. To this point, in a word, we have governed ourselves, arrived where we are in our own way and under our own power. Our progress has been automotive, almost automatic, and loudly touted as the progress of democracy.

Now the question is: Where are we? Nobody seems quite sure, least of all the masters of our political fate currently engaged in nominating the contending candidates for the Presidency of the Republic and building platforms designed to be indistinguishable one from the other and to contain no plank not broad enough for every voter to stand on. This year's conventions are like all conventions, splurges on the grand scale of competitive salesmanship, yet they are held in one of the real crises in human history, a crisis not only economic but political.

For ten years and more we have been hearing about the crisis of democracy. Until a few months ago, however, that particular crisis did not hit the mass mind of America. Our democracy has been rather like one of our automatic devices, as much a part of our regular equipment as the telephone, taken for granted as available whether used or not. But lately, from the grass roots to the glass towers, the attention of the country has been focused on government. Everything has piled up together—taxes, tariffs, the crushing cost and corruption of local machines, congealed credit in State and Federal banks, unemployment, snowballing relief budgets, hunger and thirst, rackets and panic—to fill the valley of depression with a mountainous exhibit of our dependence on politics.

At last we discover that government manages our lives; we wonder if what we suffer is not first of all a crisis of democracy. If it is not a failure of productive or consumptive power, of supply or demand, as obviously it is not, then it must be a failure of the democratic intelligence embodied in political institutions. To point to the simultaneous breakdown of other governments or systems of government is no comfort or no answer to the rudely awakened American. He insists that democracy fostered our famous spread of prosperity and that it must be proved equal or unequal to the stresses of adversity.

To a country beginning to face that radical act, the Congress now adjourning seems feeble and frivolous. The conventions seem frivolous. The whole political bag of tricks looks as cheap and useless as a deposit box stuffed with stock certificates or a counter piled with goods reduced for clearance. During this strange interlude when the national slogan is "No business as usual," repeated everywhere with a certain grim gayety, the nation's business is government. For the first time to anything like the present extent, the eyes of all the States are glued on their political representatives. Under the unflickering gaze of this new and once indifferent gallery, the political show appears something like a costume party, quaint, pre-war, full of Spencerian flourishes, of eternal gestures, of nimble sidestepping, the "à la main de" left and right of the old quadrille. "Actually they are behaving as they always behave!" gasps the audience—embittered because it cannot do the same!

The multitude does not blame the politicians for the depression. The guilt for that has been firmly fastened on the bankers. What is resented in the men of politics, and resented with a unanimity that may unseat them all, is their solemn levity, pussyfooting, resourcelessness, the unbreakable habit of "playing politics." Observe how the slump has multiplied ballyhoo magazines; watch what people read on trains and buses, in the long summer evenings on the porches of the suburbs and the small towns. Then you will understand why 7,770 Texans telegraphed

Congress to adjourn and why Iowa expressed a violent preference for a "chicken-stew" candidate as against "the same old baloney" of Senator Brookhart.

I—*Along Main Street*

On the most metropolitan main streets today people stop to talk. One of the strange signs of the times is the little groups on the downtown sidewalks exchanging rumors, views, echoes of views, on the state of the nation. There is a lot of echo; for once the talk is the same in industrial city and country town; for once both have plenty of time to talk. There is also an air of leisure long absent from the American scene. Turned colloquial, the urban streets become village-like and friendly, and the colloquies themselves bring back the lost flavor of the cracker-box, a ghostly cracker-box overwhelmed by motor traffic but essentially the same old mourner's bench of the country store.

Ten to one the talk goes straight to the new question of America: "What's the government going to do?" The tone is not tragic. It runs around in circles, as in a labyrinth without an exit, but the habit of optimism is strong in us; it never stops in despair. It is not revolutionary. The contemporary models of revolution are mentioned often enough, but as bogeys rather than as beacons. "I'd as soon be in Russia as here." "If Congress keeps on fiddling we'll be saddled with a Mussolini yet." These are common remarks, but delivered in the accent of Little Orphan Annie referring to the goblins.

Nobody yet believes in such alternatives, and none would be more surprised than the few who seriously predict communism or fascism if their words were to come true. Such prophets of doom as there are speak without conviction. America would be more reckless if it had any real fear of doom; now it presents the novel paradox of a people saving not for a rainy but for a sunny day. The talk is seldom without humor, wisecracks and sallies of heavy sarcasm. As often as not the huddles break up in a laugh, sour but hearty.

The general tone, however, is one of exasperation, directed particularly against the politicians. Wherever two or three citizens gather together, there is a political convention. In these private conventions, however, the keynoter has no encomiums for any candidate or either party. Four years ago the manoeuvres at Kansas City and Houston were followed with a mild sporting interest mixed with shrugging cynicism, the usual attitude of prosperous America toward politics; such heat as developed in the 1928 campaign was kindled from the fires going deeper than politics. In normal times we are spectator citizens as well as spectator sportsmen. Now the interest is intense to the point of anger, not a dynamic anger driving toward action but a vague irritation, mostly against hokum and cowardice, which may spend itself in turning out most of the present officeholders and replacing them with names drawn from the same hopper, by the same methods, and promising no change except a greater inexperience.

The elector does not rationalize this resentment. He is not consistent. He curses Congressmen in general for logrolling, for obstructing and delaying national measures in favor of local interests, in the same breath in which he demands from his own Congressman nothing but local representation. If there are no national representatives, neither are there any national citizens.

From the beginning the country has looked to the economy program as the real test of the sincerity of its official representatives. Here, too, it is unreasonable, since the establishment it now rebels against was built to the specifications of the voters, always calling for more government service. Nevertheless, the failure to slash costs is viewed with something like despair, as the final proof of political stupidity.

Can democracy function in an emergency? More and more this question worries the congresses of the street. It is a question I have heard many times, but not in crowds, and not in this temper, except during those fumbling preludes which in other countries lead to dictatorship.

But America is not like other countries. The reporter who has made the international round feels that strongly as he circulates among his protesting and bewildered countrymen. Something destructive has happened to us in the past few years, the same thing that happens to people under dictatorships. Here it is the combined effect of government increasingly concentrated, of mergers and chains and corporate ownership, of ownership without effort, of easy money and paper profits and losses. We were fast becoming a nation of clerks, deputies, high-priced hired men. The sense of responsibility atrophied, the sense of values was corrupted; after the gaudy 1920s we were flabby and a little the worse for synthetic gin and synthetic prosperity.

II—In the Capital

That shows up now just as Congress shows up now. This session has been better than most, anxious, laborious, less partisan than usual, more cooperative. When one turns at last from the represented to the representatives, it is only to meet in Washington a group of tired, harassed and baffled men, up against problems too big for them and unhappily aware of it. Was Congress aware that it was under scrutiny more close and critical than ever before, that the public was sick and tired of old stratagems, of stale campaign speeches, of flag-raising on top of a volcano?

Washington remains strangely secluded on its smokeless river, an Olympus hiding in clouds of talk, but I have never seen it so exposed to the harsh weather outside. It is fully cognizant of the mood of the country. Every Representative and Senator I questioned made these three points: first, that Congressional mail was never so heavy as in this session, nor so peremptory; second, that newspapers everywhere now publish daily the record of the local representatives on each roll-call and increasing pressure is brought to bear to make them mere delegates for their constituencies; third, that for two months there has been a concerted campaign of propaganda against Congress, in behalf of the business and banking interests seeking to hasten adjournment, in behalf of the administration seeking to gain prestige at the expense of the legislative body, or in behalf of both. That they are victims of a planned attack of ridicule and misrepresentation is firmly believed by both houses and members of both parties. In this session the persecution complex, so called, has moved from the White House to the Hill.

"Why should we be the scapegoat?" asked a distinguished member of the Senate. "If we had rejected some inspired plan for national recovery, any plan, in fact, we might reasonably be damned. But not a single group in the country, businessmen, industrialists, bankers, labor leaders, not a single individual, from the President down, has yet come before us with a real program, a constructive suggestion. No, the country pretends it expects nothing of Congress and now condemns us for not doing what nobody can do. We are blamed if we act and if we don't act. Having led us to ruin, the great business brains of the country can think of nothing but to berate this contemptible body for not pulling them out."

For years all honest Congressmen have lamented that there is no counterweight against the pressure of lobbies representing special interests; the people as such, they say, are never heard from. In this session the people have been heard from again and again, but in such confusion of counsel and demand and protest that they have but added another element to the general bewilderment. The truth is, of course, that democracies cannot act as democracies when there is vital need for quick and dis-interested decisions. Representative government gives satisfaction but not efficiency. One reason for the St. Vitus dance of Congress is that it is too representative, pulled by too many strings.

Emergency shows us up, shows up our system of government, and shows up with complete clearness certain processes that have been going on for a long time without much remark. One is that for twenty years we have been electing our public officials on the prohibition issue, making a candidate's sentiments on the liquor question practically the sole test of his fitness to deal with the most intricate problems ever put up to legislators. Another is that our great popular reforms, such as the direct primary and the referendum, as worked out by a heretofore wholly indifferent electorate, have weakened party responsibility without giving us better officers or fairer laws. A third is progres-sive centralization of power and function in Washington that has neither relieved nor simplified State establishments, but has radi-cally disturbed the original balance between the executive and legislative branches of the Federal Government and turned every session of Congress into a struggle of the waning against the crescent power.

Most important is what has happened to the party system. Under our rigid two-party system, with power and responsibility in the hands of the majority, there is no provision for those legislative sessions, like the last, in which no working majority exists. Usually such sessions are sterile or stormy. But aside from that, it is perfectly evident that the two parties have long since ceased to have any sustaining principles or vital points of difference. Every tariff and taxation bill provides that we are divided not into parties but into economic sections, so that the parties themselves have degenerated into little more than rival machines for electing a President and controlling Federal patronage. For effective government under our charter, the parties have to function as such, strongly led and unified. Much of our present confusion and impotence arise from the fact that we are organized under one system and operating, or trying to operate, under another; nominally we have two-party rule, but actually we have rule by group, bloc, section, lobby; we have an unorganized economic parliament without the legal machinery to regulate it.

America is not like other countries. It has not even so much logic as England, which hates formulas but moves pretty steadily in one direction without them, while we love formulas, and with them manage to proceed in any direction. Thus you cannot predict of America what you might of really rational countries that follow premises to conclusions; you cannot say that because we are in a mood to welcome it that there is the least likelihood of a dictatorship.

Our government is not like other governments. It may be doubted if any other could ride along with so many wheels within two wheels. That feat supports the hope that even democracy might work in a modern State if it were tried. Representative government breaks down in times of stress mainly because it has never been adjusted to the facts.

This is a time of great decisions. Among the greatest questions, because it involves the future of the democratic principle in government, is whether we can revitalize the parties to make them mean something, by giving them fighting programs, new names, new aims, modern machinery, and then whether we have intelligence and courage enough to build up another and more honest system of representation, strengthened by some sort of economic council, appointive, non-partisan, non-local, of such intellectual calibre and practical experience that it can function as a brain for the body politic.

No ordinary political campaign is this on which we now embark. It may be our last chance to prove that there is initiative enough left in democracy to make it worth saving and spirit enough left in Americans to turn this abstract, sentimental, agitated but unfocused Americanism into positive and adventurous citizenship. It is our representatives, after all, who personify and indict us. "I consider myself a poor Congressman," one of the wisest said to me, "abdicating most of the time my own fairly informed judgment. But you know why, don't you? I am a poor Congressman because I want to continue to be a Congressman."

John Dewey Surveys the Nation's Ills

by S. J. Woolf

WHILE THE OUTBURSTS of convention oratory were still re-echoing through the air, a retiring, slow-spoken, silver-haired college professor sat in his library and discussed political theories. No flood of imagery swept away the simplicity of his words, nor did eloquence or emotion enter into his arguments. Quietly and almost haltingly John Dewey enunciated theories that might be the planks of a third party platform. A hesitancy of manner, by its very contrast, added weight to the arguments of a philosopher who has always preferred to deal with the actualities of life rather than to search for the reality back of the material changes in the universe.

John Dewey, above all else, is essentially American. New England has left its horny thumb mark indelibly upon him. Neither the breezy Middle West, where he was professor at the universities of Michigan, Minnesota and Chicago, nor the East in the shape of Columbia has spoiled his simplicity or dulled his quaint humor. His soft brown eyes which for so many years have pored over the written words of thousands of philosophical treatises, still twinkle merrily behind their large rimless spectacles.

The twinkle was there as he told me that four years ago, when a scrubwoman had asked for whom he was going to vote and he had answered Smith, she said to him: "Oh, professor, you surely do not believe that such an uneducated man should be in the White House."

There is an intense practicality about John Dewey, a quality inherited from his Vermont ancestors, which has prevented him from being lost in the wilderness on a vain search for the Absolute. To his mind the greatest harm has come from disassociating thinking from acting and regarding it as something, for that reason, more desirable. He believes that feelings, habits and volitions are as important and as worthy of study as so-called pure reason.

These being his ideas, it follows that this Yankee philosopher has not shut himself up in his library, allowing the world to pass by unheeded. Causes of all kinds have found in him a stanch champion. More than forty years ago, while still a Professor of Pedagogy, he published "School and Society." Edison was then perfecting his electric light, the Wright brothers were attempting to solve the problem of flying, Westinghouse and a host of others were working on their epoch-making machines. Bland and Bryan were preaching the spirit of unrest that was shaking the country.

It was then that this professor of education in the University of Chicago saw students throughout the country, in classrooms in which shades were drawn and windows closed to keep out both sights and sounds, bending over old-fashioned readers and reciting fixed formulas by rote. Neither their teachers nor their books opened the eyes and minds of students to what was going on about them. To John Dewey this all seemed ridiculous. Why not connect learning with life and make education a helper in the problems of life? He proclaimed this doctrine and it helped to bring about a revolution in the science of teaching. He has carried out his theories in his own career, maintaining a vital touch with the world about him.

It was therefore natural that the first topic of conversation should be the college man in public life.

"For the last twenty years or so," said Professor Dewey, "teachers and students have been called in to solve our national economic problems. This was more or less of an innovation here; notwithstanding that in Europe men of learning have long taken a part in governmental affairs. But economics has not been the only subject in which expert advice has been sought. Throughout the country there has been a distinct trend toward employing experts in working for a solution of other questions. There have been all sorts of commissions whose members included college professors.

"The country has need of expert service of this kind, but there is one objection to it. In economic questions, in municipal problems and in State problems one is likely to find that most of the work is in the nature of compiling statistics. Statistics are all right in themselves, but unless the man of learning is competent to apply statistics to the questions at hand, they will not help matters. What is necessary is an interpretation of them. Changes are going on rapidly all about us and we must be able to interpret them.

"I do not blame the experts for this. Lack of ability to apply to conditions the information which they have gained from their investigations is not their fault. The blame lies in the training which they received in their schools and colleges. Social science at the present time has collected too many facts upon which it has not worked. It has gone about matters in the wrong way. Facts after all are not physical objects which can be caught, labeled and put in glass cases. The greatest collection of them so displayed will get us nowhere. Theories must evolve from them; otherwise there is no use in bringing them together. They must lead to control and action.

"At the present time higher teaching is beginning to broaden and to pass from intense specialization to a more direct dealing with fundamental issues. There is a distinct tendency now to connect in more ways than ever what is taught in the classroom with the problems of life.

"The present economic crisis will assist in this movement. For during the last two years our colleges have been graduating thousands of young men and women who suddenly have been brought to the realization that most of what they have learned will not help them to gain their livelihood. They are beginning to think for themselves and to appreciate the fact that they must do something to bring about a change in present-day affairs. At last they have come to the realization that they must use their efforts to alter a system which affords them no opportunities.

"This is a mighty good thing," he continued, "for the average college graduate displays a lack of interest in public affairs. Of course, when I say this I mean those in this country. But I am not surprised at this, for college still tends to an academic aloofness which has become almost a tradition. The student gets the idea that he should not pay much attention to such sordid things as business unemployment or present-day politics.

"Our higher education apparently evades serious consideration of the deeper issues of our social life. Our young people emerge from these homes of academic tradition and find that we are governed by one of two parties controlled by vast political machines in which there is a varying amount of corruption. The futility of opposing these great parties is apparent. Moreover, in all of us there is a strange feeling of wanting to vote for someone who has a chance of election; the result is that many who do not believe in either party vote under the banner of one or the other rather than, as they imagine, throw their votes away.

"How many of these new voters realize that a great modern industrial country is now being run on pre-Civil War methods? Or, if they do realize it, how many make any efforts to change it? The present division of parties is based on what happened in the days of Thomas Jefferson and Abraham Lincoln and has little to do with American life except to dodge the vital issues that beset us."

As he continued he ruffled his gray hair until it shot out in all directions. "The most important and most dangerous question in our present-day life is economic insecurity. Millions of men anxious to work are recurrently out of employment, and apart from those unemployed by reason of the depression is a standing army which at no time has regular employment. While we hardly know the number of these, we know still less of the psychological and moral consequences of the precarious conditions in which this vast multitude lives.

"Insecurity is worse than unemployment. It is the most pressing problem before us today, yet both of the great parties more or less gloss this over in their platforms and raise the question of prohibition above it in importance. I am not minimizing the importance of the latter, but I feel that our economic problems are those which require our most concentrated efforts."

"How would you solve them?" I asked.

"That is not an easy question to answer," he replied as he settled back in a carved Chippendale chair. For a moment his eyes rested on an old Chinese painting on the wall opposite. Behind his head was a bookcase in which volumes of Shakespeare's plays, bound in red, were most prominent.

"The first work must be educational," he went on. "People are beginning to seek some direction. They want to learn with what kind of policies they can successfully face the present issues of life. They are becoming desirous of finding out how they can bring about some political action that will have an effect upon their work and life. They regard the future with dread; they require reinforcement and courage that come from a sense of union with others in their position. One can almost sense this groping in the very air.

"I am not saying that popular thinking has reached a point of great clearness. It is confused and attended with less light than heat, less understanding than emotion. Nevertheless, I believe that the fundamental point is better understood than ever before. It is known that politics is a farce unless it deals openly and bravely with questions of work, commerce and finance, with things which affect men where they live. Both of the great political parties are intellectually and morally bankrupt on this question. The reason for this bankruptcy is beginning to be understood. They are both so tied up with interests that they literally cannot afford to have any ideas or policies on these questions."

Professor Dewey does not believe that the desired changes in our government could be brought by either the Republicans or the Democrats. I mentioned the so-called insurgents.

"Most of them are followers rather than leaders," he said. "They wait for enough people to create a tide in favor of a certain measure and then, and not until then, do they espouse it.

"If this were not the case you would find that they would come forward with definite plans; instead of which they primarily obstruct what has been proposed. I do believe that if their policy were constructive, instead of destructive, the result would be that men and women of this country would recognize the need of a new party."

"Do you believe that the average worker, whether he works by hand or brain, is getting a fair share of the national income?"

"I do not think that many people feel that the great mass of the American people has been getting a square deal. The great American principle of equality has become a myth.

"This is apparent more and more to the rank and file of our citizens. The depression has impressed the fact upon them to a greater degree. I can see a great party rising from all these classes, a genuine political party of opposition, based upon principles and not upon power and pelf resulting from doing errands for organized business.

"But," he continued, "even if a new party should come into power the necessary economic changes would not occur immediately. There must be something more than political action. There must be vital changes in education as well as in the attitude of men in responsible places in industry. The immediate and central issue, however, is of a definite political nature. Before desired legislative, administrative and judicial changes can be brought about, control of government must be redeemed from special interests, which have usurped it, and restored to the people. If this does not happen then political democracy is doomed."

"You then still believe in democracy?" I asked.

"I do," he answered, "provided that all those critics who claim that democratic government is a failure get down to business and, instead of finding fault with it, endeavor to direct attention to the economic forces which seriously threaten it.

"And this threat is a serious one. We are faced with a situation in which there is a conflict as great as that between the North and South seventy-five years ago. Either, the economically privileged groups are going to seize the reins of government and drive wherever they will, or else the people in general, the masses of hard-working, peaceably inclined men and women, are going to take hold and run things to promote general welfare."

Thomas Depicts the Socialist Utopia

by S. J. Woolf

SITTING IN the studio of a broadcasting company, surrounded by every evidence of the machine age. Norman Thomas posed for a drawing and stressed the failure of our present economic system to solve the problems which modern conditions have brought about. The artificially cooled room, its air fresh (though it had no windows), the microphones which would soon carry the voice of the Socialist candidate for President far over the ether, the maze of wires and other electrical contraptions were evidences of modern technical skill. Yet despite the advances brought about by new discoveries, he pointed out, man is economically no better off than when the power of his own hands, the muscles of a few animals, running water and blowing winds were the only forces he employed in his struggle for existence.

"I believe," Mr. Thomas said, "that historical evolution and the development of a machine age have brought us to a place where our only escape from disaster lies in the social ownership and management for use, not for profit, of the things necessary for the common life."

The clustered chandelier on the ceiling threw gleaming highlights on his prominent forehead, his narrow nose with its arched nostrils, and his heavy upper lip. His wavy hair is steely gray and now grows far back from the temples. This accentuates the dome-like shape of his head which is further emphasized by the low position of his small ears. He is essentially an intellectual type. There is nothing of either the fanatic or the demagogue about him. Nor, despite his sense of humor, might he be described in any way as a "happy warrior."

The woes of the world rest heavily upon him. He is above all else intense and serious, and had not fate by a strange prank turned him to socialism he might have remained to the end of his days a minister in an established church. The one trait which prevented that is his hatred of orthodoxy of any kind.

Born in Marion, Ohio, forty-nine years ago, Mr. Thomas is descended on one side from a long line of Welsh Presbyterian preachers, on the other from French Huguenots who originally settled at Southampton.

"I was not very strong as a child," he said, "and up to the time I was 16 years old my chief recollections are spells of sickness. I was tall and lanky, and, though I played when I was well, so far as I can remember the only thing for which I was distinguished at high school was the fact that I was the champion high kicker. Some of my friends say that I still hold that distinction.

"Another thing that perhaps I should mention, though what bearing it has on my later life I am not sure, is the fact that as a boy I delivered The Marion Daily Star, which was published by a certain Warren G. Harding, on a regular route.

"The summer that I was graduated from high school my father, who like most of his forebears was a Presbyterian minister, became pastor of a church in Lewisburg, Pa., and all our family moved there. This was a small town much nicer than Marion and with much lovelier surroundings. For a year I attended Bucknell College, but I had read Jesse Lynch Williams's stories about Princeton and they made me anxious to go there. A relative who had more money than my father offered to pay part of the expenses and in 1902 a rather green lad entered as a fresh-sophomore. I spent three happy years there. They opened for me many doors of opportunity."

Circumstances pointed to the ministry. Walter Wyckoff's "The

Workers," Eugene Debs's leadership in the Socialist party and the difficulty of reconciling ethics with the crude, hard-fisted economics of the "new capitalism" were obstacles, but for the time being parental example overcame them. After his graduation from Princeton and service as a settlement worker in the city's slums he became a minister.

For eight or ten years he occupied various pulpits in New York, but his principal work seems to have been in the parish houses. There men came not because of their belief in Calvin but by reason of their interest in the young minister, who was already offering new visions for an old world.

It was probably the war which caused the ultimate break between Thomas and the ministry. Unable to understand how a preacher of the gospel of the Prince of Peace could exhort men to fight, he turned toward the Socialist party as the exponent of pacifism in the troubled world of that time.

"After my resignation as a minister," Mr. Thomas told me, "I founded a magazine, The World Tomorrow, which is still being published. I was connected with The Nation for a year. I also tried to make The Call, the Socialist daily, a big labor paper, but failed in this. I also became a director of the League for Industrial Democracy, an organization which in colleges and elsewhere is trying to help men and women see the necessity for a new social order based on production for use rather than for profit. I still work for the league.

"It was not until eight years ago that I became a chronic office seeker"—here he smiled—"but since then I have run for something every year with a beautiful impartiality. It has made no difference to me whether the office was Alderman or President.

"I must not forget to tell you also that I have been arrested three times and in jail twice for short periods. This has happened in connection with my work for the American Civil Liberties Union, and I am proud of it. In every case we won our claim, which, after all, shows that although American justice is far from what it ought to be, nevertheless it is not so entirely imperfect that one can never win a righteous cause."

Today Norman Thomas sees in socialism the only hope for the world in its disturbed state.

"I believe this," he said, "because I believe in democracy, and because socialism alone of all political systems can so develop democracy as to prevent another such economic cataclysm as is overpowering us now. Moreover, I see an increasing danger of fascism unless socialism is adopted to combat it. Even the Communists, with their proclamation of inevitable violence and their tactics within labor organizations, are unwittingly aiding fascism.

"Here in America we must depend upon a genuine democracy of the workers with hand and brain, and not upon any dictatorship. But unless conditions are changed a strong man will arise and we shall see the same thing happen in this country that has happened in Italy and is beginning in Germany now.

"Democracy, providing the class struggle is ended by the establishment of a classless society, is better than any kind of dictatorship and will serve the interest of the great mass of people as against the interest of one group of them."

I interrupted to ask the essential differences between socialism and communism.

"Socialism differs from communism," he answered, "in the vital matter of tactics and in the emphasis we place upon the value of freedom now, without waiting for an ultimately perfect socialistic society. I refer especially to those aspects of freedom that we class as civil and religious liberties.

"Both Socialists and Communists are unalterably opposed to the capitalistic system and both desire to found a new one in which production will be for use and not for profit. But we desire a peaceful revolution, while the Communists feel that nothing can be effected until a dictatorship of the Communist party is set up.

"We respect the devotion and zeal of many Communists and we are in entire sympathy with the substantial economic achievements of Russia. Personally, I believe that the Russian revolution is one of the events from which men will date an epoch. Think of the economic achievements against the heavy odds; machinery is being harnessed to general service, men are working hard for something other than great profit, and a planned economy is succeeding. The educational and cultural work of the Soviets is also enormously significant.

"But the continuing rigor and ruthlessness of the dictatorship raise new problems for the future even in Russia, with its czaristic background—problems that would be enormously greater and less excusable and more disturbing in America. The Communist insistence on inevitable large-scale violence and ruthless dictatorship promises here in America not even such good results as Russia has achieved out of great suffering."

"Suppose," I said, "you were elected President. What would be your first step?"

"If I were elected President," he replied, "my first step would be to mobilize the country for war on unemployment along socialistic lines. The vital thing for which I would work would be to transfer the natural resources and the principal means of production from private to public hands, from management for private profit to management for public use."

I inquired if being opposed to private profit he was also opposed to private property.

"Under socialism," he relied, "men generally would have more private property in consumption goods. I see no reason why there should not be sure tenure of house, garden and farm on condition of occupancy and use and probably payment of a land-value tax. Hand tools would also be privately owned. But absentee ownership would be progressively and rapidly ended. So would all inheritance of the sort represented by stocks and bonds and rent rolls.

"Of course," he continued, "the ending of inheritance would depend on the progress of socialization, and in a transitional state some consideration would have to be given to a wife and to children who were dependents.

"The program may sound harsh, but I cannot too strongly insist that a proper management of our resources and machinery would mean abundance for all. Socialism proposes to build a civilization on abundance, not upon want and insecurity. In industrially advanced America that ought to be easier than in Russia.

"You must remember that under socialism great fortunes would be prevented by preventing private ownership and manipulation of natural resources, credit, public utilities and great monopolies or semi-monopolies. Such ownership and manipulation and speculation are the sole source of great fortunes.

"There would also be in a transitional society upper and lower limits on salaries and wages. In the transitional stage socialism would make extensive use of a tax appropriating for society the land values which society creates, and drastic income and inheritance taxes would be imposed not merely to limit fortunes but also to help in the transferring of ownership to the State."

"How can governments, in which there is always more or less corruption, run industries?" I asked.

"The trouble with all governments," he answered, "is the capitalistic system. That is what makes for corruption and also for inefficiency. Government is corrupted by seekers after special privilege. However, even under the present system many departments of government are more efficient than a whole lot of businesses, and for that matter more honest too. The crimes and follies of Wall Street have cost us more than those of Tammany Hall. And when I say this, you know that I am no defender of Tammany.

"We expect to set up a new sort of commonwealth, with new ideals, in which engineers will work for society instead of for absentee owners. No modern Socialist wants bureaucratic political government of industries through a set of Postmaster Generals or their equivalents. What we want is public ownership, with title vested in the nation or the State or even the municipality, but control vested in such public authority as will best look after the interests not of private owners but of producers and consumers. In every case we would put a premium on efficiency. We would temper bureaucracy, however, by a recognition of the union and direct sanction of public bargaining. And it goes almost without saying that with socialized industries should go along a development of consumers' cooperation in the distribution of goods, for distribution is as important as production."

He pointed out, when I asked how production and distribution could be coordinated, that this was implied in the Socialist conception of production for use, not for profit.

"The more equitable distribution of income," he said, "will of itself tend to promote a more steady and reasonable demand for goods. But a machine age requires national and international planning and a planning board. I believe in plan, and I further insist, as against some who talk economic planning, that the question of purpose—for whom and for what we should plan—is of positive importance."

While Mr. Thomas was speaking a radio announcer entered, and a glance at the clock showed me that in a few minutes he would have to go on the air. I hurried.

"In such a State as you propose," I asked, "would men have free choice of their life work?"

"A man would be at least as free to choose his work or profession as now," he said; "probably more so, when you consider that today accident, ignorance and dire need exercise a compelling power.

"Choice will be made on the basis of vocational fitness and upon the forecast of a regularly made public future need for workers. Influence, guidance, attraction perhaps by variation in rewards there will be. Conscription there need not be. Even in Russia despite all the industrial backwardness under communism, there is not general job conscription. There certainly would not be in America under socialism.

"We do not believe it is possible to cure unemployment without adopting socialism as a system," he went on. "We are in no sense of the word social reformers, but we are convinced that the world needs most of all a new purpose and a new philosophy and that the more widely this revolutionary new philosophy is spread the faster we shall progress. On the other hand, Russia has shown us that our goal cannot be achieved at one fell swoop.

"Of course ours is a movement of men, not supermen, and therefore disappointments and failures are bound to occur. But nowhere except in socialism do I find an answer to the great problems of our machine civilization—a solution by which men of all nations and races, who have become more and more interdependent upon one another by reason of inventions and discoveries, can meet the challenge of their day and generation."

Roosevelt's View
of the Big Job

by Anne O'Hare McCormick

THE FIRST IMPRESSION produced by the Democratic candidate for the Presidency is that of the fortunate man who is doing what he most likes to do, a man who enjoys his present office, is eagerly on his way to one he will like better, and in all circumstances maintains a "smilin' through" philosophy and a singular zest for the adventure of life. In those good old days when he nominated the Happy Warrior, he was, like the painter who suggests his own characteristics in his portraits of others, extolling the political temperament he has successfully cultivated in himself.

When I first saw Franklin D. Roosevelt, at the Cox notification ceremonies in Dayton in 1920, he was a handsome and radiant figure, faring forth on a hopeless campaign with a smile of gay good humor. Twelve years later he swooped down from the skies to accept his own nomination from the Chicago convention. In the interval he had suffered one political defeat mostly vicarious, and a physical disaster so valorously surmounted and lightly borne that it has become almost an asset. Otherwise his luck has held: the luck of being a well-born and comfortably circumstanced American, happily following a chosen career, mounting with rapid steps the political pyramid until at 50 he stands at the apex, leader of his party in a year when the winds blow in his direction.

Back in 1900 Governor Roosevelt, then a candidate for the State Senate, made the first automobile campaign. He made another precedent when he flew to Chicago, and by that characteristic touch of drama, plus the same smile, now more fixed and deepened, like his voice, he succeeded in dissipating the glumness of an assembly that toward the end had gone heavy and more than a little sour. His campaign speeches have a similarly inspiriting effect. He is not a speaker to raise the echoes and the temperature, like Governor Smith, but he does raise the hopes of the Democrats, and their eyes to the Promised Land.

It is in Albany, however, on the job and eating it up, that his gusto is most impressive. There you see him stimulated by the stir and movement, the light and spotlight, of the public tournament. He enjoys attacking the problems of administration. He relishes the stratagems and surprises of the election fight. Above all he loves the crowding contacts with all sorts of people. He has something of the indiscriminate enthusiasm, the "dee-light" of the first Roosevelt. His first interest, he says, is in the theory and practice of government; his second is in people. When he speaks of "humanizing government," a favorite phrase, he means bringing the two more closely together. If called upon to move in, he would "humanize the White House," too, and at Albany you can imagine what effect that might have on the pleasant, pitilessly public but austere domicile of the Presidents.

Stodgy and heavily Victorian in outward aspect, the Executive Mansion of New York State under the present régime is probably the most informal official residence in the country. This is also a house without privacy, but nobody seems to mind. It is a house full of life and laughter. The Governor's ready laugh rings out from nearly any room, the members of the family have a lot of fun among themselves; even the visitors are cheerful. It is a house of wide-open doors and few secrets. The Governor's study is immediately to the left of the front door and he is not only visible but apparently accessible to anyone who enters. People seem to wander in and out, glancing at the telegrams on the hall table, eavesdropping if they will, examining the books piled up on the tables in all the rooms, in variety like a circulating library of current publications. The day I was there a reporter picked up a copy of Stuart Chase's "A New Deal," and discovered fifty new one-dollar bills between the pages, so sent as a campaign contribution.

This was an off day. The Walker hearings were suspended and the Governor did not go to the Capitol. He took advantage of the first lull in three weeks to catch up with his correspondence, dispose of accumulated routine business of the State and map out the series of speeches for his Western trip. As if this were not enough, with an interview or two thrown in, in the afternoon there were hearings on the cases of two prisoners condemned to death in Sing Sing; a two-hour conference with representatives of the railway workers' unions, invited by the Governor to give their views on a perplexing public question; a discussion with two State Commissioners on new power houses; a review with counsel of Judge Staley's decision on the Walker appeal; the daily press conference. There were besides a stream of other callers, letters to sign, a dozen calls over the long-distance telephone.

All the motion and commotion, the flow of people and talk, naturally revolved around Governor Roosevelt. He moved from room to room, everywhere interrupted, but always unhurried, unworried, good-humored, interested in everything and everybody, thoroughly enjoying himself; in his element. Between-times, at odd intervals, I asked questions, which he answered with great facility. Not only is he quick-minded, but so pat and fluent, speaking in paragraphs and never hesitating for a word, that he might have written out his answers. My last interval was at half past 10 at night, and when I left, some time after 11, to catch a train, he was still untired and smiling, starting in to draft a radio speech.

An interview under such circumstances is not wholly satisfactory, but the glimpse it affords into the mind and methods of a possible President is revealing. To an onlooker, the "off day" seemed unorganized and overcrowded. At the end, however, you saw that Governor Roosevelt in his casual way had tossed off a volume of work and had exerted his well-known charm on a considerable number of people. The railway union men, for example. At first they sat in a stiff circle, reserved and quiet. In no time they were in a close huddle, all smoking, shooting questions and answers as fast as they could. The charm is interest, in Roosevelt real and inexhaustible.

Anyway, systematic or not, that is the way he works. He likes to know something about everything. He is a great "skimmer" of books, he says: books on history, biography, economics; as a hobby, books on naval affairs, of which he has the largest collection outside the Navy Department; as a diversion, detective stories and children's books, particularly the latter, in which he finds huge delight and also texts about Alice in Wonderland and the Delphic Oracle to illustrate policies of his political opponents. He admires the encyclopedic, the versatile mind. To him the four most interesting men in American history are those most distinguished for their many-sidedness, men of sufficient range and curiosity, as he puts it, to take in the whole sweep of civilization. They are Jefferson, Franklin, Count Rumford, that early New England genius, scientist, sociologist and political philosopher who spent most of his time illuminating the courts of Europe, and Theodore Roosevelt.

One guesses that "T. R.," to whom he constantly refers and whose career his own parallels in so many particulars, is the north star in Franklin Roosevelt's firmament. All the Roosevelts were Democrats until the Civil War, when they became what was known as Lincoln Democrats. Most of the clan returned to the fold in Tilden's time, but James Roosevelt, Theodore's father, remained an independent. Whether or not his progressivism derives from T. R., the example of his distant and distinguished kinsman fired the imagination of Franklin from his earliest years and probably set the course of his life. After a family caucus he voted for Theodore in 1904, "because he was a Roosevelt," but not in 1912; by that time Wilson had emerged and "T. R. had no chance of election." T. R. gave away his niece on the day of her marriage to her sixth cousin, of all Franklin's lucky days the luckiest, as everyone agrees who knows the part played by Mrs. Roosevelt in her husband's life. "Let's keep the name in the family," chuckled the first Roosevelt on that occasion.

It is a potent name, easily the most potent influence in the destiny of Franklin Roosevelt. Yet, though the Governor's versatile interests and unconventional methods are Rooseveltian, they do represent, nevertheless, his own conception of the personal and human relationship that should exist between the Executive and his State and, by extension, between the Chief Executive and the nation. He thinks that the President should personify government to the citizen, should express the ideas germinating, ready for realization, in the popular mind.

"The Presidency," he says, "is not merely an administrative office. That's the least of it. It is more than an engineering job, efficient or inefficient. It is preeminently a place of moral leadership. All of our great Presidents were leaders of thought at times when certain historic ideas in the life of the nation had to be clarified. Washington personified the idea of federal union. Jefferson practically originated the party system as we know it by opposing the democratic theory to the republicanism of Hamilton. This theory was reaffirmed by Jackson. Two great principles of our government were forever put beyond question by Lincoln. Cleveland, coming into office following an era of great political corruption, typified rugged honesty. T. R. and Wilson were both moral leaders, each in his own way and for his own time, who used the Presidency as a pulpit.

"Isn't that what the office is—a superb opportunity for reapplying, applying in new conditions, the simple rules of human conduct we always go back to? I stress the modern application, because we are always moving on; the technical and economic environment changes, and never so quickly as now. Without leadership alert and sensitive to change, we are bogged up or lose our way, as we have lost it in the past decade."

"And you?" I asked. "Is that the reason you want to be President? What particular affirmation or reaffirmation is required of the national leader of today?"

The Governor laughed. "Months before the nomination I told you I didn't know why any man should want to be President. I repeat that I didn't grow up burning to go to the White House, like the American boy of legend rather than of fact. I have read history and known Presidents; it's a terrible job. But somebody has to do it. I suppose I was picked out because the majority of the party thought I was the best vote-getter. Now that I am picked out, naturally I want to be President. I want to win." He laughed again, then went on gravely:

"The objective now, as I see it, is to put at the head of the nation someone whose interests are not special but general, someone who can understand and treat with the country as a whole. For as much as anything it needs to be reaffirmed at this juncture that the United States is one organic entity, that no interest, no class, no section, is either separate or supreme above the interests of all or divorced from the interests of all. We hear a good deal about the interdependence of the nations of the world. In the pit of universal calamity, with every country smothered by its own narrow policies and the narrow policies of other countries— and that goes for us, too—everyone sees that connection. But there is a nearer truth, often forgotten or ignored, and that is the interdependence of every part of our own country.

"No valid economic sectionalism exists in these States. There are opposed economic interests within every section, town against country, suburb against city, but as a nation we are all mixed up, fluid. All the States are in some degree like New York, a blend of agriculture and industry. The rural South is changing, the Western prairies are planted with factory towns. East and West, as we use the terms, are mostly states of mind, not localized but everywhere. What we need is a common mind, and, even more, common sense to realize that if we are not acting for the interest of the whole country we are acting against the interests of every section."

Perhaps this is Governor Roosevelt's answer to the charge that he is trying to be all things to all sections, conservative in the East, radical in the West; he simply denies that there are sections in that sense. He classifies himself as a liberal. I asked what he meant by that elastic term, how he defined the difference between the outlooks vaguely called conservative and progressive, or between his program and that of the opposing party.

"Let's put it this way," he explained. "Every few years, say every half generation, the general problems of civilization change in such a way that new difficulties of adjustment are presented to government. The forms have to catch up with the facts. The radical, in order to meet these difficulties, jumps, jumps in groups, because he doesn't count unless he's part of a group. One group usually differs from another in its program, but they are all equally definite and dogmatic about it. They lay down categorical terms—'my plan or none.' Their characteristic is hard-and-fast processes, cut-and-dried methods, uncompromising formulas. The conservative says: 'No, we're not ready for change. It's dangerous. Let's wait and see what happens.' Halfway in between is the liberal, who recognizes the need of new machinery for new needs but who works to control the processes of change, to the end that the break with the old pattern may not be too violent.

"Or say that civilization is a tree which, as it grows, continually produces rot and dead wood. The radical says: 'Cut it down.' The conservative says: 'Don't touch it.' The liberal compromises: 'Let's prune, so that we lose neither the old trunk nor the new branches.' This campaign is waged to teach the country to move upon its appointed course, the way of change, in an orderly march, avoiding alike the revolution of radicalism and the revolution of conservatism."

In this credo of the liberal is nothing new but rather the echo of something very old, the voice of the country gentleman in politics. The voice was dominant in the early history of the Republic. It is familiar still in England. And in fact it expresses what is most deeply rooted in Franklin Roosevelt. He differs from T. R. in being country-bred instead of town-bred; fundamentally he is up-State and not New York City. He farms, plants, is himself planted in what is, for America, the ancient, coercive soil of Dutchess County. When he speaks of understanding the country as a whole, he is identifying himself, consciously or unconsciously, with those who have settled this continent and who now, across the plains, are bewildered to see it passing out of their control.

Like Henry Ford, the repentant mass producer, Roosevelt goes back to the soil for his solutions. Like Ford, he believes in de-centralization of industry, sees the same loss of balance between the country and the town. Pressed for definite specifics which he would offer, or order, were he in power, as remedies for our present economic ills, he always contends that you have to begin at the base. You cannot build a healthy industrial civilization, he says, until you restore the solvency and purchasing power of the farm.

"I agree," he declares, "that our main problem is to get people back to work. All programs that fail to do that do precisely nothing. Until unemployment is cured, we're sick, and will get sicker. Unemployment insurance is necessary, but it's the second step, not the first. It cannot meet the present emergency. I believe we could spend $2,000,000,000 in construction work, partly self-liquidating, without bankrupting the country. With effective economy in government, it would hardly increase taxes. But that's not enough, either. Unemployment was increasing long before the depression. It's inevitable when half the population had lost its purchasing power. That's the fellow you've got to start building up, the farmer."

Governor Roosevelt will develop his farm relief proposals in his speech at Topeka. They include a sharp reduction in rural taxes and reforestation of marginal lands, a national program based on what he has accomplished in New York, where since 1929 the State has purchased at nominal rates and reforested more than 102,000 acres, giving employment to something like 10,000 men in each planting season. The main remedy, however, is a measure no longer called the equalization fee, a debenture plan or any of the old names, but described simply as the extension of the benefits of the tariff to the growers of the great export crops —wheat, cotton, &c.—"temporarily," he qualifies, and "on that part of the crop consumed in this country."

If that brings up the whole vexed question of tariffs, on which the Democratic record is no longer clear, it at least puts the farmer in the vicious circle along with the rest of us. Unlike President Hoover, Governor Roosevelt believes that tariff is a foreign policy. He goes a bit further, or at least further than the party platform, in proposing to call at once an international conference to discuss export and import duties. "The entire question is now reduced to such absurdity," he says, "that all nations are ready for a new deal. They all know, even while they keep on adding new spikes to the wall, that there can be no world recovery without a flow of world trade. Trade is exchange; you can't argue away that fact. We'll have to go back to some form of reciprocal barter, and we'll have to do it soon."

The way of the liberal is the middle way, the way of compromise. Compromise is the essential tool of the fine art of politics. "To accomplish anything worth while," Governor Roosevelt once wrote, "it is necessary to compromise between the ideal and the practical." He himself is an adroit politician. He has the great political gift of playing the game with spirit but without rancor. He can fight hard with good temper; all that happened before his nomination he has already forgotten.

The way of the campaigner is the way of attack, and Governor Roosevelt is a good campaigner, ready, friendly, vigorous, sharp to seize every advantage of the offensive, and to hold it. He may be expected to give a good show of fight wherever he goes and to find all the weak places in the enemy position. When all is said, the Lochinvar who rides out of the East will ride on his personality, on his zest and gusto and confidence, on his eighteen-carat American background, on the blind desire to punish and to change, which is the mood of crisis.

Three "Pied Pipers" of the Depression

by Francis Brown

DISCONTENT BUBBLES throughout America. One does not need to be an alarmist to detect the signs. A remark overheard on the street corner; talk along the bar of the neighborhood café; reports of labor troubles—all these have significance. But they count as little when compared with the indisputable mass-surging behind leaders who would sow the wind.

Who are these leaders, these "Pied Pipers"? At the moment three stand out above all others—Father Coughlin, Huey Long and Dr. Frank E. Townsend. Each is a product of the economic crisis; each has tightened his hold because of the present domestic unpleasantness; each extends the promise to abolish poverty. Their greatest ally is the radio, for with it, as General Johnson said in his recent denunciatory address, "they can pollute our great popular pool of justified resentment."

A public, which for want of work sits idly before the radio, receives almost daily from them "red pepper for its raw emotions and—for its hope—enticing promises of a money miracle—

From the *New York Times Magazine,* March 17, 1935, copyright © 1935, 1963 by The New York Times Company.

manna in the wilderness of despair." When Father Coughlin last Monday came back at General Johnson, giving measure for measure, he forgot neither the red pepper nor the manna.

The "leaders" differ in method and in the details of their promise. Father Coughlin wishes to organize a great lobby that will overawe Congress. Huey Long depends on direct political action and the ballot. Dr. Townsend employs the constitutional right of petition. Coughlin is more general in his promise than either Long or Townsend, but they are as one in their concern for monetary manipulation which, with the aid of the power to tax, will usher in the Utopia of plenty.

A promise to abolish poverty would attract followers in any age. It has still greater appeal in this time of troubles, when men and women have been told, not by rabble-rousers but by sober scholars, that America has entered upon an era of potential plenty, when poverty can be abolished. That is the American Idea which has been shouted from political platforms and into broadcasters' microphones. The Idea is as old as the country, but for the moment, twisted and distorted, it is the stock in trade of false prophets.

The Idea, nevertheless, has found its mark among farmers and skilled workers and that large segment of the population grouped under the heading, white-collar workers. These are the people who have been hardest hit by the depression, who have seen their life savings swept away by bank failures, who have lost homes purchased in the happy Nineteen Twenties. They have lived, and do live, in the shadow of insecurity, fearful that the job which exists today will be gone tomorrow. They have lost confidence in the old promise of a chicken in every pot, even as they have lost confidence in those who made that promise. These are the folk who plumped for Mr. Roosevelt in 1932 because he seemed to offer release from woe. But today they are not so sure, and countless numbers of them have gone chasing after Long and Coughlin and Townsend.

People who have experienced five years of ugly misery are in no mood to avoid strange byways if these may lead to a long-sought goal. That goal is social security. The American multitude has made up its mind that, come what may, it will not undergo again the experience of the depression. Americans want security; they have been told that it is attainable; they insist that they will have it.

In this regard it should not be forgotten that during the winter of 1932–33 the technocrats were busy sowing the idea that the country had reached a stage where agriculture and industry could produce enough to feed and clothe and house everyone in adequate fashion. In other words, the age of scarcity had passed into history. Were our economic system properly organized, the technocrats said, everyone could enjoy an annual income of $20,000 or thereabouts. That idea seeped through America, exciting women's clubs no less than workers' forums, and though the technocrats have gone, the idea of potential abundance persists. To a people in quest of security that is a weighty thought.

Security can be all things to all men. It may mean only insurance against unemployment or against a penniless old age. It may suggest the application to present conditions of fantastic panaceas. It may go so far as to require the remaking of society, or it may be achieved with the removal of particularly crying abuses. The very indefiniteness of security permits its misuse by the spellbinder.

For a long time now the bespectacled Father Coughlin with his deep, burring voice, has been broadcasting Sunday after Sunday from the Shrine of the Little Flower in the Detroit suburb of Royal Oak. Originally his broadcasts were intended to build up a feeble parish, but gradually they did much more. By denouncing the maladjusted portions of our economic system, Father Coughlin gained national influence. For a time—though that now seems long ago—he was even regarded as a spokesman for the New Deal. And he still insists that it is "Roosevelt or ruin."

Father Coughlin, like Huey Long and Dr. Townsend, is a phenomenon of the depression. His hold, like theirs, is on the battered, smarting skilled workers and farmers, clerks and petty bosses. Go into any shop on Monday morning and ask about Father Coughlin's remarks of the previous afternoon. Quickly a discussion will develop, for all have heard the stinging words that came through the ether from the Shrine of the Little Flower. A year ago it was estimated that Father Coughlin reached 10,000,000 radio listeners; today the number is probably greater.

Father Coughlin avoids specific proposals for social security, even though the exhortation to abolish want in the present of plenty recurs in all his broadcasts. Though he has sponsored a government-owned central bank and has pleaded for a "sound" currency which will not fluctuate in value over the years, he has not been so rash as to promise a $200-a-month pension or a $5,000-a-year income.

Instead, he has been content to talk about a living wage, about profits for the farmer, about government-protected labor unions. He insists that human rights be placed above property rights. He emphasizes the "wickedness" of "private financialism and production for profit." It is all quite vague, but Father Coughlin's strength lies in his vagueness, since he is thus able to play on the hopes and prejudices of various groups in the population.

Last November, a few days after he had begun his forty-fourth year, Father Coughlin formed the National Union for Social Justice. He expects to enroll 10,000,000 members, welding them into a lobby that will force Congress to bow to its bidding. That he already commands a powerful lobby he showed during the recent Senate vote on American entry into the World Court. The blizzard of telegrams which at Father Coughlin's request was loosed upon the Senators gave notice that a new force had entered American politics.

There has for months been a rumor that Father Coughlin and Huey Long had joined forces. This rumor was brought into the open by General Johnson's speech, in which the general not only characterized the priest and the Senator as "a couple of Catilines," but declared that there is an "open alliance between the great Louisiana demagogue and this political padre."

Huey Long is a demagogue; he is self-seeking and unscrupulous, but he speaks dramatically the thought of the masses. He has known how to capitalize on the general urge for security. That he is a shrewd strategist he showed when, instead of replying to General Johnson's bitter attack, he broadcast to the nation the principles of the Share-Our-Wealth Society. This loose organization, scarcely a year old, has several million members who are sure that every man can be a king. They believe Huey's bombast. He speaks their language, even to his frequent use of biblical analogy.

Huey Long's followers know that their own lot is sorry, that a vast army in the United States is unemployed, that wealth is concentrated in the hands of a few. And they also know—it amounts to that—that America is a land of plenty. When Huey Long assures them that through the Share-Our-Wealth Society every family in the country can have an annual income of $5,000,000, they believe him without further questioning. Why? In part because of the persistent idea of abundance; in part because of Huey himself.

Is not Huey Long the personification of the forgotten man's hopes? Huey began with nothing; he has become something. Nor has he forgotten the masses from whom he sprang. Uncultivated and vulgar though he may be, these are qualities which the average American finds not so displeasing. And the Senator from Louisiana is clever; he is witty; he puts on a good show. When he tweaks the beard of some pompous banker or statesman, he does only what the common man for generations has wanted nerve enough to do. Because of the events of the past five years or more, it is still more popular to disregard the likes or suggestions of those who hold economic power. And it thus becomes possible to base a Share-Our-Wealth movement upon a soak-the-rich policy.

"We do not create a state of mind," one of Huey Long's lieutenants has said, "we merely discover and recognize a state of mind that has been created by conditions." That is another way of saying that radicals do not breed discontent, that discontent breeds radicals. And it is true that without popular discontent Huey Long would never be where he is.

After Senator Long's first national broadcast on Share Our Wealth, he received 64,000 replies; only nine of them, according to reports, opposed his views. There have been other broadcasts since which have brought from ordinarily sober people the comment: "He talks like a crazy man—but his ideas do seem to make sense." The Long movement, though yet to demonstrate its full strength, is on its way, and the Presidential bee buzzing noisily in Huey's bonnet has become publicly audible.

Father Coughlin and Huey Long are loud and spectacular. Their influence cannot be laughed away, yet it is doubtful whether either man has created half as much stir as that for which the rather shadowy Dr. Frank E. Townsend is responsible. And this is because Dr. Townsend, with his old-age revolving pension plan, has appealed more directly to the popular desire for security.

Dr. Townsend, until illness drove him to California, was a country physician in South Dakota's Black Hills. For many years, as assistant health officer in Long Beach, Calif., he came in contact with the aged and ailing. These people, so he believed, worried themselves sick over their possible fate in old age; the obvious cure seemed to be the removal of the threat of the poorhouse. Out of some such reasoning Dr. Townsend, an economic amateur, developed his pension plan.

It is all very simple. All over 60 who cease working for pay and who are not habitual criminals are to receive a pension of $200 a month. The pensions will be financed by a sales tax and the $200 will have to be spent within a month of being received. Dr. Townsend—he is 68 and knows well the mind of the class to which he belongs—contends that his plan will bring both security and prosperity. The aged will be removed from the labor market, thus aiding employment; the money they spend will stimulate business. Unfortunately, the economists are not on his side. They point out that even were the rest of the plan feasible, the sales tax to finance it would have to be so large that trade would be stifled.

Yet Townsend-Plan Clubs have spread from California to Maine; signatures on petitions for the plan have been gathered at filling stations; the plan has been outlined on the radio and from the platform. Recently the lean, spare, rather withered doctor asserted that he has 20,000,000 supporters for his ideas. Small wonder that the Townsend movement was described to a Senate committee as "the finest promotion job in American history."

The naive but hopeful millions behind Dr. Townsend agree with him that "if we persist in our present crazy plan of starving in the midst of plenty we deserve to remain in the midst of depression." They find true wisdom in his insistence that "the time has come to abolish poverty." So definitely does Dr. Townsend's plan express the aspirations of the American masses that, to quote an experienced observer, "to lack faith in it is like expressing doubt of the goodness of God."

Governor Merriam of California has come out for the Townsend plan; it has interested several State Legislatures, and though Congressional committees have laughed at Dr. Townsend, members of those committees secretly fear what may happen should the Old-Age Revolving Pension Plan ever reach the floor of either chamber.

All these men—Coughlin, Long, Townsend—appeal to the emotions. They utilize prejudice, fear, hope. Particularly do they hold out the vision of a better day not far distant. What they seem to intend is to execute some clever yet simple manoeuvre, some sleight-of-hand; then, presto! the millennium. Call them spellbinders, rabble-rousers, demagogues, or what you will, they cannot be lightly dismissed in the present temper of the country.

These men belong to the Nineteen Thirties; their methods and measures are of this day. Yet they fit into the traditional pattern of American movements of protest. Another generation had its "Pitchfork" Tillman, its Bryan, its Mary Ellen Lease, who wanted Kansas to raise less corn and more hell. Social distress lifted them into leadership even as the present distress has brought Coughlin and Long to the fore. Another age had its currency cranks; this one apparently is to have its pension cranks, of whom Dr. Townsend is the first to attain national prominence. The return of prosperity in the past destroyed the power of so-called radicals, and one can be sure that if prosperity returned to the United States tomorrow no more would be heard of Coughlin and Townsend.

But if there should be no recovery—that is another question. Then the present discontent can be expected to continue, creating other "radical" leaders at the same time that it aids the fortunes of a man like Huey Long. The fact to bear in mind is the popular insistence that security be realized and guaranteed, for upon this insistence Long and Coughlin and Townsend depend for their continued influence.

Whatever may be the fate of these individuals, they are planting firmly in the minds of Americans the belief that a new era, an era of social justice and plenty, can be ushered in. It is not that the idea itself is new or dangerous, but that extravagant hopes have been built around it.

Part 2

THE NEW DEAL AS REFORM

THE STRIKING THING about Anne McCormick's interview with Roosevelt in this section is the effort to portray the President as conservative. He himself takes pains to do this, and so does McCormick in her summary. The implication is clear: in the country at large he was being viewed as a radical, someone who would seriously alter the society. Notice in the article, too, how careful Roosevelt is to eschew ideology or dogma. Always his emphasis is upon methods, not ends.

The Delbert Clark article, which appeared almost a year later, reflects a somewhat different situation, one in which Roosevelt is now adrift, not knowing exactly where he is going. This article, incidentally, is one of the earliest to set forth the thesis that in 1935 Franklin Roosevelt shifted ground from the First to the Second New Deal. (The conception has been discussed more fully in the Introduction.) Noteworthy in the article is the suggestion that Roosevelt may move against the Supreme Court because it has been so unfriendly toward New Deal measures. In early 1937, Roosevelt did precisely that with his effort to enlarge ("pack") the Court. Clark's surmise here is premature, to say the least, but it reveals a good journalist's understanding of the direction the thinking of New Dealers was taking in 1935. Once again, despite the depiction of Roosevelt as anti-business, the thrust of the article is a defense of him against charges of radicalism.

The remaining six articles in this section are intended to illuminate the nature of the New Deal's activities. Frank Hill's piece on the Indians calls attention to a neglected reform of the New Deal, for the Wheeler-Howard Act of 1934 is one of the most important pieces of Indian legislation ever passed in the United States Congress. To call it a "New Deal" for the Indians would be appropriate and accurate. Something, too, of the international context in which the New Deal operated is provided in the article by R. L. Duffus on the TVA. He pointedly contrasts this New Deal agency with the methods used by the Nazis and Fascists in their efforts at social change. Duffus' article also calls attention to one of the early objections to the TVA, namely, that all of the new electrical power being produced by the dams could not be absorbed usefully by the admittedly underdeveloped economy of the Tennessee Valley. Private power companies had predicted that it could not in order to justify their own refusal to expand the production of electric power. Today we know that the demand for electric power in the valley has far outrun the hydroelectric capacity of the TVA's dams. Most of the Authority's power is now produced by steam plants in order to meet the increasing requirements of the region which TVA has helped to develop.

Two articles have also been included on the New Deal's response to the plight of young people during the Depression. Never before had the federal government directly invested in young men and women, but as these two articles indicate, it was certainly time. VISTA and the Peace Corps are obvious descendants of the CCC, just as the fellowships under the present National Defense Education Act have their antecedents in the National Youth Administration. The reference in the article on the CCC to the banning of military indoctrination in the camps reflects the hostility toward the military that was also expressed in the society at large in the opposition to compulsory ROTC. The inevitable contrast with the Fascist and Nazi youth movements once again calls attention to the international context in which the New Deal was worked out. As in so many New Deal agencies, especially those dealing with the unemployed, the CCC is viewed as likely to continue as a permanent part of government activity. (For further discussion on the persistence of unemployment see Part 3.)

The New Deal's effort in the field of housing was merely a token, as the article by Albert Meyer makes evident. Yet that effort represented the beginning of a novel and ultimately permanent task for government, which at least the New Deal recognized, if it did not adequately attack.

Black people, as has been already noted in the Introduction, were not a direct or primary concern of the New Deal. Yet the programs of the Roosevelt administration, especially as they touched the South, where most Negroes lived, could not help altering the day-to-day lives of black people. "The Big World At Last Reaches Gee's Bend" is a dramatic description of how a completely black community in rural Alabama felt the transforming hands of the New Deal. For the historian of the period it is also more than that. It reveals something of the stereotypic ways in which the Negro was still being depicted in the press of the 1930's, even in a newspaper of the quality of the *New York Times*. For there is a superciliousness and paternalism about the author's description that today is offensive. Yet there is also a modern touch in his rejection of the idea that the blacks of Gee's Bend somehow be made into carbon copies of white men.

Roosevelt Surveys His Course

by Anne O'Hare McCormick

WASHINGTON

AS HE LEFT Washington to travel westward, President Roosevelt definitely set a milestone in his course and the course of the United States. A third of his administration lay behind him. He had signed the last of a long series of emergency measures of unprecedented scope and cost. For the first time since that bleak March day in 1933 when he took office—how far away and long ago it seems!—he paused for a look forward and backward along the chartless road he entered then. He paused, and America with him. Out of the whirl and daze induced by the strongest stimulants administered to any people in this crisis, the nation emerges in that stage of convalescence when the patient begins to ask questions and take an interest in the shape of the future.

The adjournment of the Seventy-third Congress marked the end of the first phase of the New Deal. Other, even greater, recovery measures may still be necessary, many already enacted may not stand the tests of time and experience, but in a general way the phase of hasty improvisation, of artificial stimulation, of experiments tried out in the heat of emergency, is felt to be over. The New Deal is organized, as any one can see who compares its entrenchments in Washington today with the tentative camps of a year ago. Now it moves on toward its permanent objectives.

What these objectives are the President indicated in his last message to Congress and his radio talk on the eve of his departure for the Pacific. The long-range program he sketched contains much that is new for the United States if not for other countries, but nothing Mr. Roosevelt himself has not pondered for years, nothing not already foreshadowed in the confused march of the past sixteen months. The chief cause of the confusion, indeed, the ragged tempo, the swings right and left, the advances and retreats, is the incidence of the permanent and the temporary. The rush of the immediate necessity deforms the larger plan just as the beat of the irrevocable slows up the speed and chills the spirit of the emergency helper. In its first stage the New Deal has been a collision on the job between the repair man and the rebuilder.

The second stage looms ahead, but meanwhile there is to be a breathing space. No one knows better than Mr. Roosevelt, whose sixth sense is the keenest of all his senses, that there are limits to popular capacity to digest new ideas. The country is due for a rest from edicts and experiments; it needs time either to learn to walk with crutches or to try out its power to walk unaided. It is too much to expect a vacation from partisan politics in a campaign year, but at least the blazing stage at Washington will be dark for the summer season. On 10,000 Main Streets, during the long twilights of the dog days, the America which has reached this point with Roosevelt will be able to look at itself, undistracted by the eye-filling show put on day after day at the White House.

Washington will continue to hum with old and new activities, all speeded up. The alphabetical good works will go on full tilt with increased staffs. Never since wartime has the capital been so crowded in July with perspiring young men saving their country. Only the headliners are absent. The members of the Cabinet will follow their chief into temporary retirement. "We shall have a new form of government this summer," smiles Mr. Roosevelt. "The Under-Secretaries, even the Assistant Secretaries, will be in command."

It was the fag end of a day before the evacuation. The capital was flayed by a typical blast of tropical heat. All day long the President had been besieged by last-minute visitors. He had signed or vetoed the final batch of Congressional bills. He had supervised the packing of cases full of reports to be studied and books to be enjoyed on the long cruise on the Houston. The books, he confessed, were mostly detective stories and biographies; "all other forms of modern fiction" bore him. Now he sat at ease on the circular terrace behind the White House, sipping iced tea and chatting as if there were nothing in the world to do but discuss the state of Europe with a returning traveler. Like any American gentleman relaxing on his back porch in the cool of the evening, I was about to say, but at the end of his day what other American executive is as fresh, as serene, as completely focused on the subject in hand? Or, for that matter, what lesser member of the Brain Trust?

The most remarkable and crowded year in the history of the Republic had gone by since I last saw Mr. Roosevelt. Whether or not he has been engineering a revolution depends on your definition of revolution. Certainly he has been fighting a war, a war on so many fronts and with forces so obscure that no war President had half as much to worry him. Yet here he was, apparently the least worried man in the country. Or in any country; of all the men in public life today he must be the least subject to moods, to highs and lows in the spiritual barometer. I recalled other rulers encountered in the interval, each struggling in his own way with the superhuman job of governing the ungovernable.

Mussolini, swinging between the deep pessimism of last year, when his Four-Power Pact hung in the balance, and the high spirits of six weeks ago, when he slid like a boy across the glassy marble floor of his office, big as a lake, to illustrate how he ski-ed. Hitler, running the gamut from cloudy to fair in a single interview, one moment morose and wooden, the next smiling and suave or rapt in some remote vision, the medium, so it seemed, of flickering emotions not his own. De Valera, the romantic schoolmaster, blazing with cold passion for an idea, fretting over the exact placing of an indefinite article. Dollfuss, the little Chancellor of a state of siege, depressed or elated according as the winds over Austria blew north or south. Stalin—but who knows what goes on behind that quiet mask, as even in its dark immobility as the sunny surface of Roosevelt?

A procession of statesmen, great or small, gloomy or gay, but all nervous, all dwelling in a climate sharply different from that temperate zone of the mind which President Roosevelt alone inhabits.

Evidently this ruler is not confused by confusion or overwhelmed by the overwhelming. He looks better than he did a year ago, a shade harder, browner, and as confident as ever. If there are chinks in his shining armor of assurance no one reports them. If his cheerfulness ever sags he conceals it from his intimates.

As Mr. Roosevelt looks back, it is easy to see that he appraises the New Deal as an educational method as well as a means to recovery. On the whole he is well satisfied. A year ago, facing the heavy pull ahead, he could not have anticipated, he says, that the country would be so far above bottom as it seems to him today. All the economic indices point to steady progress upward. With a long way yet to go in reviving confidence and increasing employment, the mood of crisis is passing. In his view the greatest change that has taken place is the change in the general state of mind and the most encouraging "lift" the rise in the level of public intelligence and social sense.

As a sign of the development of a new public mind, there is the remarkable expansion of the Brain Trust. Originally it consisted of only five members, the President himself, Professor Moley, Professor Tugwell, Louis Howe and Judge Samuel Rosenman. Now, according to Mr. Roosevelt, it is 250,000 strong and includes practically all those enlisted in the new government services.

Washington is full of this strange type of intellectual and enthusiastic bureaucrat. They form the army of "fine young men" that so impressed John Maynard Keynes, in contrast to the scarcity of the young in the public life of England. From the Bronx to Seattle come reports of the effective work they do in interpreting to the country the changed scope and spirit of government. Rather scornful of party politics, these Roosevelt recruits not only exemplify the nonpartisanship of the administration but they constitute forces in training which the Chief Executive counts on to supply the national leadership of the future.

The President is proud of the Brain Trust. He likes to think of the past year as a tough term in a great school of adult education. During a period when the Federal Government has functioned almost as a receiver in bankruptcy for a paralyzed economy, constant contact with the business brains of the country has convinced him that too many business executives have gone ahead "with blinders on," unmindful of anything outside their own narrow field. Compared with this one-track mind, the outlook of the average Congressman is broad and patriotic. Teaching business to think in terms of the country, in conscious relation to national policy, seems to him the most valuable effort of the New Deal, and particularly of the NRA.

In spite of criticisms, of recessions, of structural weaknesses, Mr. Roosevelt considers NRA "a magnificent success," the outstanding achievement of the administration to date. It whooped up the revival movement at the low moment. It is an invaluable experimental method, fluid and flexible, for studying and charting the unknown, anarchic states of industry. Certainly it is a storm center of controversy, but that is what it was intended to be, a frame wherein the conflicts between employer and employed can be fought out. It is, above all, an educational agency, forcing those within and without the codes to do some hard thinking on the central problems of modern life, the involved problem of the control of industry, the hardly less irritating issues rising out of its ethics and its social attitude.

Recently a delegation of striking workers in the textile industry brought their case before the President, who has become the court of appeal in an ever-widening variety of disputes. The Cotton Code Authority had met and summarily announced that it was necessary to cut down production 25 per cent during the dull season. Mr. Roosevelt told the workers that he thought the employers were justified. "Well, why didn't they tell us?" demanded the employees, with righteous wrath. "Are we partners in this enterprise or not?" The incident was cited by Mr. Roosevelt as an example of stubborn bad habits, of the Bourbon-like wrong way, more exasperating than real injustice, of doing the right thing.

When he is asked whether the policies of the New Deal tend toward fascism or socialism, the President is likely to answer that he hopes they tend toward strengthening American democracy. Though opposed as Fascist by some who a couple of years ago were yearning for a Mussolini, the industrial codes represent the American way of achieving, by what Mr. Roosevelt insists is voluntary organization, the industrial peace and order compulsorily imposed by the corporative system. As to controlling agricultural production, he points out that England exercises far more regulatory power than has ever been contemplated by the AAA. Cotton is the only commodity we produce on a quota system, but the English farmer is integrated into a production plan in which he cannot plant anything without a permit.

The vast relief program put into effect by the administration has one central aim: it works to make more people property owners, to save their property for those who would lose it without government credit, to safeguard small savings and legitimate investment. This is the idea behind the movement for subsistence homesteads, the decentralization of industry, home loans, home building, the banking and securities acts. When Clarence E. Pickett of the Department of the Interior recently returned from a housing survey in Vienna, he reported that the Socialists settled on one-acre garden plots outside the city refused to join their comrades in the urban tenements in the February rising against the government. The homesteaders had a stake in the land. The New Deal seeks to multiply the number of American stakeholders.

"Is this socialistic?" asks the President with the characteristic crinkle of his eyes and backward jerk of his head which accompany his hearty laugh.

For a long time, and on this point in accord with the well-known ideas of Henry Ford, Mr. Roosevelt has been pondering over schemes for decentralizing industry, with the specific object of preventing the development of a proletarian psychology by giving the factory worker a backlog in the land and of a peasant psychology by offering the small farmer a part-time job in a factory. When Governor of New York he requested the head of the

General Electric Company to study the problem with a view to determining what units of a big plant might be detached and profitably operated in small communities. For years he has advocated the reforestation of marginal lands and rural slum clearance by the resettlement in more favorable environments of farmers on the lowest levels.

Early in the spring of 1932 he outlined to the writer the three-point "security program"—decent housing, development of sites offering better living facilities to farmers, a system of social insurance—he now proposes as the next step in the New Deal. Some time in the fall he plans to call together the 265 executives who control 70 per cent of American industry and ask their cooperation in hammering out a plan to scatter factory units over as wide an area as practicable and at the same time to budget production in order to guarantee the worker the amount of employment he can count on for a year.

On the question of public ownership of utilities the Roosevelt philosophy is purely pragmatic. It is not easy to define a public utility, or, having defined it, to decide whether it would be in the general interest to operate it. It would be next to impossible to take over the milk supply, for instance, yet milk should be classified as a public utility. So, obviously, are railroads and telephones, but in this country the latter give better service than any publicly owned system in the world, and the constant effort of the administration has been to devise means to keep the former in private hands.

On the other side the postoffice has been operated by the government for decades, and nobody denies that in taking over the parcel post it improved on the service of the old express companies. It simmers down to a question not of ownership but of efficient and economical public service. In the Roosevelt view that is the test.

All the President's tests are simple and non-theoretic. He has changed not at all in a year in which the United States seems to have moved far and to have enormously complicated its running gear. In the labyrinth he has created he retains the faculty of making everything look simple, almost obvious. Surrounded he may be by doctrinaires, yet no occupant of the White House ever seemed so little touched by the winds of doctrine. Hoover and Wilson held theories which they defended stubbornly to tragic ends. Roosevelt has purposes and a program, under his amiable manner he is as firm as they, but his course is less shaped and determined by theory. If anything, he reacts against theories, at least against any one theory; his indifference to party labels is an instinctive response to a like indifference among people in general, but it is also a recognition that in a time of flux you cannot be bound by formulas; you must be free to try anything and to reject anything.

To Mr. Roosevelt the New Deal is a method, a combination of methods. Such planning as he does in his essentially practical and sensitively political mind is flexible and subject to revision; therefore he sees nothing strange or disturbing in the program of social legislation he means to propose to the next Congress as the sequel of the recovery measures enacted in the last session. "Where we go from here is neither right nor left but straight ahead," he says.

There is nothing new in the proposals. In fact, the agencies erected this year and the enormous expenditures they involve are more drastic innovations than the contemplated social insurances. To one who has made the rounds of the European capitals, the news that we are to move "very gradually" toward goals long left behind in nearly every other country sounds neither so upsetting nor, alas, so promising, as it seems to America. Evidently every industrial country, when it grows up, has to make public provision for the chronic industrial diseases of unemployment, disability and impoverished age. We are the last to act because we are the last to leave the happy frontier of unlimited opportunity and undeveloped territory.

Here it is planned to make the insurances compulsory and general, the payments to be shared by employer and employee and the benefits to be administered in some such fashion as in England. Subject to such social costs, however, perhaps larger slices of taxation, the profit system is no more threatened by the New Deal than is the principle of private ownership. In time, size itself may become taxable. That is one way of decentralizing, of meeting the new hazard of monopoly created by coded industries. Mr. Roosevelt has an idea that industries may be too big; he thinks they are too big when they spread beyond the possibility of supervision by the responsible heads. He remembers the executive of a great steel corporation who learned from him, with incredulous surprise, that the miners were reduced to living in his coke ovens.

If there is nothing startling in a plan for social insurance, beyond the reminder that we are passing into the "old-country" stage, neither is there anything in the philosophy of the New Deal to frighten those familiar with the accents of an earlier America. A note of nostalgia sounds through Mr. Roosevelt's utterances; even his prophecies of the future promise a return to "earlier ideals and values." In this he is like the Progressives, those faithful ancients who never forget the Founders. He talks not at all like a Brain Truster but like an old-fashioned Jeffersonian who differs from his predecessors in being willing to accent and actualize the modern implications and connotations of the old phrases about liberty, equality and the pursuit of happiness.

The President believes that the American people are behind him more strongly today than they were a year ago. He takes that as his mandate to go ahead. If his calm spirit is fed by anything outside of the sources of strength in himself, it is by the exalting sense that wherever he goes the masses of the people go with him. That may take him far—into more and more regulation as he sees more and more that should be regulated.

The path of reform has no end. But at least one thing it is safe to predict as he enters the second phase: his genius is for politics, for interpreting the vague but powerful impulses behind popular movements, for measuring the weight of the human equation in the play of economic forces; he will go no further than America is ready to follow. As he sat on the White House porch in the cool of the evening, to the home-coming American he seemed as reassuring as America itself in an otherwise unpredictable world.

Roosevelt Recharts His Course

by Delbert Clark

WASHINGTON

ROOSEVELT, MAN of many surprises, has suddenly thrown off the pale cast of thought which for the last few months appeared to becloud the executive countenance, and with sudden and dramatic force has entered upon the third phase of his Presidential career, a phase which differs essentially from, but is not inconsistent with, his first two stages.

His first phase began with his inauguration. It was a period when swift moving action, relief and recovery measures, backed up by essential reforms, was indicated to save the country from imminent disaster. This brilliant "hundred days," from March 4, 1933, up to the end of his first session of Congress, was a succession of thunderclaps and pyrotechnic display, all required, it seemed, to start the nation on the road to economic recovery and impart the assurance that "it shall not be again." The reverberations and the afterglow continued through the rest of 1933 and all of 1934.

But with 1935 began the second phase, presaged in the preceding autumn by the elaborately staged peace conference with the bankers. The Brain Trust had taken the elevator going down, businessmen and seasoned politicians took their places at the Table Round, there was less hammering at the Congress, more peaceful contemplation and apparent willingness to "give recovery a chance." Wiseacres attributed this apparent shift of front to the fact that primaries were but little more than a year away, that the President wished to appear in the role of the country's savior from the Pied Pipers who had begun to fill the mighty air with their persuasive fluting.

It seemed safe to say that, with the nation weary of excitement, confident that recovery was on the way, the President was preparing to trim cargo, run with the popular wind for a space, and, gliding safely into the port of a second term, complete his legislative program in the four years to come. There is still no reason to believe that such was not the case, but inexorable circumstance, that "divinity that shapes our ends," stepped in on May 27 and took the helm.

It cannot be stated too often that that momentous date, when the Supreme Court overthrew the NRA and delimited the Federal powers, does indeed mark a turning point in our history. From that day dates the third Rooseveltian phase, a phase of renewed activity, of hard, uncompromising driving for reform.

It is well to study this phase as closely as it is possible to study the mental processes of a man whose mind is so facile and who keeps so well his own counsel, for in it lies the key to the developing philosophy of Franklin Roosevelt.

As an executive whose continued executive tenure depends solely on the will of his constituents, an American President must listen with a keen ear for popular whisperings and rumblings; be he ever so capable, ever so wedded to a course of conduct, he must know that he can do nothing long without carrying with him the good-will of the nation.

So President Roosevelt, as close an observer of trends as ever sat in the White House, placed his ear to the ground and listened. What he heard, it is reasonable to believe, convinced him that the momentous events in Washington had had their effect, and that a nation which a few months before was crying "peace, peace!" now demanded of its leader that he stand by his guns and fight. Whether he heard aright can be told in November, 1936.

However the outcome, the impression is abroad that the President now believes action, swift and positive, is indicated. Unless the signs from the country have been read completely wrong by the President and his advisers, he is in a powerful strategic position. He has an overwhelming majority in Congress, generally ready to do his bidding to any reasonable extent. The conservative opposition is disunited, at odds as to methods and even fundamentals. The widely heralded "Grass Roots" convention in Springfield could achieve nothing better than a "full dinnerpail" platform forty years after.

But the right-wing opposition is not all. At the extreme left are the Pied Pipers, playing strange music that fascinates as it repels. By swinging definitely to what his conservative opponents term the left, Mr. Roosevelt is in a fair position to drown out the piping of Long, Coughlin and company. If the country really wants more liberalism, his advisers hold, the best opposition he can have is that of "Wall Street," and this opposition he can have and retain by such measures as the Banking Bill, the Wagner Labor Relations Bill, and the Holding Company Bill.

Postmaster General Farley realized this in 1932 when he told Wall Streeters he was delighted to find them opposing Mr. Roosevelt for President, but the latter for a time appeared to have his doubts and toyed gingerly with bankers and big business.

Indecision now appears to be discarded. Within a week the whole Washington scene changed. Uncertainty became a directness that was startling. Congress awoke to find the President hard-boiled, uncompromising, pressing ahead at all odds for virtually his entire New Deal program, and even for other legislation. The Wagner bill, scuttled last year as embodying dangerous leftism, suddenly appeared on the "must" list. The Guffey bill, a legislative code for the coal industry, emerged from obscurity to a commanding position of favor. The "death sentence" for holding companies was insisted upon. Then, as a final salute to foes and friends alike, up went the inheritance tax rocket, taking trusted legislative leaders completely by surprise.

And in the background is the purpose, confidently predicted though not yet announced, to seek fundamental changes in the Constitution to restore and consolidate the Federal powers nullified by the Supreme Court. Pervading the whole show is an attitude blithe, almost fatalistic, in striking contrast with the relative dourness and reticence of a few months ago.

What has brought all this about, and what is its significance? A reading, correct or incorrect, of the popular will, of course, but unless a man be a complete demagogue, he does not behave in high public office like a weathervane.

Behind it all, there is good reason to believe, is what may be a final shaping and coalescing of Mr. Roosevelt's philosophy, economic and social. More than ever now he appears as a man whose beliefs, not clearly integrated at the time of his inauguration, have been taking definite form as problems arose. Vacillations and tacking have resulted—the growing pains of a mind in the making. But it was inevitable that under the tremendous pressure of the Presidency in time of crisis, something should happen to the incumbent. Either he would fly to pieces and sit with his head in his hands, or crystallize and harden.

It would appear that the last named has taken place in the case of the President. The dim but discernible outlines of a Rooseveltian philosophy begin to appear. It is a philosophy refined and modernized, but not too much, from that of his Dutch burgher ancestors, the practical idealists who ruled Holland in its brief and brilliant ascendancy. There appear traces of a contempt, thinly veiled, for "grubbers," "single-track businessmen," and a desire to put them in their place.

It is difficult to divide the economic from the social, in the case of Franklin Roosevelt as well as in the case of Theodore, for at all times both his economic and his social philosophy rest on the basic desire for all men to be happy. To this end, his economic philosophy turns to what amounts in effect to a nationalization of natural resources and means of transport, through strict regulation. It implies a steadfast advocacy of the conservation of these natural resources for the whole people, not their selfish exploitation by the few for private gain.

Where Theodore wanted to preserve the forests, Franklin, a

generation later, seeks to preserve the forests *and* the sources of electrical energy, that unwearying servant whose wages the President desires to keep low. His Dutch patrician ancestry and his own hard experience drive him to a rigid regulation of the money markets and all speculative activities, with a view to protecting the small investor.

"Chiseling," that Johnsonian term which adorns the New Deal lexicon and is defined as any form of evasion of the rules of the game, becomes a hateful practice. "Let the seller also beware," early crept into the Roosevelt Book of Home Truths.

Thus the economic merges into the social and the two become indistinguishable. Happiness for the greatest number is discovered as the fundament of all the President's philosophy, however far he may appear to wander at times from its practical fulfillment. It leads to a profound distrust of the social motives of super-corporations and excessively powerful individuals, and a perverse desire at times to taunt and twit them, as when he told Charles M. Schwab, "You'll never make another million," and as in an illuminating exchange reported to have taken place with J. P. Morgan. He is in no sense a commoner who seeks to elevate his class, but an aristocrat who through native geniality and his own personal affliction has come to think in terms of the general public.

A striking summation of the President's social and economic philosophy is contained in his surprise message to Congress asking inheritance taxes, increased income taxes on the very rich, and increased taxes on huge corporations. In this message the thought expressed frequently parallels in interesting fashion that of Mr. Justice Brandeis in "The Curse of Bigness." Mr. Brandeis refers principally, of course, to overweening corporate structure and industrial domination, but it is not a long stride from great individual wealth to corporate structures so powerful as to constitute a potential menace to free institutions.

Mr. Roosevelt, then, holds to the theory of freedom of opportunity, with the corollary inference that too much concentration of wealth and economic power militates against this freedom. He is not opposed to bigness as such, in the old-fashioned manner of certain statesmen who oppose large scale operation because it inexorably weeds out the inefficient small operator. Mr. Roosevelt does not number himself among those who condemn bigness per se, or adore smallness for its own sake.

But he does hold with those who are convinced that too great size may become a curse, and who believe that it should be regulated for both social and economic reasons. To wit:

"Such accumulations [of great wealth] amount to the perpetuation of great and undesirable concentration of control in a relatively few individuals over the employment of many, many others. Such inherited economic power is as inconsistent with the ideals of this generation as inherited political power was inconsistent with the ideals of the generation which established our government."

Again, he believes in effect that heavy taxes on the very rich constitute not a "soak the rich" policy, not a penalty for the accumulation of wealth, but a small repayment for opportunities afforded by our system. Under a different system, his theme runs, these vast fortunes might well not have been amassed, so it is only fair that their possessors should help in some measure to pay for the privilege the government has given them.

"The people in the mass," he says, "have inevitably helped to make large fortunes possible," and again:

"Vast personal incomes come not only through the efforts of ability or luck of those who receive them, but also because of the opportunities for advantage which the government itself contributes."

Translate all this into general terms, apply it to natural resources, transportation systems, relations of industry and labor, relations of industry and government, and the relations of industry and the consuming public, and you have a fair statement of Mr. Roosevelt's philosophy as it is beginning to shape up.

The President's ideas when he first took office appeared extremely inchoate to many of his associates; they discerned a high and benevolent purpose, an extrovert temperament that withstood storm and stress with almost unfailing good humor, but little in the way of a well thought out plan of life or of action. They say it less these days. Mr. Roosevelt, as one puts it, for better or for worse has begun to "jell."

Of course his political philosophy "jelled" long ago; had it not he would not now be President of the United States. There have been changes, but for the most part they appear to have been minor refinements born of changing times. The one really important shift discernible is his dramatic espousal, in word and in practice, of the essential tenets of federalism as against States' rights.

Yet there is little room for doubt that many Democrats who have become very prominent in their party are convinced of the holiness of State sovereignty, principally because there has never been occasion for them to doubt it. Mr. Roosevelt may well have been one of these, repeating Jeffersonian phrases like lines from the Shorter Catechism, because he had learned them and believed them as he believed in the sacredness of marital love and the existence of vitamins. He was born a States' righter. Confronted as Chief Magistrate with a set of undeniable facts, is it then surprising that he should survey them and in line with his intellectual prerogatives alter his views?

As a political practitioner, the President is in striking contrast with the idealist of other fields. He is clearly a lover of politics for its own sake, and has the best training the country affords— a course in the hard-boiled New York school. It is in this field that he is most successful, and it is his superlative skill as a politician, undoubtedly, that has enabled him to carry through his theories of government and sociology as far as he has. For only the almost alarming skill at manipulation, the mastery of the dramatic, the ear sensitive to popular trends which he possesses could enable him to drive on as he has done along untried paths.

He is a master of the mot juste, an uncanny judge of the precise moment and how to make the most of it. Effecting nice compromises, he has a faculty of retaining most of what he wants, conceding little while appearing to give much ground, playing an intricate hopscotch with political factions, and loving it. Almost, it would seem, he is a lover of the game of compromise for its own sake. Yet he has given many an exhibition of capacity for single-mindedness, of unwillingness to compromise.

In many ways an economic and social idealist, he relies politically on such technical experts as James A. Farley, who are the horror of some polite people, tempered by the sound, unselfish judgment of men like Louis Howe. Never, however, has he appeared to be the tool of his advisers.

His personality, a potent factor in any political career, has enabled him to attract to his standard the most diverse groups and individuals—millionaires and industrialists like Gerard Swope and Owen D. Young, hard-bitten political radicals, advanced economic thinkers, philosophers of every stripe, and experienced technicians in all fields with no special political interest at all.

Finally, as a politician he is no Democrat, in the old-fashioned sense, but in this he is not without company, as the correspondence of certain Senators reveals.

As President, Mr. Roosevelt, during the shaping of his personal philosophy, has been in the not entirely enviable position of being damned as a conservative and damned as a radical. Luncheon with the La Follette boys made him a radical—a ride on Vincent Astor's yacht threw him back among the conservatives. Yet if he is conservative what is Herbert Hoover, what Ogden Mills? And if he is radical what does that make Norman Thomas?

Actually Mr. Roosevelt is as radical as certain British Prime Ministers, as conservative as Theodore Roosevelt the elder. Avowed radicals have an unpleasant way of considering him a not too scrupulous conservative, a sheep in wolf's clothing trying to fool a public which, by a species of wish-fulfillment, they believe to be ready at the drop of a hat to scramble for pure Marxian socialism. Conservatives of the Plymouth Rock variety, holding to the view that any change is undesirable, consider him a highly dangerous revolutionary who is outraging the will of the people.

Is he not, really, a moderate conservative, sufficiently without bias not to blind himself to defects in the system which has fostered him, and desirous if possible to remedy these defects, real or imaginary, without destroying the system itself? If that be radical or revolutionary, then the man who reshingles his house is a radical, and if the house happens not to need reshingling he is not misguided, he is a revolutionist.

President Roosevelt had his chance to be radical in the first few months of 1933, when, in the sincere belief of many observers, he could have decreed the moon to be made of Roquefort with but little popular dissent. But he did not take that chance. It must have been clear to him that then if ever was the time for a coup of whatever description, had he desired it. There are perhaps two excellent reasons why he did nothing of the kind. The first is that his own background and tradition would not have brooked it; the second is that he was not entirely sure himself as to detail, what he wanted, other than that everybody should be happy and he should have his way.

Now, however, he appears to be more nearly "on his way" than he did in those addresses made during his candidacy and early incumbency, his philosophy better integrated, his course somewhat clearer before him. And if it is little different, if possibly a bit more conservative, than that of his cousin the great Theodore, there is only family affinity to blame.

A New Pattern of Life
for the Indian

by Frank Ernest Hill

MORE THAN a mile above the sea level, on a plateau of the American Southwest, two hundred and fifty men are building a new capitol. It is not the capitol of a State. Its stone walls rise in shapes that are strange to most Americans; its name—Nee Alneeng—falls with a strange accent. Nee Alneeng belongs to a world far from Manhattan and Main Street. It is an Indian world, and the capitol belongs to the Navajo, now the largest of the North American tribes.

This little center is symbolic of a new way of life among the Navajo: in fact, a new way of life for the 340,000 Indians of the United States. A year ago the Wheeler-Howard Act gave to the tribes the right to decide whether they would accept important privileges in education, self-determination and self-government. A popular vote was asked; the essential question was: "Do you want to help save yourselves?" So far 134 reservations containing 128,468 Indians have voted to come under the act, while fifty-four reservations with 85,179 Indians have excluded themselves.

Thus the Wheeler-Howard Act embodies an Indian policy far different from that pursued in the past. The Federal Government could have conferred self-government upon the American Indian without asking him if he wanted it. To understand why he was asked, one must take a brief but discriminating glance at American history as it has affected the red man.

The record may be thought of as falling into three stages. The first dates from the earliest white settlements in the Southwest and in Virginia and marks the beginning of a protracted struggle between European and Indian cultures. The struggle ended with the sporadic Western wars of the 1880s—in the inevitable defeat of the Indian. The last of the aboriginals entered United States Government reservations, and a second stage began: the government's effort to control and protect the Indian and adapt him to white American ways.

For more than fifty years this persisted. The possibility of a nomadic hunter's life for the Indian was gone; as a substitute, the government sought to educate him and make him a stock raiser or farmer. It is clear now that in many ways the system failed to protect him from cruel exploitation and yet prevented him from acting for himself. It led him to lean passively on the rather precarious bounty the government extended. Presently the Indian had suffered the loss of much of his allotted land, much of his separate culture, and had developed a deep inferiority complex with an accompanying resentment. Disease and bitter poverty menaced him. The days of his vitality seemed numbered.

The third stage may be said to have begun with a growing conviction among many thoughtful Americans that Indian life had latent strength and important cultural values and that the Indian if given the right opportunities could do what the government had failed to do: he could arrange a place for himself and his customs in this modern America. The appointment of John Collier as Commissioner of Indian Affairs in April, 1933, brought into power a leader of this trend of opinion.

Mr. Collier, slight, almost scholarly in appearance, at his desk in Washington describes what the administration is trying to do for the Indian and why he believes the new policy to be enlightened.

"In the past," he says, "the government tried to encourage economic independence and initiative by the allotment system, giving each Indian a portion of land and the right to dispose of it. As a result, of the 138,000,000 acres which Indians possessed in 1887 they have lost all but 47,000,000 acres, and the lost area includes the land that was the most valuable. Further, the government sought to give the Indian the schooling of the whites, teaching him to despise his old customs and habits as barbaric. Through this experiment the Indian lost much of his understanding of his own culture and received no usable substitute. In many areas such efforts to change the Indian have broken him economically and spiritually.

"We have proposed in opposition to such a policy to recognize and respect the Indian as he is. We think he must be so accepted before he can be assisted to become something else, if that is desirable. It is objected that we are proposing to make a 'blanket Indian' of him again. That is nonsense. But if he happens to be a blanket Indian we think he should not be ashamed of it. We believe further that while he needs protection and assistance in important ways, these aids should be extended with the idea of enabling him to help himself. We are sure that he can and will do this. But he must have the opportunity to do it in his own way. This is what we have been trying to extend to him. It is an opportunity he has not had since he entered the reservations, where he has been discouraged from thinking and acting for himself.

"It is all an educative process. Perhaps the most drastic innovation of the last two years has been our effort not only to encourage the Indians to think about their own problems but even to induce them to. Our design is to plow up the Indian soul, to make the Indian again the master of his own mind. If this fails, everything fails; if it succeeds, we believe the Indian will do the rest."

The people whom the Commissioner is trying to reanimate, and to incite to this crusade for self-survival, are in one sense heterogeneous. There is no typical Indian but rather a hundred different types. These are scattered. The 220 tribes that comprise the race are to be found here and there in twenty-two States. They are of many different stocks physically, and they speak dozens of different languages.

Their cultures vary, and so does the degree to which they have adopted the white man's ways. The five civilized tribes, now in Oklahoma, were farming when De Soto discovered the Mississippi. So were the Pueblo Indians, who were also skilled weavers and master potters. On the other hand, the roving tribes of the Northwestern plains did little cultivating, and, though skillful in crafts, were esthetically far less developed. Similar differences persist today. Some Indians are competent farmers and stock raisers; others are less happy and successful in the settled life.

Some speak no English, are inexpert with tools and live in crude shelters; others have acquired modern houses and automobiles and serve as teachers, doctors, lawyers and storekeepers. Some tribes find a personal "planned economy" difficult; others, like the Hopi, are thrifty and far-seeing. Unquestionably Indians generally are willing to use much of the white man's equipment and means to knowledge, but often are backward because their economic grip on life is a precarious one. Many of the tribes hold grants of land that is inferior or insufficient in extent, yet manage well with their facilities, and are deft as artisans and mechanics, sometimes eager for better tools, machinery and methods.

Underneath all their differences lie identical, unifying instincts, habits, aptitudes and spiritual feelings. Fine qualities are to be observed in almost any Indian group: artistic cleverness, tenacity, courage, dignity and a decent pride. Under the parochial control of the past, with its effort to make the Indian a white man, these qualities have shown but little. They have come out best where the Indian, as in the Southwest, has lived his own life.

In attempting to "plow up the Indian soul" and put these qualities into action, Mr. Collier has not depended on the Wheeler-Howard Act alone. This law is important; it may justly come to be regarded as an Indian Magna Carta. It repeals the Allotment Act of 1887 and so makes the further loss of Indian lands impossible. It provides for the purchase of additional badly needed land for the tribes up to a valuation of $2,000,000 a year.

It creates a revolving credit fund of $10,000,000 against which the Indians can borrow (if they accept the new law) when they have governmentally approved farm or industrial projects. This is wholly novel: the government had never previously recognized, in Mr. Collier's phrase, "the cold fact that capital in some form is needed to transform even a piece of raw land into a productive farm." There is a fund for scholarships also, and preference is given to Indians who seek positions in the Indian Service. Finally, there is the right of every tribe accepting the act by majority vote to adopt a constitution and take over most of the powers now exercised by the Federal Government.

All these privileges are important. Those providing economic and political sinews are especially significant because of the independence and self-reliance which they may develop. Yet the Indian Office regards the Wheeler-Howard Act as a step only. "It is merely a beginning," Mr. Collier points out, "in a process of liberating and rejuvenating a subjugated and exploited race living in the midst of an aggressive civilization far ahead, materially speaking, of its own. Even that beginning is oppressively difficult."

This difficulty has been recognized by the creation by the Indian Office of an organization unit of field agents and special men who will cooperate with tribal councils, business committees and special tribal commissions in framing the constitution now permitted. The organization unit will advise the Indians, seeking to make the governments they set up both effective and legal. Definite educative work will be done to give the Indians an understanding of their new civic powers.

The possibilities in economic and political development here are dynamic. However, they follow a spirit and practice fostered since the spring of 1933. This called for a much greater use of Indians both as officials in the Indian Service and as routine workers outside the permanent staff. The results have been notable.

In the case of the permanent staff, changes come slowly, for all positions are subject to civil service rules. However, while in 1932 the Indian Office used 6,172 employees, of which 1,296 were Indians, its reduced force of 5,322 today contains 2,037 Indians. The Indians have derived other benefits by being utilized on ECW and CWA projects. Last year these workers swelled the total of government Indian employees to 19,616. This figure takes no account of the quota of 14,000 Indians in the CCC camps.

The work that Indians have done in the last two years in building roads, dams, bridges, trails and improving forest lands has been impressive. More than half the supervisory force consisted of Indians. Mr. Collier regards as important the demonstration they have given of skill, initiative and responsibility.

Beyond its successful effort to give the Indian a fair trial as a worker, the Indian Service has undertaken several specific projects of considerable importance to him. The most comprehensive of these has been going forward in the Navajo country. It touches all phases of Navajo existence: the preservation of the soil, its better use for farming and grazing, the character of the stock used, self-government, health, education, and, indirectly, art and spiritual life.

The Navajo nation, the largest of all Indian tribes, was confronted two years ago, and still is, with an economic crisis. On its great reservation in Arizona and New Mexico, with an area equal to Maryland, Massachusetts and New Hampshire combined, the tribe had developed sheep raising. In 1870 a population of 10,000 Indians was existing on its arid plateaus. From their sheep they got mutton, their chief food. From them also they took the wiry wool for the best known of native loom products —the Navajo rug. They raised a little corn. They hammered silver ornaments from Mexican silver dollars—creating the best known of all American Indian metal work. These activities sustained the tribe.

But meanwhile the Navajo increased from 10,000 to almost 50,000, and the sheep, under government encouragement, increased with the population. Carefully used, the range might have supported 1,000,000 head. But in 1933 there were 1,300,-000. Furthermore, the land had long been overgrazed; experts reported its actual capacity had sunk to 550,000 head. Cropped too intensively, grass and bushes were losing their strength and were pulled up by hungry animals. Then the wind churned the uncovered soil into drifting hillocks. Rain, which falls seldom on the Navajo reservation but then usually in torrents, ran off the denuded land, carrying soil with it.

In order to live the Navajo must have his sheep. Having his sheep, he seemed doomed to economic ruin. Into this situation stepped the Indian Office. It had Emergency Conservation funds for work in the Navajo region. The office said:

"Reduce the number of your sheep. We will study how to control the destruction of the soil. We will employ your young men on government projects. We will show you how to use what water there is for irrigation. Gradually you will be able to increase your herds again. We will develop better stock for you, consuming no more but producing two-fold. In the end the land will give more than it has ever given."

In separate meetings and in their tribal councils the Navajo debated. What if the work gave out before the range was restored and the herds built back? This question is still in their minds. They have reduced their stock to 900,000 head; now they hesitate to reduce it further.

Meanwhile they have cooperated in the establishment of work projects and demonstration projects in various areas. Some are under the farm agents of the Indian Office; the greatest number are under the control of the new Soil Erosion Service. About 200 square miles of Navajo territory are now being managed as demonstration areas by this agency alone, sixty-seven of them about Mexican Springs, N. M.

In addition to the work with the land there are health and education and governmental projects in process. Schools are being built for the first time in the Navajo country. Navajo teachers will constitute the greater part of the teaching force, a new experiment. The staff of the first ten schools will consist of fifty Indians and five whites. Some instruction will be given in Navajo. The "Longhairs," the older men of the tribe, will be asked to teach the children tribal tradition, folklore and conduct of life. In health work Navajo girls are being trained as nurses to carry the fight against tuberculosis and trachoma into the remoter districts. Finally, at Nee Alneeng, twenty-five miles from Gallup, N. M., 250 Navajo workmen have been raising the walls of a new capitol which will make a center for Navajo political life.

All activities are going forward with the agreement and participation of the Navajo, and their cooperation means a training in modern methods of work, in management, in government.

The activities of the Indian Office have nowhere been so intensive as in this many-sided development and conservation of

Navajo resources. But they have been country-wide. The school program has sought everywhere to bring the Indian children into a closer relation to their homes by increasing the number of day schools and reducing the number of boarding schools. Many new schools for day use are rising—in California, in Montana, in Minnesota, in North Dakota. Economic and soil erosion work on a large scale is being pushed by the Indian Service and the Soil Erosion Service on the Rio Grande watershed, and the Indian is sharing in it.

All this is a part, with the Wheeler-Howard Act, of the new policy of setting the Indian to save himself. On the whole the response has been a revelation as to his capacity as a worker and his eagerness to lead. He has shown independence of spirit —often to the point of rebellion. The Navajo, by a narrow margin, have rejected the Wheeler-Howard Act because of unbased allegations that it would unduly curtail their herds.

But Mr. Collier, regretting such actions, prefers rebellion to dry rot. "The Indians may be confused and thrown back for a time," he says, "but it is a part of their life and education. They will win through in the end, in their own way."

If they win through it will, in the Commissioner's opinion, mean a victory for both Indian and white man. Economically independent, the Indian will cease to be a financial burden to the nation. And spiritually and culturally he will bring something valuable too.

The new policy has already started a renaissance in Indian arts. Young Indians are painting murals on the walls of schoolhouses and government buildings. They are studying the ancient pottery of their tribes in museums, and devising new designs and textures in their workshops. The young people are flocking to the ceremonial dances, which for a time they had avoided. This cultural revival goes hand in hand with an interest in self-government and economic independence. In Mr. Collier's opinion, it is equally valuable.

"The Indian," he says, "can use white technologies and remain an Indian. Modernity and white Americanism are not identical. If the Indian life is a good life, then we should be proud and glad to have this different and native culture going on by the side of ours. Anything less than to let Indian culture live on would be a crime against the earth itself. The destruction of a pueblo is a barbarous thing. America is coming to understand this, and to know that in helping the Indian to save himself we are helping to save something that is precious to us as well as to him."

A Dream Takes Form in TVA's Domain

by R. L. Duffus

NORRIS, TENN.

THE STORMS which have whirled and whistled through the New Deal agencies during the past year have left one—the one of which the President is probably proudest—intact. Despite hurricanes, whether political and figurative or shockingly real, the TVA's banners still wave over the ramparts of great dams from Norris, on the Clinch, above Knoxville, to Pickwick Landing, in Southwestern Tennessee. Where armies marched and fought in the War Between the States TVA linemen are stringing wires. Where the flatboats of the pioneers slid down muddy, swollen streams, where two or three generations later the Union gunboats crawled, cranes and steam shovels are at work. The thunder of the cement mixers would drown out all but the heaviest artillery.

The TVA is a dream taking tangible form, of surpassingly more importance than any bickering between government and private enterprise as to which shall furnish electricity. It is the first organized attempt in American history to manipulate the destinies of an entire watershed and its people.

Whether this attempt is wise or unwise, a menace or a rainbow,

From the *New York Times Magazine,* April 19, 1936, copyright © 1936, 1964 by The New York Times Company.

depends entirely on one's point of view. The facts are visible for friends and opponents alike to see. There can be little dispute as to what the Tennessee Valley has been or as to what is now happening to it. If the power issue is for the moment laid aside there can be no question that the essential thing that is happening in the valley now is not coercion but education. The famous power "yardstick" does exist and will certainly compel power companies in the valley to lower their rates and scratch gravel for new customers. But the stick that the observer on the spot is likely to think about, whether the spot is a gigantic dam or an electrified village, is the school teacher's pointer.

Nor was there ever a class or a laboratory quite like this, over which preside Dr. Arthur E. Morgan, president of Antioch College; Dr. Harcourt A. Morgan, former president of the University of Tennessee, and David E. Lilienthal, lawyer and rate expert.

The classroom includes parts of seven States, or a total area of more than 40,000 square miles—about the size of Kentucky. It looks out on a much wider area over which TVA electricity and TVA gospel will be distributed. The class is 2,000,000 strong, with 4,000,000 more outside the valley but within TVA influence.

The laboratory demonstrations set up for the edification of the TVA's pupils are tremendous in magnitude. Six great dams are completed or being built. Power plants in operation before the year is out will yield 205,000 kilowatts twenty-four hours a day and 365 days in the year. Future installations may raise this total, on existing and proposed dams, to 660,000 kilowatt hours.

In its recent report the TVA suggested five new dams—at Fowler Bend, on the Hiwassee, in North Carolina; the Fontana Dam, on the Little Tennessee; and dams at Watt's Bar, Gilbertsville and Coulter Shoals, all to be completed by 1944.

Dams and dredges will deepen the river until a boat drawing nine feet of water can safely steam from Paducah to Knoxville. Mighty reservoirs will hold back the flood waters and maintain the channel depth at slack seasons. Behind the reservoirs, on mountain farms, on fertile or once fertile lower slopes, the processes of erosion are being arrested by proved methods. From the old nitrate Plant No. 2 at Muscle Shoals phosphate fertilizer is going out to demonstration farms to bring moribund acres back to life. Near dam sites new model villages have sprung up, some of them destined to be permanent.

But these physical things are tools, not ends in themselves. When the Tennessee Valley Act was passed three years ago most people, even in Washington, were thinking of the valley in terms of electric power. Those terms are still valid, but the objective has broadened until it has become the revivification of the life of a people. Whatever the validity of the means adopted the conception has elements of splendor.

Large areas of this region have been blighted by wrong uses of the land, by the wash of a myriad of little streams carrying away the fertile topsoil, by the long after-effects of an old war, by that war's destruction of an old social and economic system which was never adequately replaced. Traveling through it one comes again and again on the traces and monuments of 70-year-old battles; at Nashville, Franklin, Chickamauga, Chattanooga and many other less familiar fields. From bloody Shiloh, near the new Pickwick Dam; from Corinth, in Mississippi, where old trenches can still be seen, eastward to the heights of Lookout Mountain, the armies reeled and flowed, leaving their débris of dead and dying men, trampling down crops that in one sense never grew again. Then silence fell and not until recently, over large areas, was it broken.

The valley is one of tremendous contrasts, in the shape and nature of the land, in climate, in the education and general welfare of the people. It has modern cities, like Knoxville and Chattanooga. It has bleak cabins on dreary upland acres, where life has changed but little since some pioneer wagon broke down, some horse or mule went lame and a family's migration was halted, a century or a century and a half ago.

Corn holds sway in the mountains of the northeast—sometimes as grain, sometimes as illicit liquor; in the center and in the west the land of cotton thrusts into Tennessee out of Georgia, Alabama and Mississippi. In the east streams tumble down wildly out of the hills, the Tennessee hurries past Chattanooga and Shiloh but at Paducah it moves quietly enough, broad and muddy, into the Ohio.

Some symbols run clear across the valley, from east to west, from north to south. One is the mule, descendant, perhaps, of a stock which used to be bred in old Mexico and brought eastward and northward over the Santa Fé Trail. The number of mules in the Tennessee Valley is prodigious. Over almost every road, from the muddy byway, where motor cars venture at their peril, to the concrete highways ambles the mule, sometimes ridden, sometimes attached to a rickety cart. Too often he is an emblem of poverty and of slow, heavy time, to which no value is attached.

Another symbol is the "breeze-way" or "dog-trot" cabin. Long ago, a pioneer whose family was expanding built a second log cabin end-on to the first, connected the two with a floor and roof but no walls, and produced the first "breeze-way." The idea was good, for its day. But the "breeze-way" has come to stand for a poor way of living, on poor land, with little or no stock, on a limited diet, without sufficient schooling or adequate medical care, without plumbing, without electric lights, without telephone, with a narrow and constricted social life.

Good land, well cultivated, grows better houses than this, as one sees readily enough when one goes north from Florence, in Alabama, near Muscle Shoals, through the Tennessee Blue Grass country, toward Nashville. Here the fields look as rich and the common farmhouses as neat and comfortable as those of Iowa, and many a gracious and dignified old plantation house, with lofty porticos and well-kept grounds, still stands. Is this part of the valley inhabited by a more intelligent and industrious race than other parts? No, it is underlaid by phosphate deposits which elsewhere are lacking and which here enrich the soil.

The valley is a pageant, sometimes sad, sometimes smiling, nearly always beautiful. Often, following down along the bottom-lands of some yellow river, one is amazed at the loveliness of hills and plains. Here one would look for happy farms, for fat herds of cattle, for orchards bursting with spring into blossom, even for vineyards ascending the sun-soaked slopes. And more often than not these blessings are not there.

The smoky vistas are sweet in the soft spring light, but in rickety and unpainted dwellings, in the absence of cattle, in the deadening sense of discouragement, one finds proof that something is wrong. At dusk many a cabin is dark or lighted only by the flicker of open fires. The roads—even those marked red on the automobile maps—vary amazingly, from concrete to macadam, from macadam to dust or mud.

The trouble is not that people in the valley prefer mules to automobiles, wells and springs to plumbing, darkness to light, mud to concrete. They want these good things, but they do not grow in a depleted soil. They do not grow on cruelly gullied hillsides, on slopes where red and gray patches show that the topsoil has washed away, on land that has lost its nitrates and phosphates. They cannot be grown by a discouraged people, no matter how good the human stock from which those people are bred. And good stock it is—90 or 95 per cent of the TVA's labor force has been recruited from the neighborhoods in which it is employed, and no one who sees it in action or sees what it has accomplished will sneer at it.

The traveler must not yet look for miracles—and yet he will find a few. He will find the practically completed Norris Dam, twenty-five miles above Knoxville, set as precisely as a jewel between two high banks that were virgin three years ago. At Joe Wheeler, a few miles above Muscle Shoals, he will see another new dam, also practically completed, stretching like a white causeway across the wide stream; at the old Wilson Dam, at Muscle Shoals, he will hear the whir of generators and see smoke rising and drifting in the misty air from the tall chimney of the fertilizer plant.

Fertilizer is not a poetic subject, but there is poetry, of a modern sort, in the grinding and mixing of rock, in furnaces where flames surge to temperatures of 2,850 degrees Fahrenheit, in yellow dust going out to give life to dying soil. There is poetry in a sack of phosphate that will make rich crops grow where scrawny ones grew before.

The traveler will see three dams in the making, at Chickamauga, just above Chattanooga; at Guntersville, in Alabama; at Pickwick Landing, in Tennessee. He will see that the making of a dam is a miracle. North Chickamauga Creek is in the way: the engineers will give it a new channel and bring it out below their dam. They want to know what there is under the water to hold up their earth and concrete bulwarks; they drill fanatically, bringing up many thousands of feet of rock cross-sections. They draw roads, culverts, switches, buildings, locks, embankments on a map, and in time those things are there—on the surface of the earth.

At Pickwick, this spring, one could see a dam-building bee in full career. Dam building is a man's job. The huge concrete mixer towers perilously. The machines are stopped. Men sluice them out, then crawl inside. They merge. The thunder begins again.

Down below the engineers have constructed a cofferdam of steel sheet piles driven in sixty-foot circles, filled in with sand. Inside this dam a massive lock is being built—the highest single-lift lock in the world. The cement comes out into huge buckets, a crane lifts them as a farm boy would swing a milk pail, flits them just above the heads of men working in the lock. A Negro jumps to a lever at the bottom of the bucket, throws his full weight on it; the bucket disgorges and men settle its contents into place with vibrators driven by compressed air.

The April high water topped the cofferdam. Warned thirty-six hours in advance, the engineers took out all equipment that water could damage and let the river in. The flood crest, two feet above the walls, did no harm, and as the river dropped the engineers were ready to pump out and resume work.

Over the hills, straddling down from Norris, comes a line of tall towers. They will carry Norris power down the valley. Three important cities—Knoxville, Chattanooga and Memphis—have voted to use TVA power. Dayton, where the famous "monkey trial" took place and William Jennings Bryan died, is a TVA patron; Florence, Sheffield and Tuscumbia, near Muscle Shoals, will take TVA power when some legal difficulties have been smoothed out; Corinth and its county of Alcorn already have it; Tupelo, in Mississippi, a tragic storm center in the recent hurricane, has it and uses it in amazing quantities.

In or near Corinth you can see some demonstrations of what electricity on the farm can do: a poultry raiser enlists it to keep even temperature in his brooders and incubators; a gardener heats his seed beds with it, and makes sweet potatoes, tomatoes and eggplant grow at a season when nature never intended them to do so; a farmer uses it to kill harmful bacteria in his soil. This is a beginning, a mere inkling of what electricity can do on a farm. It can pump, grind, refrigerate, saw, milk. It has scores and scores of uses.

Agricultural colleges, experiment stations and county agents in parts of the seven States are studying furiously to see what can be done in the valley with new supplies of electricity, fertilizer and hope. Six thousand farmers' clubs are conducting experiments under expert direction.

Three years ago critics of the TVA had a standing argument. Electricity, they conceded, would be a fine thing on the farm. But could the Tennessee Valley farmer pay for it? One had only to look at the farmer and his home to realize that he had little cash. How could he take on a new luxury?

The TVA's answer to this argument, which is here offered for whatever it may be worth, is that electricity on the farm is not a luxury but an economy. First, says the TVA, you fill up your gullies, terrace your land, strip-plow your slopes, and let the water flow down as slowly as possible. You collect the water behind dams and produce power. You use part of this power to make phosphate fertilizer, and with the fertilizer you grow legumes which enrich and hold your soil. You use some of the rest of the power on the farm itself. You diversify your farming, especially if you have been depending on the soil-murdering cotton as your one crop. You raise vegetables, berries, fruits; you raise fodder crops and feed them to dairy cows and meat cattle.

Electricity makes your labor more productive: the one-mule farm becomes an electric farm. You build a big walk-in electric refrigerator, either alone or in cooperation with your neighbors, and in it you store your meat and other perishable products until the market will absorb them at a good price.

As your cash income increases you can spend more on your land, and on yourself and your family. You will be able to pay your taxes, and your community can support better roads, schools and other public services. The vicious cycle of crop failures, defaulted taxes, poverty and community decay will be reversed. In time industries can be brought in. At the beginning, at least, they will process the valley's own agricultural and mineral products, furnishing more employment and keeping more money at home.

To carry out this program the TVA must educate the farmer, or, better still, persuade him to educate himself. Perhaps the word education suggests indoctrination. Perhaps it suggests millions of Russians being turned into Communists by not being allowed to hear any other gospel. Perhaps it suggests millions of Germans compelled to goosestep from the cradle to the grave, millions of Italians getting their view of the world through Mussolini's eyes.

This isn't the sort of education the TVA has in mind. The TVA rests its case on giving advice as to the best ways of doing things and leaving it to individuals and communities to decide for themselves how the advice works out.

The TVA doesn't even pretend to have arrived at final truths. It is trying to bring to the valley a new technique of running farms and using electricity in towns and cities. Such a technique cannot possibly be final.

Mainly the TVA believes in learning by doing. It is convinced that demonstrations of better farming, of wiser and more ample use of fertilizers and of the services of electricity will prove irresistible. It looks to see the leaven spread naturally through the valley.

If this leaven does spread in the valley of the Tennessee, it cannot help affecting other American valleys. Consider the basic reasoning behind the TVA: A river valley is the most perfect geographical unit. Its people are interested, as a whole, in the control and use of the river. Piecemeal planning will not provide for such control and use. A river as large as the Tennessee cannot be developed by private enterprise—the job is too big and there are too many uncertainties in it. Therefore, government must do the developing and private enterprise can step in where government leaves off. Between government and purely private enterprise there will be a natural growth of cooperative associations, particularly in the rural regions.

Other river valleys would furnish other problems. The Ohio, already practically canalized by its chain of locks, and heavily industrialized, would require an altogether different treatment; the

Missouri and the Arkansas, flowing for long distances through dry and sparsely settled country, would be still another sort of picture puzzle to put together.

But the principle of dealing with rivers and river valleys as wholes is undoubtedly involved in the Tennessee experiment. If that experiment succeeds, it will certainly be tried elsewhere.

A Crisis for Our Youth:
A Task for the Nation

by Aubrey Williams

IT IS NATURAL to think of the unemployment problem as that of men and women who once had jobs and have now lost them. The bulk of unemployment is of that kind. The picture is not complete, however, unless we paint in the situation of the boys and girls who have reached working age since 1929 and who have not been employed at all or have been employed only intermittently and in dead-end occupations.

The fact is that there are an estimated 2,500,000 young people in America looking for work. Their numbers have been growing and must grow until society opens its ranks to make places for them. Pressing close behind them are the younger ones. In the three short years between 10 and 13, when a boy is still a child, his parents, his teachers, his pastor are hopeful about him and his chances in the outside world. They speak of what a fine boy he has become, of how well he has done in school, and either by word or implication lead him and themselves to believe that he will find his place, that society will put a value upon him, and that he will merit it and continue to merit it.

Soon he joins his older brothers, and realizes with them that there is no job for him. He has no money. He has no decent clothes. He finds other boys in the same plight as himself. By degrees he comes to the realization that he is outside the group that have things, that go places, that dress well, that somebody speaks well of, and that somebody finds valuable. He must have come from something, but as far as he can determine he is going nowhere.

That is the position of a large fraction of American youth today. It feels as if it had been very nearly pushed off the edge of the world. Break down the totals and the picture becomes even more appalling. Take the whole of our young people between the ages of 16 and 24.

More than one in seven are heads or members of relief families. Of the 600,000 who live in urban areas and are of school age 300,000 are not in school and are not working or seeking work. Considerably more than half have had some work experience, but three-fourths of these are unskilled or semi-skilled, and only 5 per cent of the whole unemployed group of young people consists of skilled workers.

Perhaps 60,000 have had some college education. At the other extreme 12,000 have had no formal schooling at all. Some 55,000 have broken loose from home ties.

About one-fourth, following the normal instinct of ambitious youth, have married. Almost 10 per cent are heads of families and a considerable proportion of these families have children. Thus there are wide variations within the general framework, yet the plight of all these young people is similar in that they are being denied a chance to make their way in the world during the very years when their enthusiasm, energy and desire to learn would make them highly useful to themselves and to society. The best of them should be in training to be leaders of their generation, the others to be capable followers. This great opportunity in human conservation is in danger of being lost.

How shall we avoid this calamity? What sort of treatment and assistance can be given to these innocent victims of a situation which they had no part in bringing about? If these youths had been well fed and housed in childhood, which most of them were not, they would now be at the peak of health and energy. Even so, they exhibit in every move, plan and instinct that these years, since they are their mating years, are in a sense their fiercest years. Fiercely competitive, fiercely ambitious. They want the best sweethearts, the best clothes, the best records in sports and social accomplishment that they will ever want.

They are, or should be, strong enough to mix concrete or run typewriters all day long, and still dance half the night. But they are haunted by desperate questions. Consciously, unconsciously, subconsciously, through every hour of their days, must run distracting uncertainties. What is to become of them? Can they marry? If marriage has already been achieved, how can they support their families?

It is not easy to be philosophical about this situation. It will not interest a young man who is hiding because he needs a haircut to be told that he is neither at the beginning nor the end of American history, that American youth has been crowded off the edge of cultivation repeatedly since the Colonies were settled, and that though geographical pioneering has ended it is still possible for the older members of the social group to move over and make room for the younger.

There still is plenty of work to do of a sort that youth can do best. Yet somehow we do have to convince millions of our young people that we have not yet come to a social domesday, and that there is something better for them to do than to jump off the deep end—a phrase common among them which apparently covers everything from lawlessness to resignation, despair and even suicide.

If we look back, the nature of previous solutions of this problem is plain to read. From the time when we ourselves were a frontier of Europe until 1890, when the Director of the Census ruled that this country had ceased to have a frontier line, the frontiers of American youth were physical frontiers. Going beyond the Alleghenies, past the Mississippi, past the Missouri where it runs north and south, westward to California in the Gold Rush, east again to the Great Plains, then to the woods of Northern Michigan, Wisconsin and Minnesota, American youth physically conquered the continent. Its electric connective to the future was the vitalizing alliance of new men with new ground.

Now we are forty-five years away from the last geographical

frontier. Millions of men registered as children in the census of 1890 have been superannuated less by age than by newly invented machines. Up to 1890 a strong young man seeking his fortune could still find good and unplowed soil. It may have been less the lure of new lands than the thrust of restricted opportunities at home that sent him forth.

In most cases he probably was not a born explorer and adventurer—if we read the personal chronicles of the westward movement we find few Daniel Boones. But the land was there. Restless and penniless youth had an outlet. A little later, the new lands gone, the mountaineers were coming down from their eroded potato patches to dig in the mines for wages, and the sharecroppers were seeking in the factories a better lot than they could find in somebody else's fields.

From conquering land American energies were turned to the conquest of nature in other ways. In the very decade that marked the end of the historic frontier 208,000 patents were granted in the United States. The velocity of invention was accelerated until in the decade ending in 1930, 421,000 patents were granted. This kind of pioneering made jobs, but it also pushed men out of jobs. For those who were pushed out, for the newer generations as they came of age, there were, with scant exceptions, no new homesteads.

The attitude of the nation toward the young had not changed. They were still expected to fend for themselves and the tradition that they would be well able to fend for themselves outlasted the conditions which had produced it.

The youths born in the years near 1890 did a job that has changed the face of the world and reconstructed the meaning of life. From them, essentially, came the automobile, the radio, the airplane, the improved and widely used telephone, the internal-combustion engine, the steel skyscraper, the linotype, together with the skill and knowledge to keep all this intricate apparatus running.

They taught us to send photographs by wireless, to cast a lens for mapping new universes; they enabled housewives to make ice in their kitchens, to build fires under the pot by turning a button; they released for nearly everyone chamber music once heard only in palaces and symphonies once heard only from the pits of orchestra halls; they telephoned across the ocean and flew around the world; they even lengthened the span of life.

Their achievements were not all positive. Sometimes they were stupid and neglectful of the rights of men and even of the expediencies which might have oiled the production machine which they were setting up. Their frontier manners were often more ruthless than any ever seen in a gun-toting mining camp.

The workers too frequently stood in line of the firing and went down in wind-rows before poverty and insecurity. In a sense the accomplishments of the generation of 1890 created the troubles facing the generation of 1936. Youth pushed itself out of its own country. It enclosed land against its own children. It grew two blades of grass where one had grown before, replaced hemlocks with peach trees and skunk cabbage with lettuce, opened up the ether as though it were a corner cupboard—then found suddenly that its estate was bankrupt.

So much, of good and bad, the youth of 1890 achieved. There is no reason to fear that the youth of 1936, if given a chance, cannot do at least as much that is good. There is reason to hope that the youth of 1936, if given help and guidance during these critical years, may avoid some of the mistakes made by its predecessors.

But guidance and help are needed. Our era is not totally different from that which preceded it, for eras do not abruptly close down over night. The world, which is at hand for the young to conquer, the world of economic rearrangement and readjustment, is neither new nor irrelevant to what has gone before. None the less, new elements have come into it.

Our production process, once a simple relationship of man, tools and materials, has now become a mass process, with masses of tools, worked upon by masses of men, to create masses of products. It can no longer be operated on the theory that the process of distributing the products must be individual, that, as an individual, a man can buy back what he makes.

Men grow rich, or merely comfortable, only because the collective forces are on their side. We can no longer ask wage-earners to fight poverty single-handed. We can no longer turn our young loose in the national pasture and expect them to grow fat. We cannot consider our youth problem as one of individuals, some of whom will be lucky, while others will fail. We must give all youth its chance, and to do this a certain amount of cooperative social action will be necessary.

The aims and possible accomplishments of the National Youth Administration must seem small and niggardly when placed against the canvas of this enormous task. We can do nothing but grubstake a few pioneers, tide them over, see that some of the same ones that start out over the high passes are the ones that reach the fertile valleys on the other side.

The Youth Administration can deal only with those among the young people who are in material need. It is doing something for them. So far it has succeeded in keeping in high schools and colleges approximately 300,000 students. More than 4,000 graduate students are being permitted to pursue their studies with NYA aid in 136 colleges and universities. Their stipend may not go over $30 a month and in most cases it is $25 a month, but it may make the difference between destructive idleness and training for a useful occupation.

For 100,000 undergraduates in nearly 1,600 colleges and universities there is a monthly allowance of $15, earned by a real contribution of work to research, library, museum or laboratory service, or to community projects off the campus. Finally, there are nearly 200,000 high school students, who receive only $6 a month—a small sum, but one which frequently makes the difference between school and no school.

In addition to these individual aids, steps are being taken to organize work of collegiate grade where no higher educational facilities exist, so that college work will be accessible to boys and girls who live at home. On our whole school program, small and thinly spread out though it is, since it touches only a tenth of the unemployed youth of the country, we are spending $27,-000,000 out of our budget of $50,000,000.

Other young people are being helped through work on WPA projects or on NYA projects organized especially for and designed to fit into the needs of those between 16 and 24. The question of how many can receive such opportunities is primarily one of the amount of money available. We could find useful and necessary work far beyond the boundaries of the present limited program.

Beyond these main functions of our program we are undertaking a whole group of efforts designed to benefit young people directly and indirectly. The first of these is the furnishing of additional personnel to the United States Employment Service to help find jobs which are universally recognized as suitable for young people.

Needless to say, we are exercising extreme caution to make sure that cheap and unskilled young workers are not enlisted to force out older and better-paid workers at the top. We are financing the Federal Committee for Apprentice Training, set up a few years ago in the Department of Labor, and through that agency, approved both by organized labor and organized employers, shall try to place young people from both relief and non-relief families in apprentice jobs where they can learn regular trades. Apprentice wages are paid, of course, by the employer and not by the government.

In addition to this we are everywhere attempting to make available a large number of practical activities for young people who have nothing on their hands but time. In State after State the Youth Directors are activating agencies to organize latent goodwill and interest in underprivileged boys and girls. Churches, Y.M.C.A.'s and literally hundreds of associations for the young are cooperating. All are helping us to see to it that these youngsters shall be included as a living and functioning part of their communities.

Looking beyond the immediate task we can perform with $50,-000,000 we see a vast field yet to be cultivated—a real national undertaking to conserve the morale and the as yet untested capabilities of the coming generation.

I believe that we must broaden our school system until we reach some arrangement whereby we can make education meet more nearly the needs of life. We have got to make clear that the services of farmers will never be used up in farming until every child has enough of the right sort of food to eat; that the services of industrial workers should always be in demand until we reach the place where the poor can be as warm in winter as wool and fuel can make them; that the services of economists and accountants, of clerks, salesmen, delivery boys, railroads, trucks and highways, of telephone and mail services, will never be over-employed until the necessaries reach every home; that the building trades, or the housing factories which may in part replace them, will never reach overcapacity until every family has a home of its own; that writers, painters and musicians are not too many or too prolific until they make available to all the expression of what life can mean.

This is a task which we may begin for youth but which must be carried on by youth. The urgent need in this crisis is that we shall not throw away or spoil our human resources, and par-ticularly that we shall conserve the health and the enthusiasm of the young. Youth must rebuild what has been destroyed. It is the nation's most precious asset, now and in the years that are com-ing. We must not let a single spark of that splendid fire go out, in the boredom, hopelessness and actual want that unemployment brings to those who meet it at the threshold of their active lives.

The CCC Marches Toward a New Destiny

by Frank Ernest Hill

AS THE Civilian Conservation Corps marches toward its fourth birthday next month it bids fair to achieve a secure place as a training school for American youth and a peacetime force for the husbandry of national resources. Director Robert Fechner, in a letter to President Roosevelt, definitely proposed such a rôle for it and the President has said that his governmental reorganization program includes a permanent CCC. Meanwhile, provision has been made for its continuance to June 30.

Millions of Americans have had glimpses of the stream of young men passing through the CCC camps—the total number is now mounting toward 2,000,000. They have on occasion seen these young men at work in the city, State and national parks; they have noted roads, bridges and recreation buildings constructed by them, have heard of their fighting floods and forest fires; planting trees and working on farms and watersheds to protect the soil from erosion. But they have not seen what goes on from hour to hour in the 2,084 camps of the "tree army" which dot the mountains, prairies or deserts of almost every American State; and it is here, perhaps, that one may discover what value

From the *New York Times Magazine,* February 21, 1937, copyright © 1937, 1965 by The New York Times Company.

lies in all this activity for the nation and its youth. Let us walk out into the shadowy air of morning as the bugle rouses the 200 men of a camp from their night's sleep and follow them through their day's work.

We are in the Georgia hills. An officer in uniform stands beside the bugler. The "enrollees" emerge from the low buildings half hidden among the pines and stand at attention as the flag runs to the top of the staff. There is a brief report on attendance, a world of dismissal, and the men saunter individually (never in military formation) to the mess hall for a breakfast of prunes, corn flakes, eggs, bacon and coffee.

They are boyish but rugged in appearance. Mostly from Georgia, and many from these very hills, they have the "Anglo-Saxon" look of most Southerners. Sun and brisk weather have tanned and ruddied their faces. In the kitchen, with its great range and serving tables and electric ice box (operated by the camp's own plant), a corps of enrolled cooks is busy, and enrolled waiters carry the food to separate tables where leaders survey its orderly distribution.

Outside, after breakfast, several trucks draw up near the administration building, in the center of the little flat among the trees where the camp lies. The men pile into them, pack them full, and stand holding one another and the side rails of the trucks. They wear caps with ear-flaps, mackinaws, heavy shoes— all government-issued. They stamp and whistle or chaff the enrolled drivers: "Step on it, Tom!" "Let's go!" And soon the trucks move off with a grinding of gears to the "work job" five miles distant.

Now the camp has emerged clearly in the morning light. Most of its dozen oblong buildings are on the flat; a few peer from the trees on the surrounding hills. They are of unpainted wood, but the door and window frames are touched with color. White-washed stones border the road that comes to an end in this remote work settlement.

Before the headquarters are the ghosts of garden plots that bloomed in summer. Walks paved with stones taken from the hills connect most of the structures: infirmary, recreation hall, officers' quarters, garage. The goal posts of a basketball court and the seats of a crude amphitheater set in the curve of a hill suggest some of the activities that occupy the men after their day's work. And there is a log schoolhouse built from the trees of the forest by the labor of the men.

Inside these buildings you will find wood-burning stoves for heat. In the washroom there are showers and tubs for laundry. The barracks show their two rows of army cots with chests at the foot of each for the men's belongings. An "overhead" detail of half a dozen men takes care of the buildings and grounds. Another detail taps typewriters and files papers in the camp office. It is a self-manned unit, this camp, simple and in some respects almost primitive, but neat and efficiently manned.

A short run by car takes one to the work job. Some of the men are doing forest improvement—clearing dead wood, thinning trees, running a trail. Another detail is completing a stone bridge. There is a variety of labor: some workers drive and man a truck bringing rocks; others swing picks and shovels; others are masons. A watchful foreman stands by, and occasionally a man comes to him for directions. Once he bends in brief consultation over a blue print.

They will work here until noon, then into the trucks and back to the mess hall for a hot lunch, then to the job again until the eight-hour day closes in the late afternoon. Supper is over by 6 P.M. and there is a long evening ahead for talk or reading in the barracks (every camp has its library, often running to a thousand volumes), or ping pong or letter-writing or gossip at the counter of the post exchange, or work in one of the classes which make up the camp's education program.

This is a typical camp—so far as any is typical. In New York and New England the men are often of Italian, Irish, Polish and Jewish stock; there are more Germanic and Scandinavian contingents in the Middle West; there are French in Louisiana. And the buildings and grounds and facilities vary with the ambitions and energies of the army officers who administer, the forestry or park or soil erosion experts who guide the work, the camp adviser who presides over education, and the men themselves. But a common spirit pervades all the camps, and there is a certain common denominator of appearance and action.

These reflect the philosophy of the CCC officials as it has developed in more than three years of experience. In flavor this spirit is democratic. Those in charge of the camps and their work regard the men with whom they deal as fellow-Americans and individuals.

There is also a strong pioneer aspect to the CCC philosophy. The sites of the camps, nearly all in untamed parts of the land, almost necessitate this. So do the limitations of the CCC budget. "Making something out of nothing" is a problem with officials and men, but both have faced it with an almost joyous courage.

The astounding and almost elegant appointments of the best camps—recreation halls with hardwood floors, schoolhouses (not provided for in any budget), motion-picture projectors, museums, theaters, athletic fields—all are made possible by savings from the post exchange profits, by volunteer labor, or by "chiseling" on the good-will and pride of near-by communities. But the democratic and pioneer aspects of camp life are in turn part of an emphasized purpose to "rebuild" the young men who enter the CCC.

This purpose was not dominant at first: relief and work were the original objectives of the CCC. But President Roosevelt, its founder, early stressed the "moral and spiritual values" which lay potentially in the organization, and experience has made these of greater importance. These young men are jobless, often ill-educated, often without training, often physically below par. The corps has gradually widened and deepened and made more conscious its program for their rehabilitation.

Its specific goals are now (1) to build up the physical man by giving him clean, comfortable surroundings, good food and healthful work; (2) to develop work skills in all interested men as they labor at their daily tasks; (3) to discover by personal conference their abilities and inclinations; (4) to further these through the field work or through educational courses of a practical nature; (5) to give each man some sense of his duties and privileges as a citizen in American society, and (6) through all these processes to breed new confidence and a desire and capacity to go back to active work in home communities.

The educational program has formed a kind of center for CCC philosophy. The camp adviser holds individual conferences, ascertains "the needs and wishes of the men" in planning courses, and brings in the officers and park or forestry officials to further the general plan.

Men interested in the road building they do during the day will find their superintendent or foreman teaching masonry or surveying at night. Officers and technical staff members and teachers employed by State relief agencies, and the adviser and some of the qualified enrolled men give courses like automobile mechanics, business English, woodworking, American history, current events, tree identification, office practice and journalism.

The classes are informal groups, and the academic flavor is discouraged. They stick close to prospects for employment or conditions of life which the men may face when they leave camp. And their popularity is shown by the fact that, while going to "school" is voluntary except for illiterates (some 9,000 of whom yearly are taught to read and write), more than 60 per cent of the 323,000 men now in the corps are engaged in some kind of study.

What does all this activity mean to those who receive its benefits? One way of finding out is to ask the men. But the answer may be had more succinctly from one of the editors of Happy Days, the unofficial camp paper for the entire corps, who has probably observed more CCC camps and men than any other outsider. He made an estimate that from 15 to 25 per cent of the men are really "rebuilt."

"They find health, training, new knowledge, new ambition in the CCC," he said. "The great majority make definite but smaller gains. The rest get little"—besides the $30 a month each receives in addition to his board and lodging, of which about three-fourths goes to his family. This estimate tallies well with my own observations in more than one hundred camps in all parts of the country.

But CCC officials claim no more than that they stimulate many men, show them possibilities in themselves, give them preliminary training. The maximum of eighteen months is indeed too short to do more. However, they can point to foremen in the organization who were once enrolled men, and to the fact that from 25 to 40 per cent of the men get and keep jobs after leaving the corps.

Certain charges have been made against the CCC which are considered in weighing its benefits. The most important of these has been that the camps are a camouflaged military activity. The army administers the corps, but the officers in charge of camps function under severe orders to impose no military training on the men; and the army carries out orders. The army insists on standards, but enrolled men will walk up to a commandant with a "Say, Captain," as fearlessly as they would approach an employer or the principal of a school. And the officers have no control over the boys while the latter are at work. The park or forestry or soil erosion officials supervise the work jobs, and their influence is perhaps the dominant one in the camps.

Other criticisms run to the effect that the food is bad, that living quarters are poor, that officials are domineering or inert, and that there are restrictions upon freedom of speech. One or more of these may be true of individual camps at times, but except for the last all are essentially without foundation.

There is a real basis for the charge that free discussion of social and political matters is not permitted in many camps. Army officers fear "Communists" and "agitators" and zealously discourage them. Many of the educational staff protest; some camps boast that any radical may speak his mind freely. But in general he may not.

Consideration of the CCC involves not only the atmosphere of the camps and its effect on individuals but a look at the balance sheet of work done and expense involved. The figures are impressive in sheer size. About 1,900,000 men have passed through the corps since April, 1933, including the 350,000 now enrolled. They have accomplished much both in amount and variety. They have built, for example, more than 82,000 miles of truck trails and minor roads; planted 1,000,000,000 trees, constructed 3,000,000 check dams and treated 3,800,000 acres in soil-erosion control work. They have fought fires and engaged in many other activities.

The cost of the camps to Jan. 1 is estimated at a little more than $1,400,000,000; during the fiscal year ended last June 30 it was $492,000,000. Appropriations made by the last Congress were $308,000,000 from July 1, 1936 to March 31, 1937; and the deficiency bill signed recently by the President included an item of $95,000,000 for CCC work from April 1 to June 30.

Those who advocate the permanence of the corps set against the necessary outlay certain intangible but important social advantages.

It is, they point out, an institution peculiarly American in character—wholly different in spirit and practice from European experiments in work camps such as Hitler's labor battalions. And by its combination of work and study it has reached destitute and underprivileged boys as no other agency could. The bulk of these have been "through with school." But the CCC has found a way of carrying on where the schools could not, of converting relatively poor material into useful and sometimes very valuable material.

They argue also that not only the underprivileged will profit by such training as the camps give. Boys from various economic levels fail to make a right adjustment to life in the conventional surroundings. With such an approach to their problems as the CCC affords, many would find themselves.

Finally, they assert that the CCC has come at a time when the nation is in need of such a force for dealing with its public domain. The national and State parks and forests have increased in number; the forces that care for them are insufficient. Soil erosion has arisen as a new problem; here too is a service ground for youth. The nation will profit, they argue, by retaining the CCC, adjustable in size to economic emergency, as a means for saving its youth and its domain.

Undoubtedly the CCC has exerted a vitalizing force on the young men of America. It has taught many of them the meaning of work, something of citizenship, and pointed the way to the skill and knowledge which make citizenship more worth while. It has given many of them new health and new courage.

And no less has it contributed toward saving or improving the wilder part of the American land—mostly the property of the

American public. The park and forestry services have been able to indicate what could be done with a force of young workers: valuable conservation work which they say could not otherwise have been accomplished in a quarter of a century. And they report today that there is an indefinite amount of important protective work still to be done.

The Nation Weighs a Vast Housing Program

by Albert Mayer

ON A VISIT here last year, in which he observed our housing progress, Herbert Morrison, Labour member of the London County Council, remarked that the then pending Wagner bill was somewhat milder in its provisions than the English Act of 1890. The Wagner bill did not pass. This may be taken as a gauge of the status of housing here as compared with that in European countries.

However, a revised Wagner bill is now up for action, with apparently much stronger support, and some things have happened here in the last few years. Some public housing has been done. We need no longer rely altogether on statistics, blue prints, photographs of architects' models and of European examples. We can actually see—and a few lucky families can actually live in—communities with lawns and trees, spaces where children can play without one eye on the traffic. A fine job is more stirring than tons of literature.

Conceivably, the time may be near at hand when, in the characteristic American way, we shall suddenly dart forward at a given moment and begin to cope with an accumulated situation which elsewhere would have been coped with in a more concerted, gradual way. Bills are being introduced in Congress and in the State Legislatures to give public housing a permanent status.

The new and probably compelling factor is the dwelling shortage. It is the one element in the housing situation on which everyone agrees. It is being brought daily into dramatic focus by evictions and tenant strikes and vociferous but as yet futile public hearings. Rents are rising markedly. While the shortage in its upper economic reaches is a matter for private enterprise, this is not true at lower income levels, because the workers cannot afford to pay enough for satisfactory housing to yield a profit.

The other factors—our indefensible slums and our inadequate building industry—have long been with us, but have been generally recognized only in the last few years. Whether the incidence and recognition of these factors will fuse into a determination to meet the whole problem in a reasonably integrated way, or whether we shall allow it to drift along in the haphazard hands of the speculative builder remains to be seen.

It is worth examining what has happened in housing since 1933 and what light this may shed on the future. Nineteen hundred and thirty-three was the year in which—except for the war housing—public housing was initiated. Emergency funds—ultimately some $130,000,000—were allotted under the Public Works Act, of which 45 per cent was grant and 55 per cent in the form of loan at low interest rates. It was also shortly thereafter that relief workers began extended surveys all over the country, indicating the shocking conditions in which our low and even higher income population were living.

Of course, some things had happened before that. Remedial and restrictive legislation had been passed at long intervals, improving the more flagrantly bad details of existing laws. Zoning had swept the country—zoning of a type that scarcely changed housing or city patterns, but rather defined them in accordance with existing practice. The war housing had influenced technical thought, but had not aroused public interest.

Probably the most significant and influential pre-1933 development was the report of the New York State Commission of Housing and Regional Planning in 1926 which resulted in the creation of the New York State Housing Board. A most painstaking and comprehensive critique of our whole system of inadequate housing and non-planning, it stimulated various isolated projects for low-middle incomes. Some, like Radburn, Sunnyside and Chatham Village, had considerable influence in preparing for the large-scale government efforts of 1933 and the following years. Practically 100 per cent of the houses before 1929 were built by speculative builders, uncoordinated with each other or with any rational larger planning. All were built for the upper-third income group.

The long gap of the depression ensued. Practically all housing construction stopped for a period of some five years. In 1933 the PWA Law was passed, the first of a series of efforts to make public housing serve as one of a number of emergency re-employment measures. Many of its difficulties arose from the fact that housing was conceived as merely a minor employment measure rather than a frontal attack on the problem, with strong popular backing. A number of government agencies at one time or another have planned and constructed housing—the PWA, the TVA, the FERA—later succeeded by the Resettlement Administration. In each case the organization existed in the main for other purposes, and only a minor part of its funds and energies were devoted to housing.

While there was no real coordination among them, each of these organizations had its sphere. PWA operated in cities, TVA did one big housing job in the garden city of Norris, FERA started subsistence homesteads. The Resettlement Administration took these over and added to them in its rural resettlement program. It also initiated three satellite or greenbelt towns for industrial workers—near Washington, near Cincinnati and near Milwaukee.

A rough figure of the number of living units built, building or immediately planned by these agencies would be about 40,000. This in the face of 500,000 families in New York City alone living in old-law tenements, in the face of an estimated minimum of 10,000,000 families living in substandard dwellings in the country and in the face of a physical shortage of 10,000,000 dwellings in the next ten years.

About 10,000 dwellings are completed. The remainder should be completed within a year. For PWA this means a period of over four years. The other agencies—some of them established later—proceeded more rapidly. Causes for delay were the shifting of emergency funds back and forth from housing so that the departments never knew just how much to plan for; legal questions both within the departments which made their degree of authority doubtful and external legal obstacles in the form of injunctions by which property owners sought to prevent the work altogether. PWA suffered from personnel clashes at the start and from an early policy which attempted to build on slum land in multiple ownerships, which delayed land assemblage and caused cancellation of projects or later shift to readily obtainable land.

Despite the disappointingly small number of houses, despite delays, despite the fact that in general rentals have not been brought within range of the lower-income groups, this public housing has great positive significance. For the first time we are able to see and grasp what is meant by large-scale housing in planned communities; planned with respect to adequate light and air; with respect to recreational, social and educational facilities; with playgrounds and parks either within the project or near at hand.

The PWA will have erected some fifty of these in thirty-five cities. Here for the first time is a pattern for living scarcely available at all in our cities at any income level. To have seen such communities in Europe, to see the early examples here is to know that their plan, their size, their physical equipment furnish the frame for the good life within one's community and for spiritual pride in it.

The greenbelt towns are based on the observed tendency of population to decentralize to the periphery of urban regions. Their prototypes are the successful English garden cities. Where the usual suburbs spread indiscriminately much as our cities have done and are often finally indistinguishable from them, the greenbelt town is a planned community whose ultimate size is limited by a permanent green belt of farms, meadows and woods. It is a complete town with its own government and ultimately its own industries, but located near present industry to assure a free labor market.

These towns together with TVA's Norris demonstrate three immensely significant points. They are the first large-scale urban examples of a planned land-use program in place of the helter-skelter lack of policy that has hitherto characterized the growth of our cities and suburbs. They make for urban-rural interrelation, both cultural and economic, in place of the hitherto increasing separation. They offer a pattern of the large-scale integrated units which the building and especially the home-building industry must eventually follow.

What has private industry done during this time? Its incipient revival has been made possible by two government agencies. The Federal Home Owners Loan Corporation to the extent of $7,000,-000,000 bought the frozen mortgage loans of financial institutions, making possible the reloan of these funds for private construction. This compares with the total of some $250,000,000—about one-thirtieth—made available for all the government's public housing.

Second, in 1934, it established the FHA, which insures loans by private institutions to 80 per cent of their appraised valuations, and did much to spur the sales of new homes by its tremendous propaganda. Examination of these houses, their costs, their methods of construction and sale, indicates that the private building industry has not made significant progress in community planning, in the quality of the house itself, or in inherent cost, over the last thirty or more years.

Costs vary simply with wages paid and quality of materials used, and have not been lowered by significant improvement of process. This applies to all our homes at all income levels. These facts are largely due to the fantastically small and irresponsible units through which the assembly and distribution of houses takes place. Prefabrication alone will not change this picture essentially, unless the wastes of distribution are cut down. Indeed, it is the reluctance of manufacturers to disturb the small-scale speculative distribution method that is delaying the introduction of prefabrication, rather than technical unreadiness.

Two improvements are visible. More individual mass-produced appliances are available, that is, refrigerators, oil-burners, thermostatic control. Second, the twenty-year single mortgage with amortization has succeeded the short-term first and second mortgages with bonuses for renewal and replacement. Unfortunately, the FHA in its eagerness to push construction has been unable to insist on standards of planning and quality of construction which would improve the security for the mortgage and make such mortgages less vulnerable investments. It has more or less taken the industry as it found it and confined itself to suggestive advisory pamphlets.

Generally, speaking, neither public nor private housing has yet reached really low-income groups. PWA's predicted rentals vary from about $7 a room, including heat and electric current, to something like $8.50—depending on land costs and locality. Seven dollars, with heat and current, corresponds to about $5 a room base rent. Cost of and monthly financial tax-maintenance-heat charges on private homes are not available. But from FHA's loan figures, it would appear that the average home costs just under $5,000, that only 6 per cent of homes cost less than $3,000. The average monthly charge, including maintenance, would be about $40 a month without heat, to which must be added interest and amortization of $6 on investment.

While public housing enjoys financial subsidies and lower interest rates, private housing receives subsidies in the form of non-union wage scales, often inferior materials and workmanship. In addition, private building has in general not provided communities, leaving the provision of parks, recreation areas, &c., untouched.

Private housing on comparable standards of wages and product has not shown itself more efficient and has made no conservative contribution. Public housing is initially proving expensive for various reasons—in some cases high-priced slum land, in some cases excessively elaborate standards and specifications, the use of inefficient relief labor, the purchase of extra land necessary for future community growth. But it is showing the way in community planning, in long-range land-use programs, in site planning, all of which are possible only in large-scale units. Such trends indicate ultimate economies in first cost and in yearly charges by way of operating economies and lessened obsolescence of homes and of neighborhoods, which in turn increase safety of mortgages and should decrease interest rates.

As to the house shortage, estimates vary from a figure of about

9,000,000 to 14,000,000 as the construction requirement for the next ten years. The great variation depends both on the uncertainty of available figures and on viewpoint. The low figure contemplates no improvement in existing substandard houses; the high figure contemplates some replacement.

We may assume a necessary building rate of 1,000,000 houses a year for the next ten years. This compares with about 180,000 publicly and privately built last year, and an all-time high of some 600,000. Every agency, public and private, will have more than it can do.

The bulk of housing is going to be done by private enterprise in any case. As the boom increases and prices rise, it will be possible to make a profit either on more and more costly houses, which only a smaller and smaller group can afford, or on skimpily built houses for which the house-hungry public will pay excessive prices. The permanent presence of the government is required not only to supply housing for low-income groups but to set standards that will in every community serve as challenges to private enterprise and as examples to the public of what it may legitimately seek.

The Wagner bill (the Wagner-Steagall bill) as now introduced, provides for a United States Housing Authority appointed by the President, to assist local public housing agencies and cooperatives and other limited dividend enterprises to establish decent low-rental housing. To public agencies it may make loans for the total project cost at the going Federal interest rate, and grant fixed annual subsidies to a maximum of $12,500,000, which is supposed to bring rents to less than $6 a room. A total of $100,000,-000 is authorized, to be raised by bond issues guaranteed by the Federal Government over a four-year period. It is granted broad powers over erection and construction of projects, and may build projects where no competent local body exists.

The Wagner-Steagall bill provides a very minimum of public housing; its funds would cover only about 50,000 dwellings a year. The best obtainable measure, it should pass so as to assure an immediate permanent status for public housing, for the emergency agencies are being dismantled. While decentralization and local initiative are essential, it would be folly or insincerity to rely on local initiative exclusively. Local governments lack the funds, in many cases they lack even the political mechanism, and, above all, that would mean further delay.

For example, a bill has been offered in the New York State Legislature authorizing a vote in next November's election on whether $100,000,000 worth of bonds should be raised for low-rental housing. Certainly it is a minimum, and certainly such laws should be passed. But to rely on it exclusively would mean a year's delay as compared with passage of the Wagner-Steagall bill. Once it is passed, public opinion must see to it that it is promptly put to work and that the subsidies go toward lowering rentals, not toward indemnifying slum-land holdings at high prices or into the profits of material manufacturers.

Though erecting only a small proportion of the total of houses, the government will be the largest concentrated factor, and as such can point the way to rationalization of the productive and distributive aspects of the industry.

The whole housing problem then takes two immediate forms. How much public low-rental housing shall we get in the next period of prosperity and boom? Will the housing at whatever level be the same speculative helter-skelter product that had to be rescued to the tune of billions in the last depression, or will it begin to measure up to our acquired knowledge in planning, in technique, in social stability and usefulness?

The Big World At Last Reaches Gee's Bend

by John Temple Graves II

MONTGOMERY, ALA.

BELOW MONTGOMERY the yellow Alabama River on its way to the Gulf wriggles like a water moccasin. In one of the wriggles is Gee's Bend and its community of 700 Negroes with a single name and a way of life. Approachable only by gullied roads from one direction and a precarious makeshift ferry from the other, the community has been isolated for generations from the motley of civilization and is a relic of something that both includes and antedates the Old South.

Romanticists and realists who vie now in the business of examining the South, recovering its lost places, finding its new ones, making poems of its past and problems of its present, may sense here the whole gamut of Southern Negro history, from tribal jungle to antebellum plantation to New Deal alphabetics. They may sense it in the point of view, the way of life and in the nature of the three Negroes who lead this remote and extraordinarily autonomous community.

They may watch the one called Little Pettway as he goes about the Bend with other Pettways at his side, hear him pray in a language no one knows, wonder at his authority, and guess that without benefit of nose ring or paint he is the chieftain of a primitive tribe. They may go with the one called John Henry to the big house and to the place where "Marse John" is buried, and see in him the plantation man, the trusted slave turned overseer. And then they may listen to old Patrick Bendoff's smooth talk under a chinaberry tree, his gossip of what the Government is going to do, and be reminded that for better or worse this is the twentieth century, after all, and that a New Deal is watching Gee's Bend.

The drums of Africa, the banjos of antebellum plantation times, the dreams of Rexford Guy Tugwell—all are tokened there on the plateau above the curving river where half a hundred little cabins surround a great cotton patch, and the big house of one-time white masters looms apart, guarded by two giant pecan trees, an elm and an ancient water oak.

The big house is a ghost, paintless and in unsightly disrepair, but the fanlights over front and rear entrances, the beautifully proportioned rooms, the high ceilings, the fine detail of cornice, woodwork and plaster, speak of its day that was. The cabins are shabby and poor as they lift their tattered tops above the cotton rows, but the logs that wall them are hand-hewn; the hand-split shingles that roof them are weathered to a gray so silvery and soft that Eastern architects would sell themselves down the river for the sight of them; the bare yards are clean and sandy-white, and the picket fences are all in place.

From front to rear of each cabin, dividing it after a superstition that no two rooms shall have a common wall, is the dog-run —an open hallway through which not only dogs but pickaninnies and pigs and chickens run as occasion calls. Within most of the yards, after the same superstition, there are several separate one-room buildings in addition to the central cabin. It is all crude, backward, poor, but the great point is that human beings have been happy and productive, self-serving and self-governing and healthy there for a long time, and, given half a chance, may continue to be.

With few exceptions the Negroes at Gee's Bend are descendants of the hundred or more slaves Mark Pettway found and bought when he came from Halifax, N. C., in 1845 and purchased the plantation from Charles and Sterling Gee.

All of the descendants are surnamed Pettway now because that was the only surname their forebears knew when, after the war between the States, freedmen found it necessary to have a second name. There are plenty of first names, but not enough good ones to go around, apparently, for one hears of a Tom Pettway and then of a Tom-O Pettway and a Tom-I. Austen is so favorite a name that its suffixes ran through more of the alphabet than most Pettways know, for education is something that has come late to the Bend. But intelligence and character are not late. They have been there for generations, and so have love of the land, faithfulness to the community, willingness to work hard and look ahead. And so has orderliness. The Sheriff of Wilcox County will tell you that no one from his office has had to make an arrest at the Bend in thirty years.

So quiet, so self-contained are these Negroes, so little inclined to leave their community or to take newcomers into it, that they might have gone on happily lost to civilization if the depression had not come. If cotton hadn't dropped to 5 cents a pound they might have gone on being what the world calls primitive, keeping their Negro blood pure, surviving the annual freshets, growing their cotton and corn on good land for a good return, getting their stores and their only contact with outside life from the "furnishing merchant" in Camden across the river.

After Mark Pettway died soon after the Civil War, his son John ran the plantation until his own death in 1900. The Negro families made a simple living as tenants, raising most of the foodstuffs they consumed, selling their money crops for supplies and occasional cash at Camden, building their own cabins with nothing but nails to be paid for. There were other owners to occupy the big house for a while after "Marse John" died, but finally there were no white men at all and one of the Negro families was put into the big house.

Life went on much as usual through these changes. In the years of rising prices before the World War there was real money at the Bend, over and above the amount owed to the "furnishing man" for supplies. In 1916, though, came the terrible "July freshet," when the river flooded the whole Bend, with crops in full, and brought a winter of hard times. After the war, when the boom began, Gee's Benders did better than ever in their lives; some of the larger families who owned mules rather than oxen received checks for as much as $1,000, even after heavy interest charges and supply bills had been deducted by the Camden merchant.

History rolled by them like their yellow river, something beyond the Bend, only occasionally interrupting their routine or spoiling their smooth way with its flood moments. Their land was rich and they raised foodstuffs on it as well as cash crops, generally coming out about even when they had purchased what outside supplies were required. They sang in the fields, in the cleared space down the lane from the big house, in the unpainted old church. The families worked together on their acres, plowing, planting, hoeing, picking, pulling.

When there was a marriage the men of the community would build a cabin for the new couple as a gift—a gift of work rather than of money. When there was a death the burying would be without ceremony if it came at a time when the men could not be spared from the fields. The ceremony would take place several weeks or even months later, when it could be enjoyed to the full and in good conscience. Sickness was rare; isolation from the outside world held contagions to a minimum. The white masters became white landlords and then disappeared altogether. Nobody came, nobody went. Gee's Bend was a world in itself.

Then the depression came. Cotton fell so low it wasn't worth selling. The merchant agreed to hold it for better prices, crediting each family and advancing supplies on the credit. He was a pleasant man and Gee's Benders trusted and admired him. He was the source of everything they needed from the outside world and they had no complaints of the good profit he took on loans and sales to them.

For three years he made these advances against unsold cotton. Then he died and trouble came to the Pettways. His business had to be liquidated and, with cotton still low, the security wasn't worth the supply bill. That meant a wagon train at the Bend, with white men taking everything in sight—feed, implements, live stock, whatever could be sold for cash. When the families gathered in their queer, dilapidated old church to worship and pray, their songs were "moanful" as never before. Gee's Bend had become a charity case.

During the winter of 1932–33 the community existed miserably on small supplies of meat, flour and meal provided by the Red Cross. The white owner of their land, Mr. Vandergraff of Tuscaloosa, agreed to let the families remain without rent, but he was unable to provide necessary supplies. The owner of a neighboring plantation gave a few beeves and an occasional day's work at clearing land, but cotton was still low and no one was willing or able to risk the considerable sum needed to outfit the Bend again for normal production and living.

In the summer of 1933 the men worked on county roads for 50 cents a day, although there was one day when they failed to report and Little Pettway had to explain that they had lived on wild plums for four days and hadn't the strength for road work. This seems to have been about the only time in history that Gee's Benders ever complained of their lot, and even this was not a complaint. It was an explanation. In December the CWA gave part-time work at 30 cents an hour and throughout the following year the Alabama Relief Administration helped, while cotton prices were rising again.

Since 1935 Gee's Benders have been "clients" of the Resettlement Administration. Their improving economic lot results not only from general business improvement and from the intelligence and sympathy with which Regional Director R. W. Hudgens has handled their case, but also from their own eager and cheerful loyalty to whatever fate's best offer may be.

Equipment, feed, fertilizer, work animals, medical aid and supervision from the Government have restored them to economic life. Rehabilitation loans are being paid in full as they fall due. Mules have been substituted for oxen on three-fourths of the farms and there is a great increase in cows, hogs, brood sows and chickens. The average net worth per family was only $28 in 1935 and is $385 now. Supplies come once more from Camden, but no longer from a single merchant—and Little Pettway does the buying for everybody.

He is the head man. How he comes to be the head man no one knows. Perhaps it is owing in part to the extraordinary quality of his praying when the families assemble, as they do so often without apparent schedule or call, weekday and Sunday alike, for religious worship. He prays in a tongue unknown to linguists or to Gee's Benders either, a series of eloquent and moving sounds that excite his hearers as recognizable words never could. A slight man in his middle forties, bare-footed, baldish, soft-mannered and very black, he does not impress the outlander with leadership at all. Some of his authority comes of his business repute, for the Pettways are proud of the trades he drives at Camden now as community buying man. With white people he is amiable but uncommunicative. He is the tribal chieftain, and his confidences seem reserved for the group of male members of the community always at his side.

Much more the white man's Negro is John Henry Miller, another of the leaders, who lives with his sociable, substantial wife and an invalid child in the big house, surrounded by the faded relics and fine woodwork of Gee, Pettway and Vandergraff masters gone with the wind. It was John Henry's job to collect rents for the white owners as far back as Marse John Pettway, and it is his job today, and pleasure, to play host to white visitors —show them around the Bend, take them through the house, answer questions. If Little Pettway is the tribesman, John Henry is the plantation man.

Harder to place is the third leader—65-year-old Patrick Bendoff, who lives with his wife and many children and grandchildren in the best cabin, wears a tucked-in white pajama top gracefully in lieu of a shirt, has seven additional one-room buildings within his picket fence and a grove of peach trees beyond, and who makes a distinguished occasion of it when he welcomes visitors under the big chinaberry tree that flourishes in his clean front yard. Patrick is a conversationalist, a man of humor, a philosopher —and a clearing house of up-to-the-minute information. Gee's Benders come to him now for word of what the Government is planning to do and for somewhat uneasy consultation on what the bountiful but revolutionary planning from outside may bring to them individually. The Government's people seem equally to look to Patrick for word of what the Benders are thinking and feeling.

His authority in the community comes in part from his personality, but also from his affluence. And his affluence comes of his extensive kinfolk and progeny. One of his daughters is John Henry's wife. He has other married daughters and sons living in cabins all around the cotton patch, and in his own home are still others who, without having attained marital status, are parents. As a moral man and a leading citizen he expects to see each of these married to the other party as soon as economic conditions permit.

Patrick wasn't born at the Bend and that is why he does not bear the Pettway name. But by grace of his marriage to a sturdy Pettway and his prowess as a father he is kin to more Pettways now than anybody in the community and has more sons and daughters to work for him. That means wealth, for at the Bend it is manpower that counts.

The Resettlement Administration has bought Gee's Bend now from the Vandergraff estate and there are plans for redistributing the land so that everybody can have some upland for cotton and some lowland for corn, installing a medical unit, improving the roads, building new living quarters.

To all of which the Pettways are unstintingly responsive. They are not a progressive people so much as they are a faithfully accepting one. They accept what comes their way and make the very best of it, work hard and happily with it. Some of them are a little worried, it is true, about giving up their old cabins and changing their land. Even Patrick Bendoff wants to know if he can't keep his old cabin after the new one is built. He might need it, he says jokingly, for "somebody to run away to," and he is concerned, too, lest "some nigger git my peach trees who ain't never eben planted a chainaberry tree."

The slight uneasiness is contagious, for visitors themselves wonder if the well-intentioned plans of the Government for rehabilitation of these picturesque and normally happy, independent people are going to make a regiment of them, put them into standardized houses, bring them into contact with a world that will spoil and dissipate them, rob them of self-reliance, individuality, peace.

Mr. Hudgens swears he will not let this happen. He agrees that there are things worth saving. He means to have the families build their own houses, as of old, he says, with only a few limitations and standards in the interests of health, security and economy. They can have lean-to kitchens if they like, he says, and he will encourage them to build dog-runs. That will be good news, for every Bender knows that a house without a dog-run, where rooms have only one wall between them, is marked for a death.

But not even the excitement of visits from a paternal government gives anybody nervous indigestion at Gee's Bend. The Bend is dried out now from the economic freshet and is at peace again. The men are building a new church, exchanging their services at a neighboring sawmill for some special lumber while the women obtain money for nails and other incidentals through the sale of eggs.

In the cleared space near the big house is a huge out-of-door brick oven under a wooden shed where the women, in bright-colored gingham dresses and gay bandannas, gather sociably to prepare their fruits and vegetables for canning against the winter, while their children pick wild plums and blackberries in a near-by thicket. The women murmur in soft-voiced undertone. In the cabin yards at mid-day large black iron pots are boiling with food for the men who will come from the fields, and hoe cakes are being cooked in the ashes. There are plans for a big community fish fry and barbecue.

Meetings in the church are crowded as ever, and pencil scrawls on the wall beg worshipers to "pleas be quied" and "pleas dont spit on the flore," but this spelling will improve, for an average of 100 adults attended a school conducted for them last year. Soon there may be new machines and implements to be purchased and used under what the Government calls a "cooperative plan"—a cotton gin, a peanut picker, a hay baler, a grist mill, a cane mill, a canning plant, tractors and terracing machines. But cooperating is nothing new to Gee's Benders. They have been doing it all their lives, doing it because so many of them are kin and because they all like and trust one another.

No one can visit Gee's Bend without an appreciation of racial virtues preserved there which are vastly worth preserving and which tend to disappear in more civilized quarters where the ambition of the Negro is to become only a carbon copy of the white man. It is not necessary to wish the Negro's destiny confined to what these families enjoy to believe that the families and their way of life and point of view are of value as a storehouse of original racial qualities, a laboratory in which the most excellent characteristics of a people may be isolated for example's sake.

Renwock C. Kennedy, the Camden minister who first called public attention to Gee's Bend, believes that the Negroes there feel superior to other Alabama Negroes, "and probably are." But it seems to me that their self-possession is lodged not in superiority so much as in a great serenity. They do not seem capable of understanding either superiority or inferiority. They are themselves. They are objective. They are serene.

And they are affectionate. They love everything that gives them half an excuse for being loved. Most of all they love their land. "I'se got more confidence in my land eben than I has in my wife," one of them told me. And that is saying a lot, for the Pettways of Gee's Bend are a very moral people—after their fashion.

Part 3

THE CENTRAL TASK

VARIED AND NUMEROUS as the reforms of the New Deal may have been, its primary task, as New Dealers themselves defined it, was to rid the country of the blight of unemployment. The articles in this section are selected to provide some conception of the responses made by the New Deal to the massive unemployment of the 1930's. The sad thing is that conscientious as these efforts were, they did not do the job. Only war provided sufficient stimulus for those without jobs to be absorbed into an expanding economy.

The article by Harry Hopkins, who in 1935 became the head of the principal work relief agency of the New Deal, the Works Progress Administration, is revealing on several counts. Noteworthy, for example, is Hopkins' interest in the decentralization of industry with the intention of reversing the movement of population from country to city. Roosevelt, too, in the early years of the New Deal expressed a similar goal. In his first Inaugural he called on the nation to "frankly recognize the overbalance of population in our industrial centers and, by engaging on a national scale in a redistribution, endeavor to provide a better use of the land for those best fitted for the land." Hopkins' recommendation of subsistence gardens around factories also reflects the rural bias that is often unrecognized yet so characteristic of the New Dealers.

They liked to think of themselves as hard-boiled social engineers, yet they were obviously soft on the agrarian myth that considered green grass and a plot of earth as particularly soul-satisfying, if not actually regenerating. Of equal importance in Hopkins' article is his conviction that work relief was already a permanent part of the government's responsibility. Indeed, the conclusion to be drawn from all three of the articles in this section is that the problem of unemployment had become permanent. That there would come a time when the job would hunt the man was beyond the fondest expectations of these men. Full employment was more a wistful utopia than a realistic social goal. There is no better measure of the deep impress that the Depression made upon Americans in the 1930's.

One of the consequences of the massive unemployment, as Jacob Baker's article shows, was that government began to recognize it could put men to work in a variety of ways other than on the usual road-building and construction jobs. Once again the sphere of government enlarges. Yet even in 1934 it was still necessary, Baker's article makes clear, to defend the unemployed against the charge that they were in some way different or deficient. The recognition that a man could be without work through no fault of his own is probably the most significant change in attitude brought about by the Depression and the New Deal. Until then it had been axiomatic among Americans that in this land of abundance anyone who really wanted a job could find one.

The challenge of persistent unemployment as well as the resistance it offered to solutions come through with luminous clarity in the R. L. Duffus interview with three national leaders concerned with the problems of labor. As one reads the solutions proffered by each of the men, the inadequacy of their answers to the problem is almost painful. Their chief remedy, basically, is to piece out the available jobs among as many people as possible; none of them seemed to recognize that the true answer lay in finding ways to expand the economy. At that time, unfortunately, there were few people who understood how to stimulate economic growth. Heretofore "natural" forces had been counted upon to bring depressions to an end, but in this economic debacle those forces seemed no longer to be working. The author's statement that he believes a constitutional amendment is necessary to provide government with the extraordinary authority required to end unemployment is yet another measure of the novelty as well as the intractability of the problem.

The article by Rexford Tugwell, former head of the Resettlement Administration and long-time adviser to Roosevelt, provides an example of the more advanced social thought emanating from the New Deal. Wrestling with the question of farm tenancy, Tugwell dissents from the easy solution that advises the lending of money to sharecroppers so that they may buy their own land. Quite properly he sees the question as one of rural poverty, which demands a more profound as well as a broader attack. Notice, too, his awareness of the need to adjust social goals to the changes brought about by new technology—an acknowledgment not always common even today, but all too rare in the 1930's. His article also illustrates one of the significant departures of the New Deal, namely, its recognition of the powerless and the very poor in American society. The New Deal did much to bestow power upon organized labor through a law like the National Labor Relations Act, but it did little to grant power to the unorganized poor.

Today we know that the answer to unemployment lies in the expansion of the economy. In a sense, the Roosevelt administration was on the right track when it turned to compensatory spending by the government as the principal means for lifting the economy out of the slough of depression. The essential defect in the New Deal's efforts was that the expenditures it could countenance were never large enough to do the job. The New Dealer most closely identified with the idea of compensatory spending was Marriner Eccles, who is interviewed in Francis Brown's article. Once again the reader is impressed by the author's need to defend Eccles, who was a Utah banker, after all, against the charges of radicalism. The only reason for such charges, of course, was that Eccles thought government ought to play an active role in raising the economy out of its slump, and many people were still not willing to accept such activity as legitimate for government. Quite rightly, Eccles defends his approach as a strictly capitalistic method for saving capitalism. The conception of the government's role in a time of depression that Eccles here outlines is, of course, the philosophy embodied in the Employment Act of 1946 and that which has been followed by all administrations since the New Deal in countering recessions.

Beyond Relief:
The Larger Task

by Harry Hopkins

THE DAILY PICTURE presented by those of our people who are in distress makes philosophizing about the relief situation very difficult. Rather it forces one to develop practical means for quickly alleviating that distress and preventing its recurrence. The pressing need of the unemployed and their families pushes everything else aside.

For example, we have on relief rolls now nearly 7,000,000 children under 16 years of age. What that means to you will depend upon how much you have seen of relief. It means to me that we have nearly 7,000,000 children who are not living in such a way as to grow normally, to keep normally well or to enjoy those advantages to which they are entitled.

In the face of such a situation one is inclined to leave philosophizing about relief to others and proceed to a conviction shared, I strongly suspect, by all my associates in the administration of relief. This conviction is our working principle, or, if you please, our working philosophy. Every act, and there are many, that we are forced to perform for expediency or speed which is not predicated upon this principle is unsatisfactory to us.

From the *New York Times Magazine,* August 19, 1934, copyright © 1934, 1962 by The New York Times Company.

This conviction is that relief as now extended to the unemployed does not exercise sufficient curative effect and is generally unsound and undesirable as a permanent activity. There is no insurmountable reason why we should continue to give it. There is nothing inherent in the direct relationship of people to the necessities of existence—land, air and water—which should prevent their having a good life. There is enough air to go around. There are five oceans from which to recruit rain and replenish our rivers. There is land and to spare.

I feel we need to know more about this business of unemployment and its hazards. Members of our relief organization are assembling for the first time an itemized statement of poverty in the United States. We consider the work of our division of research and statistics to be of equal importance with the administration of relief. Not until we have in our hands the bill of particulars as to our habitual levels of living can we reckon the extensiveness of American poverty or figure out its specific causes. When analyzed the information we have gathered is immediately useful to us in the plotting of our relief expenditure. It also reveals to us causes and trends, such a fact as, for instance, that the five heavily industrial States of New York, Pennsylvania, Michigan, Ohio and Illinois contributed almost 40 per cent of the total families on relief.

We have studies begun or contemplated to tell us which of the industries carry their social weight and which of them are supported by the taxpayers; what relationship relief incomes bear to habitual wage incomes; and what relationship, if any, either of these bears to a decent standard of living. We are beginning to learn to what extent relief is an answer to joblessness and to what extent it is used to supplement inadequate wages. The findings on these questions will be of extreme importance.

Since we unavoidably learn these facts while we are trying to do our job, at what point does our responsibility as relief administrators toward them cease? We have been asked politely by some to stick to relief and leave the causes of it alone—in other words, to mind our own business. We follow up trouble. If we want a perpetual job as relief administrators, it would be shrewd to take this advice and let trouble alone.

I think that under the circumstances we can be absolved of conceit if we say that we are practiced diagnosticians of trouble. We have sharpened our wits on it. From aggregate cases to individual misery, mounting into millions, we have found certain social and economic deductions to be inescapable. Like doctors, we see case after case of sickness and learn the causes.

There are three courses for us to follow. Personally, I believe we can do no less than to follow them all as far as we can take them. They do not run at cross-purposes.

We are now operating under the mandate that the economic system should be responsible for its needy victims—that as long as industrial employment shall persist in tossing human beings out into unemployment government will pick them up and relieve their destitution. This is the first course and this is the true conservative's concept of the function of a relief administrator. Only when the resuscitation process becomes too expensive and requires too many relief workers, too much food, too much clothing—all paid for, so he believes, out of his own private pocketbook— does the conservative protest.

A long step beyond that, but still undeniably within the province of any department charged with providing the victim with security, is a program of unemployment insurance. This has an affirmative value both to the individual and to the industry. It puts industry on guard against waste and it rescues the individual from certain of the most degrading forces of public alms. In this bailiwick of public welfare lies also another aid to secured life—health insurance with medical care.

All of these things can be achieved with only minor disturbance to the present pattern. With private hospitals financially distressed, doctors on relief, sick people forgoing care and a national crop of tuberculosis and rickets sown and ready for harvest a few years hence, people are beginning to realize that the problems of health coexist with economic disruption. So this becomes a logical objective for any commission charged with public welfare.

The second path lies through disputed ground. This is where relief takes on the functional character of work and aspires to do more for the recipient than to give him a week's rations. It aspires to give him a job, self-respect and at least the momentary sense of security that comes with employment. So far, where this sense of security has been achieved at all it has been illusory, since we have not yet been able to project our works program far enough into the future or to work it out in sufficient detail to make it a real stabilizer for private employment.

This is ground that the Federal Government has been traversing for a year. I say it is disputed ground because it inevitably touches upon the claimed rights and purposes of the industrialist and the farmer. The activities under this province which, it will be seen, do not all attach to FERA, are the Emergency Administration of Public Works, Civilian Conservation Corps, Subsistence Homesteads, work relief, cooperative self-help societies and rural rehabilitation. They occasionally affect private wages and hours. They have created little disturbance. Talk occasionally comes up about the inroads of the subsistence farmer upon the commercial farmer's market. But the subsistence farmer is not transferring his trade. He is merely eating, whereas he was hungry before.

Even should the self-organized cooperatives of the unemployed go into an extensive production of goods for the unemployed, existing markets would not be drained. The unemployed would be making things for themselves which hitherto they had gone without. Wherever local existing wage levels have been disturbed by work-relief wages so that, as is occasionally alleged, workers refuse private employment because they can make more from relief, the true state of affairs is apt to be that the local wage level is no level at all, but a subcellar.

However, it is easy to see that effective relief methods—that is, practices which will take us out of the necessity for relief— will eventually have to change certain practices of our economic system. As we follow this third part of the course we can point out the trouble and possibly the way out. We know where poverty is, and where it will continue to be, so long as certain practices of our economic system are allowed to persist. We know what congestion does to standards of living, what lack of sun and air does to health. We know that the complete reliance on cash income, peculiar to the city dweller, is his chief trouble when he loses his job. In April, this year, in New York there were 1,187,439 persons on relief, or as many as in the whole city of Los Angeles. The percentage of this number to the total population of New York is unimportant. The quality of their destitution is the important thing, and the evil thing that it makes out of life.

I believe the time has come to decentralize as much of industry as possible, and I do not say this either as a follower of Gandhi or of Longfellow. The alternative to the big city is not an Arcadia. Our rural slums are as bad as our city slums. But somewhere between the squalor and poverty in both of them there lies a suitable existence and a good existence for men. It is becoming clear that, if a very sizable number of people whom industry is now failing are to be again included in its benefits, adjustments such as decentralization must be effected.

So far, big-city industries have given us much bad housing, small chance for outdoor recreation, no security, but both cash incomes and the company of fellow-beings. The cash and the company are essential. The land yields neither of these. But it gives room, air, sun, food, a back-log and a root-cellar against winter. A combination of these virtues seems desirable enough to work for. The goal is to balance small units of industry, to provide some cash income, in communities capable of yielding a pleasant existence on land capable of producing a part of the workers' necessary food.

Decentralization cannot easily occur in all industries. The heaviest industries seem logically centered on fixed points. It is ludicrously evident that it would be impossible to farm out the making of locomotives, for instance. A man can scarcely put a roundhouse in the vegetable patch to take up his spare time. Neither can the steel industry be uncoupled from cheap transportation or its materials. But it would not be difficult to list the industries in which labor plays a more important part than materials, and in which the maximum efficient unit is smaller than that so common today.

Much of the present concentration of industry is the result of accident and inertia. The old excuse of power no longer holds. Power is widely—and could be cheaply—disseminated. Neither must the old idea of being near to market have such a tenacious grip. A redistribution of work would redistribute the market. Better wages would increase it.

This is no moving-van job. We shall have to relax the economic tensions which produce big cities. If we moved all the people in Chicago to the Promised Land, they would snap right back to Chicago again. Freight rates, money rates, wage differentials, land values, farm markets are but a few of the considerations involved. Furthermore, the housing administration of New York is discovering that the poor are unwilling to leave the city. They feel that the close-crowding intimacy gives them social defense against unknown dangers. They have been the support of each other.

The idea of decentralization of industry and the encouragement of smaller units in smaller communities, dependent in part upon wages of local factories, and in part upon subsistence gardens, comes to us as a means not only of inducing people to leave congested areas but as a solution for people stranded without work because mills have moved away or mines have closed down. In their case, the arrival in their community of a unit of going industry would prevent their having to be moved elsewhere. Decentralization of industry may also have significance for people stranded on deficient land.

From an examination of these rural stranded we learn that 36 per cent of our total relief families live in rural areas. This gives us either the right or the responsibility, as you wish, of insisting upon a reform in the use of the land. We are obtaining a new concept of the use of land. The most ambitious dreams of early conservationists, who hoped the country would some day become conscious of the perils of stripping the land of forests and farming it for maximum crops, have become tragically true.

If any good can be said to have come out of either the drought or of this acute phase of a chronic farm depression, it will be that we are willing to consider the land as a national utility, to be defended against greedy exploitation, and even more especially from ignorant use. The man who is in the business of farming has to be guided and protected in that business. But, in addition to this, we have learned that land is not idle when it stands either in forest or grass to protect our water supply, and that land put into vacation areas gives a manifold return on the money.

When, finally, if ever, we shall have attempted to cover each problem with an answer, we ought to find relief at the bottom of the structure rather than at the top. At the top should be industry and agriculture so geared as to give the maximum employment and the maximum wealth in goods to each of its workers and to take a responsibility for a maximum number of our population. Beneath this great roof of private employment should be a permanent structure of public works, responsive to the increase and decrease of the private labor market. It must be organized to contract and expand easily. In order to have integrity either for the individual employed or for the government which creates the employment, the work done must have real social utility, in addition to the fact that it creates jobs. By social utility I mean it must increase the national enjoyment in existence, whether the project is one of slum eradication or cancer research.

This will be the big net under private employment, designed to catch the workers dropped from industrial payrolls. Of finer mesh than this will be the social safety devices of unemployment and health insurance.

It is inevitable, until we become physically a better race than we are, that there will be many to sieve through all these safety devices. These will be the unemployables and the social dependents. These social dependents have status and protection under the State laws. Government must take care of its unemployables. We shall probably never be able entirely to dispense with relief. But it can and should be relief with responsibility assumed by the people as a whole and administered for and by the people through their agencies of government—Federal, State and local.

Work Relief:
The Program Broadens

by Jacob Baker

IN THE WORDS of Harry L. Hopkins, Relief Administrator, the widely circulated idea that people would rather accept straight relief than work for it "is an Elizabethan notion, and 100 per cent wrong." Our works division is another answer to this fiction.

What we have been doing during the last two years we have been compelled to do, to a great extent, by the will of the people themselves. Our merit, if we have accumulated any at all, lies chiefly in the fact that we have tried to interpret that will in terms of deeds.

Our work program is based upon the recognition that the vast majority of the unemployed prefer work to straight relief. Last winter the civil-works program was launched by the President largely to meet this demand, and 4,000,000 needy unemployed are on work relief, and month by month this total is growing. In found employment under it. At the present time nearly 1,500,000 this whole matter we are doing what the unemployed themselves want.

Indeed, long before the CWA program was started, many of the unemployed had already taken the matter in hand themselves, and started self-help cooperatives, the object of which was to make their members self-supporting—take them off the relief rolls. Like so many things that happen in America, the movement was started by individual initiative. Only after it was well launched did the government, through act of Congress, come to its assistance. There are 207 cooperatives receiving Federal aid. We figure that they have saved the government at least $1,000,000 in relief expenditures, without taking into consideration at all the moral values they create.

A number of cities claim the credit for having been the first to set up city work-relief plans. We in the Federal office have never attempted to determine whether it was Indianapolis, or Milwaukee, or one of several other cities. We do know, however, that by the time the Federal Emergency Relief Administration was formed the pattern of work relief was well established, and it has been the function of the Washington office of the FERA to preserve this pattern and strengthen it, not to substitute a new one of its own invention.

To this end it has acted as a clearing house which has set up standards of procedure and practice; but the responsibility for the proper use of the grants allotted by Washington rests with the States, and to them belongs most of the credit for the achievements in work relief.

Out of experience a few general principles have been evolved. One is that work relief should in no wise interfere with normal employment. People on work relief should not be doing jobs that cities, States or school districts ordinarily hire men to do. It is not sensible to take a janitor or clerk out of his regular job and put him on relief.

Work relief should in no wise injure the standing of other workers. Wage rates, for example, should not be lower on work relief than elsewhere. Also, we assume that the rate of pay declared by the President to be the basic minimum for decency should be paid to persons on work relief. Last year, after the President's Recovery Agreement was issued, we set our minimum rate of work relief at 30 cents an hour.

A still further principle is that work relief should not be made so attractive as to induce people to stay on relief rather than take jobs at their regular occupations when they can get them.

We let a man on work relief work only as many hours as are necessary to keep himself alive and clothed.

Besides general principles, some general practices have been established. In each country a wage-rate board composed of representatives from organized labor, the business public and the Relief Administration, decides what is the prevailing rate of wage in each craft. A further machinery exists for the hearing of complaints about wage rates and working conditions. A careful and continuous program of safety education is carried forward, stimulated from Washington but worked out in detail in State and local organizations.

There is practically no type of construction that the unemployed do not undertake. Most of the State capitols have been rehabilitated and redecorated. Relief workers have built waterworks, sewage systems and garbage-disposal plants, irrigation ditches, hospital buildings, swimming pools, stadiums and athletic fields. They have moved tracks for municipally owned street-car lines and rebuilt cars. They have built power lines for community-owned electric services. They have built and are now building several thousand airports.

Construction work exactly suits the American temperament. That is one reason why it developed. We have had splendid technical resources at our command. The competence and eagerness of American engineers, employed and unemployed, is amazing. Nothing can delay or hamper them.

From actual construction, work relief proceeded quite logically to service projects which contributed to the health of the public. Some 25,000,000 rats were eradicated in a campaign against typhus. Millions of acres of malaria-breeding marsh lands were ditched and drained under this program. In a campaign to check intestinal diseases, such as typhoid and hookworm, other projects were undertaken throughout the rural districts. Much of this work has been carried on for the workers themselves, because their unemployment has given rise to special needs for medical and health care. They have also needed more recreational and educational opportunities than people with jobs.

This is where the unemployed professional people have had a chance to contribute their special abilities rather than be put at work foreign to their experience. It has been recognized that when an artist or musician is hungry he is just as hungry as a bricklayer and has the same right that a bricklayer has to be employed at his own trade. For the first time in our history, our government has become a patron of the arts, officially and quite unashamed. Unemployed musicians play in free orchestra concerts. Actors give free performances of plays, artists paint canvases or murals in public buildings. Unemployed teachers have classes for unemployed adult pupils. Scientists are put to work at research.

Naturally, in most cities many of these methods had already been employed before the Relief Administration came into the field. We simply aided already operating local agencies to expand their work. But in the less highly developed rural districts the cultural program came as something new and inspiring. There it had more than a quantitative value.

Rural community centers were built by work-relief employees and staffed by them. Here women could come to discuss and learn about child hygiene and nutrition. Rural visiting nursing services were established in many places. In a number of States an enthusiastic campaign to wipe out illiteracy in the back country, as well as in the slums, was undertaken. Books and magazines were contributed by people in the cities to extension library services in back-country districts and sent out to isolated mountain settlements. Where there were no railroads they were carried by what are known as bookmobiles, and where there were no passable roads they were carried by pack-horses.

The men and women of these rural districts, for the first time perhaps, had a share in health, cultural, recreational and social welfare facilities hitherto, for the most part, accessible only to city people. This part of the program, we feel convinced, has left a lasting impression on these communities and will not be dropped altogether when times grow better and the relief program is finally liquidated.

Also in nursery schools the Relief Administration has been able to make lasting contributions to educational theory and practice. About 2,000 such schools have been set up under the Relief Administration procedure in the last year. The whole pedagogy and theory of nursery-school and infant education is in process of formation. Within a year we multiplied existing institutions by ten, and created a groundwork for study of the habits of young children and of the relationship of nursery education to family life.

The construction phase of our program was spontaneous. We not only had the temperament and facilities for it: it was the traditional kind of public work. But the unemployed themselves found it insufficient.

It is they who have contributed to the trend away from pure public construction and toward the creation of goods and services of which they themselves, being the needy ones, will be the beneficiaries. Schools, plays, concerts and health services have been one phase of this transition. Production by the unemployed for the unemployed is another. This tendency arose at the end of the civil-works period, when small groups began to gather in workrooms to try to make things for themselves.

There is a simple logic in an unemployed man's attempting to produce and distribute things for his family needs. Beyond that, there is a great financial saving to the public when a man on relief is allowed to lower the cost of his maintenance. Finally, there is a future advantage to the community in giving unemployed workers a chance to keep up their discipline and skills, so that they may keep in condition to resume their old jobs when opportunity offers.

Before the drought, in practically every State the unemployed were producing vegetables in individual or community gardens, consuming the produce according to their needs, and conserving the surplus. In some States they had canneries mounted on trucks operated by relief workers. These traveled from place to place putting up vegetables and fruits which had been brought in by the women of the neighborhood. The drought meat-canning program proved to be only an extension of an activity already well developed.

In the same way the proposal to consume 250,000 bales of surplus cotton by making mattresses and bedding found a number of sewing and mattress workrooms already going in various States. At present there are throughout the country some 689 mattress-making and sewing projects. It is hoped these will provide 1,000,-000 needy families with mattresses, comforters, sheets, pillow-cases and towels.

We who are in a position to replace our household equipment from time to time have scarcely an idea of what five years of destitution can do to household goods. A broken glass in such a household is an irreparable loss. Any number of people in the country are sleeping on bare slats or bed springs. To fill this almost bottomless need household goods are being turned out by the unemployed on a limited scale for distribution among the unemployed.

Thus far, many of the goods and wares have been hand-made. Hand-woven rugs, furniture worked by hand, hand-modeled pottery —these are some of the products which are being turned out in relief workshops. The workers seem, certainly, to get more creative enjoyment out of this sort of production than from oper-ating machines. Since our object is not to save labor, but to create it, their preferences can easily be indulged. Some of the self-help cooperatives have gone in for handicrafts. One organi-zation, for instance, turns out very beautiful hand-cut and en-graved glassware.

There is really no ground for the concern expressed in some quarters that we are going in for wholesale manufacturing. A relatively small percentage of the 1,500,000 individuals on relief work are actually engaged in production and distribution. Most of them are still employed either in construction or in the cultural and educational and service fields. Moreover, we have no equip-ment in our workrooms for high-speed mass production. In order to create jobs, the work is done as far as possible by hand or with very simple machines.

In some States there has been worked out a more comprehen-sive scheme for production by the unemployed. Sometimes it is called the Ohio plan because it has been actively developed by the Relief Administration of that State and has received more publicity than similar activities in other States. The arrangement is to lease some of the idle factories, re-employ as many of their old man-aging personnel as possible, and then let the unemployed work full time in producing goods for their own needs.

They propose to cover the minimum budget of each worker by cash payment of wages; all wages over and above that amount to which he is entitled, he will receive in goods produced in these relief workrooms. Relief workers engaged on non-production projects will also be paid over and above their budget needs in these goods. An important feature of the plan in Ohio is that all rented factories are on short-time leases. If the owners get any commercial orders the plants can be turned over to fill them.

Since for the present relief production must develop, of necessity, rather slowly and remain always on a limited scale, the chief problem still faces us. How are we to divert the trend of construction work from public luxury improvements to projects that will prove of more immediate benefit to the unemployed themselves?

There is one field where this is still feasible, namely, housing. The greatest need of the American people at present is for new low-cost housing. Estimates place the deficiency at 1,500,000 inadequate quarters. In order to make decent dwellings available for them, rents must not exceed $4 or $5 per month per room. Decent housing at these rates cannot be supplied by private capital. If it had been possible to earn even a modest return, private capital would have undertaken the task long ago. Inducements of various kinds, tax exemption, loans at low interest by government-backed agencies, and even outright subsidies have brought no rush of building. The job must be approached differently.

All over the country, relief administrations are looking more and more to the employment of relief labor for solution of this housing problem. Already we are engaged in demolishing old and unfit dwellings at the request of the owners; we are also using relief labor for rehabilitating and modernizing old houses. The owner repays us for the work done in various ways, the most customary being an agreement by which he permits families on relief to occupy the renovated building rent free until the improvements have been paid for.

But what are really wanted are plans by which the unemployed can be put to building new houses. The workers now receive their subsistence from the relief administrations. They are already on either direct relief or work relief. The direct cost of the houses would therefore be only the amount paid for materials and land. By this method housing can be amortized over a long period and the rentals kept under $5 a room.

The houses belong to the communities in which they are erected, and the men who work on them become the tenants while they are on relief. As long as they are unemployed the rental payments are made from their relief allowances. As soon as they get jobs they become rent-paying tenants in their own right. Here is a wide field of relief employment which has barely been scratched and that in less than a half dozen cities in the country. It carries with it many collateral benefits through the supply of material with consequent advantage to the heavy industries and the agencies of transportation.

All of the foregoing perhaps sums up in this: that the unemployed constitute a cross-section of the United States; they are the same kind of people as the people who have jobs, they have the same kind of skills, they can do the same kind of work. Conditions of life for these great masses of our fellow-countrymen would now be unbearable had no measures been taken in recognition of their needs and in compliance with their desires. Out of their work great public benefits accrue.

Our work program is an extension of the ordinary program of relief. Relief furnishes the food and keeps men and women and children alive. It is the work that satisfies their sense of independence and keeps them a part of the industrial and social system in which we live. The unemployed demand the right to work for what they get. The relief administrations of the United States have assumed the responsibility of providing suitable tasks of economic and social merits—tasks that result in a gain to the community and in direct benefit to the men and women who work on them.

Unemployment: Must It Be Permanent?

by R. L. Duffus

WASHINGTON

DESPITE SOME EVIDENCES of recovery more than 11,000,000 Americans are still believed to be out of work. How much will this figure be reduced if and when the full tide of prosperity returns? Will it entirely disappear? If it does not, what provisions shall be made to care for it? Even if it becomes negligible is it necessary to plan far ahead for the unemployment which will probably come when the economic cycle has completed its next full swing and business again reaches a low point?

Three men in Washington, each intimately associated with the unemployment problem, each coming to his conclusions by a different road and out of a different experience, are in substantial agreement as to the answers to these questions. They reflect, probably, a large body of opinion in the fields of public life, of social work and of organized labor. They are in line with the beliefs expressed by such disinterested bodies as Governor Lehman's Commission on Unemployment Relief, which recently recommended a long-term State program.

Senator Robert F. Wagner of New York, author of the Economic Security Bill and the new Labor Disputes Act, with a long

From the *New York Times Magazine,* August 25, 1935, copyright © 1935, 1963 by The New York Times Company.

experience as lawyer and jurist, is one of the three men. Harry L. Hopkins, head of the FERA and of the new Works Progress Administration, social worker of more than twenty years' standing, is a second. William Green, former mine worker, president since 1924 of the American Federation of Labor, is the third.

What the three have to say on the subject must be interpreted according to what is meant by unemployment. Men engaged in seasonal industries are only nominally unemployed if they can earn enough during a part of the year to maintain a reasonable standard of living all the year round. Technological unemployment—the displacement of men by machines—is only a transient phase if machine products bring about lower prices and so increase the general buying power of the public.

Finally, a man employed on a worthwhile public works project must be subtracted from the totals of the unemployed, even though private industry has no place for him and even though the money with which he is paid comes out of an emergency appropriation. Thus, if the new Federal works program were to realize its announced objective (a goal which may or may not be reached) there would be no employable unemployed. The unemployable unemployed would be a charge on any society. Their numbers can be reduced only by minimizing the forces which break men down: industrial accidents, occupational diseases, preventable sickness and disability, and the permanent collapse of morale which comes to many men after they have been a long time out of work.

Of the three men, Administrator Hopkins, who has come closest to the problem of relief, is possibly the least optimistic as to the ability of private employers to keep everybody at work. Essentially, however, his position is not greatly different from that of the other two. He discusses it in his FERA office at the end of an exacting day's program—for, whatever may be said of other people, Administrator Hopkins is not out of work. He is lean, nervous, concise in his way of speech, at times half-humorous, half-sardonic.

"Of course," he says, "I think unemployment is a permanent problem. There is nothing new about it. It has always been a problem. There were great reservoirs of unemployed in particular districts even in such boom times as 1929. The problem has been greatly aggravated since then. In my opinion we will have a larger number of unemployed in the years to come than ever before."

Senator Wagner, taking a breathing space in the spacious committee room adjoining his office before meeting his morning swarm of letters, puts the case differently.

"Large-scale unemployment is not inevitable," he declares. "If it were a necessary attribute of our present economic system, then no proposal for change could be too radical to command respectful attention. But I am convinced that our system will endure, and that within the framework of existing institutions the man-made evil of unemployment will be destroyed by the application of human intelligence."

President Green is just as confident. Sitting in his shirt-sleeves in his unpretentious office on the top floor of the A. F. of L. headquarters, in the heat of a Washington summer noon, he explains the position of organized labor.

"To regard unemployment as permanent," he insists, "is to assume a defeatist attitude. We refuse to accept such a gloomy philosophy. We maintain that unemployment—widespread though it has been during the past four years—is an economic abnormality and cannot be regarded as unavoidable. Unemployment is a social and economic problem which industry, labor and government can solve if they will work together."

But how? Shorter working hours, social insurance, planned public works, better planning of private industry are the suggested ways out.

"Obviously," says Mr. Hopkins, "certain things must be done. The stabilization of employment in industry has made substantial strides not only under the NRA but through private pioneering. Firms like Procter & Gamble in Cincinnati have done work in this field which proved that industry could adjust its output in consideration of the employment needs of its workers. Undoubtedly many better adjustments could be made and I know many industrialists who are now working on the problem.

"In spite of this stabilization, in my opinion, there will continue to be large numbers of people who will be idle through no fault of their own. Since this idleness is usually due to national or even world economic conditions, the problem is one that must be handled on a national basis. The Security Act is the first step in providing unemployment insurance benefits out of reserves which are accumulated through taxation. I have no doubt the act will be amended many, many times, as have all social insurance bills in Europe. America will gradually develop new techniques and methods in this field which are adaptable to our needs and conditions.

"This will mean a well-organized, non-political employment service throughout the nation, which will be closely identified with the unemployment insurance administration. But it seems to me that in America we must go one step further than this— we must develop a permanent works program for persons out of work, especially for those whose insurance benefits have lapsed. There is work to be done in America for years to come which is entirely outside the province of private capital, which will in no sense interfere with private business, and which will contribute to the wealth and happiness of the people of America.

"These projects are not only the great Federal projects identified with land utilization, but State and city undertakings, such as housing, sanitation, public parks and the development of great recreational facilities. It simply means that a share of the total national income each year must be taken to provide for these essential social needs—of which that created by unemployment is probably the most important.

"Sickness, old age, accident insurance must, of necessity, be part of the program. It is unthinkable that in a great nation as wealthy as ours the capital structure cannot provide a share of the national income for those persons at the bottom of the economic ladder, whose lack of income is due to economic forces and conditions over which they have no control. No nation can consider itself civilized which does not provide these essential opportunities for minimum security."

Like Mr. Hopkins, Senator Wagner lays emphasis on the role of the businessman as well as on that of government.

"If we want to get at the nub of the problem of unemployment," he argues, "we must promote industrial stability. This involves first of all the encouragement of rational cooperation among business men in order that they may produce and sell goods with an adequate knowledge of market conditions and with full protection against unfair and degrading competition. It involves secondly the nation-wide synchronization of economic activity in a pattern which preserves private enterprise and which at the same time provides basic governmental supervision and permits the constant adaptation of judicial processes to ever shifting social conditions. If our public procedure and our legal machinery become inflexible and heavy the task cannot be done.

"To my mind the prime prerequisite to industrial stability is such coordination between production and wages as will maintain a steady market for factory output instead of provoking repeated depressions by the collapse of purchasing power. This necessitates at least a modicum of governmental regulation of wages and hours, certainly in the major industries. But if we are to achieve this balance while avoiding the pitfalls of a despotic State, we must clear the way for free and full cooperation between industry and labor. That is why the cultivation of collective bargaining is not merely an abstract matter of freedom for the worker, but rather a concrete foundation for the general welfare.

"Despite the prospects that such a program holds forth, those of us who are not utopian philosophers expect to be confronted by some periodic let-downs in private business activity for at least a generation. Industry cannot run with the mechanical perfection of a gyroscope. Out of simple caution we must devise some method of dealing with those who may be severed from their normal work despite our best efforts.

"For seasonal and sporadic unemployment the most feasible remedy seems to be unemployment insurance. For more chronic and technological unemployment the best remedy that we know is public works, which may be expanded when private industry is prostrate and contracted when the wheels of private industry begin to move more swiftly.

"The application of the public works idea has scarcely passed beyond its infancy.

"But I trust that with the sure advent of better times the full significance of planned public works will receive recognition. The responsibility of government to help those who cannot help themselves must be as enduring as civilization itself, and coupled with that responsibility there should be a well-conceived utilization of human energies and natural resources that will benefit the entire country.

"I have no doubt that our society can eradicate unemployment. The only question is whether we are willing to pay the price in intellectual exertion and material cost."

In approaching the same enigma, President Green emphasizes the organized labor policy of the shorter working period. He sticks to the thirty-hour week as coming as close as possible to the maximum which would permit the absorption of all chronically unemployed labor. Into this estimate enters a balance between the growing use of labor-saving power machinery and the growing demand for goods of all sorts which will be produced by a rising standard of living.

"We must resign ourselves," he admits, "to a certain amount of technological unemployment. There will be displacements due to the constant increase in the use of power. That point has never been emphasized enough. But if we accept the inevitable and make such adjustments from time to time as the needs of the nation require, we can deal pretty effectively with technological unemployment.

"Then we must consider also seasonal unemployment. Even at the height of the boom the army of the unemployed ranged from a million to a million and a half. This army could be reduced, I believe, if the task were approached in a systematic way by all concerned. In so far as it cannot be eliminated, we must think in terms of an annual, not a daily or weekly, wage. It is what the worker earns during the twelve-month period that determines his standard of living.

"I look on unemployment insurance as a means to an end. It should be used to accelerate employment. The cost should tend to inspire employers of labor to find work for people rather than carry the heavy financial burden of insurance costs of unemployment.

"The government should make a systematic, long-time plan for public works, which it has not yet done. What is needed is a program, well thought out, well considered, that can be applied without delay when the emergency comes. We prepare in great detail and with great thoroughness for war. Why shouldn't we prepare for unemployment?

"The employer must cooperate. So far he has tended to react negatively to proposals made by labor. Employing interests have objected to the movement for the elimination of child labor. They opposed workmen's compensation and many other social welfare laws, all of which the more enlightened among them have since come to accept as being in their own as well as the public's interest. Their spokesmen have been suspicious that organized labor was trying to put something over. The record should prove that that is not the case. Unemployment and other economic evils do not merely concern labor. They hurt everybody."

How large a body of public opinion these points of view represent can only be guessed at. There would be little serious questioning of them, so far as they go, among the 2,600,000 members of the American Federation of Labor or the 1,500,000 to 2,000,000 workers in organizations not affiliated with the federation. They are to the left of the conservative opinion which sees the only possibility of relief from unemployment in the free play of economic forces. They are obviously to the right of the smaller body of opinion which sees no hope except in sweeping change.

Social security, the compulsory shorter work-week and long-range planning of public works are within the democratic framework of existing institutions, though it is possible that they cannot be fully realized without constitutional amendment. A few years ago they would have been called socialistic. In the minds of all three of the men quoted in this article they are clearly a means of preserving private initiative and private enterprise, not of destroying it.

Behind the Farm Problem: Rural Poverty

by Rexford G. Tugwell

THE WAY toward improvement among the underprivileged farmers is not to ask ourselves what we want but to ask ourselves what we can get. Sociological ideals in this matter can do little more than confuse issues. Any defensible standard for all of the underprivileged farmers is so far from possible achievement that it might better be forgotten.

There are many people who find it hard to conceive of family life with a cash income of one to two hundred dollars a year. Because they cannot grasp the reality of living on these terms they are unable to measure the achievement represented by adding 10 or even 50 per cent to such an income. But the truth is that the doubling of a hundred-dollar income represents an infinitely greater victory over nature's obstacles than does the doubling of a five-thousand-dollar one. And its meaning, detailed in a hundred little, and seemingly uncounting, items of a budget, is apt to fill the understanding heart with pathetic satisfaction.

We have fallen so far, our lowly country folk can have so few of civilization's prizes, that the only practical course open to us is to forget our figured diets, our slick advertised standards, and begin all over, in the kitchens and stables of real people

From the *New York Times Magazine,* January 10, 1937, copyright © 1937, 1965 by The New York Times Company.

rather than imaginary ones, working toward obvious small betterments—and they are terribly obvious; there is no chance to go wrong!

For instance, one of the achievements the Resettlement Administration set for itself this year in Alabama was to see the last of its clients graduated from bulls to mules as farm motive power. This seems like a small gain, perhaps, but it is really a very great one in percentage. Similarly, twelve hundred cans of home-grown vegetables may seem like small provision against an uncertain future; but to an Arkansas farmer's wife it means the certainty of a whole winter's food—and there are many to whom this represents the multiplication of security for her family by ten, by a hundred.

These mules, the tools to go with them, and the seed and fertilizers as well; these gardens with their yield in home-canned food; the shoes and clothes of respectability, represent a first inching toward the future. What has this to do, it may be asked, with the problem of "tenancy"? The answer is, of course, that "tenancy" is not the problem. The problem is poverty from whatever cause—and frequently the cause is not the landlord-tenant relationship.

In the current outpouring of talk the usual misinformation is being made available and the usual optimism concerning administration is showing itself. To have the whole problem misconceived is distressing enough; but to be on the verge of permanent legislation, and to feel that it cannot possibly be effective because of this, is doubly so.

It may be, of course, that we are not talking about the same thing. Perhaps the current concern for "farm ownership," "independence," "free men on their own land" is one thing; and the rural poverty which has grown so serious is another. To many of us they seem impossible to separate.

If this is so, then a so-called "tenant bill" will need to concern itself relatively little with "tenancy" as such, and relatively much with a gradual attack on the causes of poverty. The simple process of making debt-ridden owners by the thousand would create more problems than were solved; and reversions to tenancy would be likely to be more rapid than any public program could keep up with.

The Resettlement Administration has been attacking poverty among rural folk with a vigor which is unprecedented in this country. It has incidentally been doing a good deal about tenancy. but its tentative objective there has been "security in possession with a more adequate family living," rather than "ownership." In the face of reality, that has seemed more practical. Squalor and degradation, malnutrition and disease, ignorance and unhappiness, insecurity and exploitation—these are the realities to be dealt with.

We feel that we have made a beginning when we have substituted mules for bulls, replaced cans of pickles which satisfy malnourished cravings with cans of vegetables which are a necessary part of an adequate diet. They fall short of the inflated goals which make better appeals to the uninstructed sentiment, but they strike at the genuine weakness.

For those who are ready for it we have provided some thousands of families with going enterprises or shares in them, with the higher standards which are reasonably defensible, counting cost unimportant if it can be balanced by certain income. There has been more publicity about these last, because it has suited our critics better, but we know that their defense is easy and that, anyway, by far our greatest efforts have been much further down the scale and that these ought to continue for some time to be the center of emphasis.

We have dealt with these problems, using emergency funds, hour by hour and day by day, out in the counties, in field, home and stable, until only the persistence of fatigue has held our devoted men and women to their task. Devotion may sound like an exaggerated word to use in this connection; there is no other which seems to me to fit so well.

Days and weeks I have traveled with these people, farm and home plans in hand, as they schemed for better living and checked accomplishment. Down the lanes and in the byways, wherever the forgotten rural folk have found themselves a spot which the better farmers did not want, the county and home supervisors travel. Finding better land or better landlords, helping to plant and harvest, making cash money go farther toward providing store goods, showing the way to greater self-sufficiency, holding out the hope of eventual resettlement in high-producing enterprises for the few who show the greatest ability. And on top of this expected task, so satisfactory in its results, we have been unexpectedly asked to fight drought and dust and flood.

In spite of all that our critics have said, we know that to have done what was done with emergency funds and against the handicap of McCarlism was nothing we shall ever be ashamed of. None of us grudges the effort it cost. Some of us may have spoken a little bitterly among ourselves at the editorial conception of "an easy government job at the taxpayers' expense," but not many of us and not often. The only source of real bitterness any of us has is the thought that our hammered-out knowledge of reality may be abandoned for a well-meaning but thoroughly irrelevant generalization on which to base future policy.

We hear it said that "something must be done about tenancy" and we shudder. We are doing something about it and about what lies in and around its roots. And we know that essentially what we are doing is sound and right.

As a matter of fact, there is no more wrong with tenancy than there is with ownership in this country. Neither, as a tenure arrangement, has been well managed here. Tenants have to shift too often; when they do they lose anything they may have contributed to capital investment in the enterprise, with the result that little is contributed and much is wasted; they suffer from credit disabilities; most lack any supervision, and without it they are no more capable of managing a farm than a workman would be of managing a paper factory or a steel mill.

But small owners are no better off. They carry the weight of a mortgage and consistently sacrifice to the god of interest; they face foreclosure with every fall in prices; their management suffers from the same or greater disabilities than that of tenants.

One trouble with tenancy is landlordism; one trouble with ownership is the mortgage. But the trouble with both is lack of direction. Neither yields security, efficiency or conservation. But both might if they were informed. Setting out to abolish one in favor of the other merely avoids the deeper issue. Anyone can see that ownership provides a certain incentive; but anyone can also see that a man is better off to occupy land he does not own provided the terms on which he can keep it are less onerous than purchase—and also provided his possession is just as secure.

During the next few months the field men of the Resettlement Administration will be actively searching for good landlords. Several hundred thousand tenants who are rehabilitation clients will have to move; their county supervisors will try to improve the tenant status by lengthening the contract from one year to three or five—no more seems possible yet—by favoring the landlords who appreciate improvements and by furnishing the active supervision which tenants need.

During these same few months about 1,000 tenants will finally be set up on farms they can hope to own. They will have a five-year trial lease with option to buy at the end or to enter into a long-term lease. Buying will cost 1.3 per cent per year more than leasing; this is a forty-year amortization charge. Each tenant can figure for himself whether ownership is worth that much. His interest rate will be 3 per cent. He can therefore have a five-thousand-dollar farm for twenty years for $150 a year. Or he can buy it for $65 a year additional.

But no doctrinaire commitment has been made to any tenure system. The belief is that no "system" is good. It is the way it is worked which counts. With Resettlement management supervision we believe that either can be worked. One advantage of this is that it leaves the whole choice of his permanent status to the individual. It gives him alternatives; it does not foreclose them. But this is not so important as the fact that it takes attention away from system or principle and centers it on operation, which is where it ought to be. The atmosphere ceases to be confused by conflict of ideas; and the problem becomes an administrative one, which we know how to handle.

This is the way in which the Resettlement Administration has made its approach. With loan or grant it has gone into some 800,000 farm homes. About 400,000 have what are called "standard rehabilitation loans." With every one of these loans went a promise from the farmer and his wife to manage their homesteads in such ways, as the county farm and home supervisors and the county citizen's committee (which passes on all loans) thought would bring the government's money back. The purpose of the loan was not that: if it were, some credit agency might as well have made it. The purpose was to rehabilitate—a long word which soon got country-shortened to "rehab." And not even that, usually, with one loan; for the first loan was a trial, a start, which, if it succeeded, was usually followed up by others.

This gradual lifting policy followed up year by year with supervision is anything but spectacular. The people who are being worked with do not count greatly in their communities. They are the poor and the outcast, or such of them, to be accurate, as have discernible skills, energies and ambitions to be recovered; for there are those who cannot be rehabilitated as things are, and these can only be kept going rather miserably by Federal grants or with local aid.

Many of these clients cannot, or at any rate do not, vote, and so, especially in the South, the politicians can afford to call them lazy, shiftless, no-account. The efforts toward farmer-aid can more profitably go to the better citizens among rural folk who can be expected to suitably repay political efforts made in their behalf.

This, of course, accounts partly for the emphasis on "tenancy" legislation. Any help which might be given under this name would inevitably go to these better farmers. The necessary work at the foundation can be escaped by savage phrases of dismissal. If this is done, the reason for it ought to be kept clear. If we have no intention of attacking poverty at its source, if we only intend to make owners out of a few of the better tenants, the administration ought not to have credit for helping really forgotten families; only for doing what democracies have usually done—helped those who needed help less because those who needed it more did not count politically.

Some rehabilitation families doubtless have a shiftless father. If so, they cannot get by the first small loan. But many who might have been thought at first to be shiftless have turned out not to be. Some were sick—a long, familiar list of rural diseases, hookworm, pellagra, malaria, venereal troubles are multiplied in incidence on the RA rolls; many had been exploited—by landlord, furnishings merchant or banker—until they had lost hope of ever getting a real start; many had lost their soil through erosion or because it did not pay them to maintain its fertility; many had been the victims of disaster, price-depressing surpluses, depressions, floods, droughts. They were sick, discouraged, hurt. They had a kind of psychosis or shock. And they have to be nursed back to health and ambition. They cannot be flung over a wall to Utopia.

Farm ownership? Yes, some day, for some, under the right conditions, at their own choice and with a clear view of its costs and after they have demonstrated their ability to rise. But now, most importantly for the many, treatment for disease, better diet for children, a mule, some seed and fertilizer, clothes to lift the shame of going ragged to town, some hope for the future, a friendly hand to help in every farm and home crisis.

For the 5 or 10 per cent who have already come through their ordeal, possession of a farm enterprise or full share in a cooperative one. For 90 per cent, medicines, food and a crop; for 10 per cent, new homes and barns on reconditioned acres, because we know they can be kept up out of the yield of the land. For 90 per cent, a little lift in level, a gradual accommodation to something better; for 10 per cent, full participation now in the American standard of living. This is what Resettlement has been and is doing. What it fears is the forgetting again of its 90 per cent and concentration on its 10.

This is a program we can afford to see through and one which avoids the great technological difficulty which faces a simple program of small ownership. These two considerations—expense and changing farm practice—have not been considered with sufficient realism by most of those who want something spectacular done at once.

When we speak of tenants we are not talking about people remote from our own neighborhoods or even over in the next county, much less people confined to the South or any other geographical region. Tenants are everywhere; they are, in fact, nearly half our farmers (42 per cent), about three million in number and well distributed. Where the land is best tenancy has increased most in recent years, so that in Iowa, for instance, exactly half the farmers are tenants (which is more than double the percentage in 1880); and this fact, in itself, complicated the proposed ownership solution.

If we set out to finance all our tenants into ownership at $5,000 each (which cannot be done because tenancy is now so prevalent in areas of high-priced land), we are deliberately contemplating an outlay of $15,000,000,000—which would increase the national debt by about half if done through borrowing. But it seems incredible that it could be carried out at a rate more rapidly than $500,000,000 a year; it would, at this rate, take thirty years to transform present tenants into owners if no others appeared. By that time the technical changes which are preparing in agriculture will have come into significant effect. A forty-acre farm may well be a survival of inefficiency by then even if the land is good.

When machinery was being introduced into the textile industry it was inveighed against by workman and professor alike; it has been so with most important technical developments which disturbed a going system of production. The current pious declarations of allegiance to the "family farm" (the last Republican platform was an astonishing document in this respect) are probably indications of uncertainty as to its future rather than otherwise.

Politicians sense these uncertainties, but they seldom have the foresight to stop the technical changes which cause them. The reorganization of agriculture will be forced by what is happening in laboratory and factory; it can be prevented by the financing of small owners. That can also make the investment unsafe.

It would be easy to exaggerate the rapidity with which changes are likely to happen in agriculture. Furthermore, they will certainly not happen everywhere alike. An Iowa farm is not like a Delta plantation any more than it is like a Great Plains ranch. Yet the need for more skilled management and the speeding up of machinery, as well as the more complicated chemical control necessary to assured production will put more and more of a handicap on small independent units. It seems doubtful if these can survive in any number although there may always be room for some as subsistence farmers especially where cultivation is extensive.

The picture of the future is so uncertain that what is called for is clearly a cautious, experimental approach. Experience of the sort which is being accumulated by the Resettlement field forces in each area is a far safer guide to policy than a doctrinaire commitment by legislation even if it is blessed by every professor of farm management in the land. This cautious approach, curiously enough, is unorthodox. The professors who wrote the Republican platform would recklessly commit us, if they could, to the policy of small ownership regardless of cost, and regardless of the plain intimations we have of future change.

Those of us who have had to administer the program and actually try to make it work, not as an office conception but as something through which our farm people can continue to function for at least five decades, have had ground into our minds two enlightenments in this connection which we are glad to share with everyone.

One is that the present system has destroyed the health and ambition of two million (more or less) farm families and taken the strength out of their land until nothing but hard and unspectacular rescue work for a decade or two makes any administrative sense at all. The other is that the future cannot be made on the pattern of the past unless we are to expect exactly the results. Resettlement is figuratively holding its breath, to see what is going to be done to it by the theorists. An honest and careful beginning has been made, but that beginning is entrenched neither in orthodoxy nor political favor. No wonder it trembles.

The Storm Center
of the Banking Bill

by Francis Brown

DEBATE OVER CHANGES in the banking system, long discussed and long postponed, has reached the floor of Congress. "The revolutionary Eccles proposal," as some describe the Banking Bill of 1935, has split the members of the Senate Banking and Currency Committee; it has stirred up argument in the House, and it has disturbed old-line economists and bankers the country over.

Marriner S. Eccles, Governor of the Federal Reserve Board, sometime Utah banker and industrialist, is the principal author of the bill. In many quarters he is regarded as a radical; his ideas, whatever else may be said of them, are admittedly unorthodox.

Eccles maintains that "laissez-faire in banking and the attainment of business stability are incompatible." What he means is that man-made laws must replace the natural laws of classical economy. He would, therefore, invest the Federal Reserve Board with responsibility and authority for controlling bank credit, the life-blood of business. With that in mind he has written into the hotly contested Title II of the pending bill provisions which would give the board a whip-hand over American banking policy. It is held in some quarters that this section of the proposed act,

From the *New York Times Magazine,* May 5, 1935, copyright © 1935, 1963 by The New York Times Company.

when reduced to simple terms, grants powers which would go a long way toward establishing a planned economy.

The new Governor of the Federal Reserve Board grew up in a part of the country where respect for convention is not great. In the West that he knows there has always been a dislike bordering on hatred for Eastern banking and bankers. His part of the country is a debtor region which has traditionally looked to the government in time of trouble. It has regularly been of the opinion that the collective power of government must be exerted to relieve economic distress and has had little sympathy for the school which puts its trust in natural forces. Some of this tradition may help to explain Eccles's readiness to advocate a socially controlled capitalism.

Eccles is defined by those who know him as the sort of person who accepts economic policies so long as they work. "Our economic, monetary and social problems," he says, "cannot be treated as an exact science." Experience alone can determine what is the right and what is the wrong way of doing things. Here also is a reflection of the West and of a pioneer heritage.

Since the day in 1914 when President Wilson picked the first Governor of the Federal Reserve Board, men who speak the language of the Eastern banker have monopolized this particular job. They have not all been Easterners—Roy A. Young was found in Minneapolis by President Coolidge—but their attitude and point of view have always been friendly toward what the West bitterly insists are Wall Street interests.

Last November there was a change. President Roosevelt chose a man who came from the region where financial heresy has always flourished, who had preached heresy himself, and in public places. This was Marriner Eccles.

Back in the days before the New Deal, Eccles had appeared before the Senate Finance Committee. "I am a capitalist," he told its members, and forthwith he proceeded to surprise them. He advocated high income and inheritance taxes as a means of controlling the concentration of wealth; he urged a unified banking system under the aegis of the Federal Reserve System. He came out for the domestic allotment plan which was later incorporated in the AAA, for a large-scale public-works program, for relief grants to the States, for the refinancing of farm mortgages, and for similar proposals.

All these measures, the Utah banker told the startled Senators, were designed not to soak the rich but to save them. That testimony branded Eccles as a radical and it had not been forgotten when, after eighteen months of relative obscurity, he bobbed up again in the governorship of the Federal Reserve Board.

When the Federal Reserve System was established more than twenty years ago, it was believed that the Federal Reserve Board would be a sort of supreme court of finance. It has never been that, either in power or in prestige, but it has served as the capstone for a banking pyramid. At the base are the local banks which belong to the Federal Reserve System; above them are the twelve Federal Reserve Banks; over all is the Federal Reserve Board, eight men in whom is lodged broad but vaguely defined authority.

The system was intended to introduce order into American banking. It was expected to make possible the control of credit and to provide a sound basis for financial operations. That all the hopes of the framers of the Federal Reserve Act have not been realized can be attributed to many things, not the least, according to some critics, to the failure to endow the Federal Reserve Board with sufficient authority. The purpose of the Banking Bill of 1935 is to provide that authority.

"The great difficulty with the monetary system now," says Mr. Eccles, "is that we haven't placed responsibility on a definite body and given that body the power and responsibility to act." He would, therefore, give both specifically to the Reserve Board.

Open-market operations impress him as the most logical means of control, for if the power to conduct such operations were properly exercised it would to a large extent determine the country's supply of money.

When all the mystery is stripped away, open-market operations are nothing more than the buying and selling of government securities in the open market. When the Federal Reserve System begins to buy, the price rises and individual banks, which in large part hold these securities, sell. The sales leave idle money in the till, which the banks, if they are to show a profit, must lend to businessmen; thus an expansion occurs. Reversing the process contracts credit.

The board now has power over open-market operations, but in a restricted manner; this power would be greatly extended under the bill. The board's authority over reserve requirements and over general credit policy would also be increased.

Eccles wants a strong, unified banking system, although he is realist enough to understand that for the present there is no chance of persuading all banks to join the Federal Reserve System. He has said this publicly; he has repeated it privately. Yet, he asks, is not the hesitancy of State banks to place themselves under Federal Reserve supervision the result of ignorance and misunderstanding which ultimately will be cleared away?

Meanwhile, the country must get along as well as possible with a banking structure which is neither wholly national nor wholly local. But he clings to his belief in social control and declares that "we can never exercise through monetary policy the requisite control while a substantial number of banks, which create money the same as member banks, are subject to no regulation or control by the authority responsible for monetary action."

During the months since he assumed office Governor Eccles has conferred constantly with his fellow-members on the board; he has kept closely in touch with Treasury policy; he has appeared often before business associations to explain his views of banking and to defend moves made by the administration. But his primary interest and effort have been focused upon the Banking bill.

The Federal Reserve Board has offices in a building on G Street, a stone's throw from the Treasury, where in the beginning the board was tucked away. Marriner Eccles's own office is large and square, its windows on the west looking toward the White House and Lafayette Square. There is little to distinguish this room from thousands of executive offices—little, that is, except for the Governor's commission, signed by President Roosevelt, which hangs behind Eccles's flat-topped desk.

The Governor is a slight man with hair brushed back from a high forehead. Swinging about in a swivel chair, he talks easily and willingly about banking and its place in a stable economy.

There is nothing of the stuffed shirt about him. He is vigorous and original; he speaks slowly and quietly; occasionally, his eyes sparkling, he strikes the arm of his chair to emphasize a point.

He likes to talk about economics and his ideas are clearcut. "I am no altruist," he says, "I am a conservative, ultra-conservative." Nevertheless, he understands that when the public interest is flouted, business and finance suffer.

Ruthless exploitation may have been well enough in days gone by; quite the reverse is true when the economy tends to turn in upon itself. Then it becomes necessary to guard the principle of purchasing-power or, as the Governor terms it, consuming-power. Let consuming-power lag and trouble starts in industry, leading, unless something is thrown into the balance, straight to a depression.

His reasoning runs along lines somewhat like these: A rise in unemployment is the first alarm-bell that consuming-power is falling. We must then start without delay a public-works program which will cushion both unemployment and industry until private spending can once again support business structure. If private employers are unable to provide jobs for workers, the government must shoulder the burden.

Though he would go very far with a public-works program and is willing, all else failing, to advocate direct government loans to industry, he is opposed to government competition with private enterprise. Whenever the government does enter into competition, he maintains, "private investment in the field stops" and the government thereupon must socialize this particular field of enterprise.

Public works, as he sees it, would act as an auxiliary engine to keep the business machine running during an emergency. If possible, of course, the emergency should be avoided altogether. The Federal Reserve Board's ability to contract or expand credit would go a long way, he believes, although Eccles would be the first to admit that monetary policy alone is no guarantee of business stability.

Income taxes, used as a device for regulating the distribution of the wealth produced, are very important, in his opinion. Under laissez-faire there is always a tendency toward overinvestment in the means of production, with the result that there are more goods for sale than people can buy. When this occurs we soon see the first signs of a depression—unemployment. High income taxes would help both to restrain overinvestment and to provide funds with which to start public works.

It is the Governor's contention that these three controls—public works, income taxes and monetary policy—would, if properly co-ordinated, assure stable business, stable price levels and steady employment. He is well aware that each of these proposals runs counter to traditional practice and theory. He recognizes that they will restrict what have always been regarded as the rights of business men and that they will limit profits. While conceding all these things, he insists that the policies he outlines are necessary.

"We capitalists," he says, "have got to decide how much we are willing to pay for capitalism."

Governor Eccles has brought to the Federal Reserve Board considerable practical experience as well as a definite social philosophy. He knows banking, for he has been president of the First Security Corporation, which operates twenty-five banks—their resources total $55,000,000—in Utah, Wyoming and Idaho.

He has been the moving force in the Utah Construction Company, the Sego Milk Products Company, the Stoddard Lumber Company and the Amalgamated Sugar Company, and while most of these enterprises are not even names on the Eastern seaboard, their annual turnover runs into seven figures. He has had fingers in other pies—in hotels and chain stores, for example—which further justify him in calling himself a capitalist.

Though during his forty-four years he has come a long way by his own wits, he is not a self-made man. He is the son of David Eccles, a wealthy and important Utah citizen who started with nothing and amassed a fortune which at his death in 1912 reached something like $7,000,000. David Eccles passed on to his son the Mormon precepts of industry and whatever of value there may be in Scottish ancestry; he gave him in addition an ordinary amount of formal education and a large store of experience gained by working in the variety of undertakings which comprised the Eccles empire. This training was topped off by two years as a Mormon missionary in Scotland, whence, in 1913, Marriner

Eccles returned to manage the family properties and to build up interests of his own.

Today he might be managing his affairs in Utah had not a snowstorm in the early days of 1933 caused Stuart Chase to be late for a Salt Lake City lecture engagement. While the audience waited, Eccles was called upon to fill in the time. This role of pinch-hitter led naturally to a meeting with Chase; it led also to the suggestion that Eccles when next in New York should call upon Chase's friend, Rexford G. Tugwell, who was slated to be a close adviser of the incoming Roosevelt administration.

Tugwell found in Eccles a banker whose ideas seemed to fit the philosophy of the New Deal, and when in January a year ago Eccles was asked to become an assistant to Secretary Morgenthau, men in the know nodded wisely and remarked that another Tugwell protégé had found a government berth. But Marriner Eccles is no man's protégé. He stands on his own and owes his place primarily to himself. He has made that clear since his appointment last November to the governorship of the board.

Part 4

THE QUESTION OF REVOLUTION

THE FOUR ARTICLES in this section are general interpretations of the New Deal, focusing on the extent to which it marked a break with the past. Two of the writers, Harold Ickes and Donald Richberg, were members of the Roosevelt administration; Ickes was Secretary of the Interior throughout Roosevelt's four terms, and Richberg was chairman of the board of the National Industrial Recovery Administration as well as executive director of the National Emergency Council in the early years of the New Deal. At the time he wrote his article here, Richberg was no longer in the administration. Allan Nevins is a well-known historian of the United States, who at the time he wrote his article was at the height of his powers; two of his books had received the Pulitzer Prize only a few years before. Delbert Clark was a member of the Washington Bureau of the *New York Times*, commenting frequently on New Deal affairs. His article suggesting a Second New Deal appears in Part 2.

The Nevins article, though written in 1933, the very first year of the New Deal, nonetheless recognized the unprecedented character of the new administration. Nevins, however, was at pains to minimize the departure from past activities and to place the New Deal well within the democratic tradition. Like a number of other contemporary writers on the New Deal, Nevins favorably compares the activities of the Roosevelt administration with those of the fascist states in Europe. The novelty of the New Deal is played down in the article, with Nevins assuring his readers that the President's power will subside once the emergency is over. On this score he was wrong. The emergency—if by that is meant the Depression—did not end until 1940, and the power of the presidency grew rather than diminished all through the thirties and forties as the Second World War and then the Cold War provided new emergencies. Perhaps Nevins' most prescient comment is his observation that the NRA, based upon curtailment of production, could not endure because it violated the powerful American belief in production.

Although Delbert Clark's article is written in the midst of the recession of 1937, his purpose is rather to sum up the nature and achievement of the New Deal at a time when, as historians would now agree, the New Deal was essentially ended. It is principally for that reason it is included here. Sufficiently critical of the Roosevelt administration to recognize its failings, Clark nonetheless offers a judicious assessment as to where the New Deal stands in the history of reform in the United States. He can recognize its debts to the past while acknowledging the progress it has made "along an unblazed trail."

Since outside observers like Nevins and Clark disagree as to the extent of the New Deal's connection with the past, it is not surprising that two participants in the New Deal also diverge in their assessments. Harold Ickes' attempt to explain the New Deal is valuable for several reasons. For one thing, Ickes was an old Bull Moose, that is, a supporter of Theodore Roosevelt in his campaign for the presidency as the Progressive candidate in 1912. Thus Ickes views himself as working toward the same goals under Franklin Roosevelt as he did with Theodore. He even assimilates the New Deal to the old nineteenth-century liberal goal set forth by the English philosopher Jeremy Bentham when he writes of striving for the "greatest happiness for the greatest number of our people. . . ." One cannot help noticing Ickes' scornful reference to the frothy 1920's, an expression that neatly epitomizes the thirties' contempt for the earlier decade of prosperity and individualism. Perhaps the most interesting aspect of Ickes' article is his describing the goals of the New Deal as utopian, for that, too, measures the novelty of the Roosevelt achievement. Like Roosevelt himself, however, Ickes wants to place the New Deal, different as it may be, in the broad tradition of reform in the United States. Hence he speaks of it as "government of, by and for the people." As always, the fear is that a conservative America will reject a New Deal that is too innovative.

Clearly aware of the great underlying social and economic changes of the century, Donald Richberg's discussion is much more sophisticated and persuasive than Ickes'. To Richberg the central issue is the necessity for government action to regulate and control the economy. In retrospect that is undoubtedly the New Deal's major impact on American thought. Like Franklin Roosevelt himself, Richberg sees the New Deal as a middle way, carefully treading a path between communism on the left and fascism on the right. The New Deal, he points out, is being achieved without class-conscious upheaval or violence. To Americans of the turbulent thirties, that in itself made the New Deal a remarkable achievement.

1933–1934:
Two Momentous Years

by Allan Nevins

THE YEAR that now draws to a close has been marked by extraordinary fluctuations and changes. It has been on the whole a year of storm, with nations struggling in the waves left by the World War. Many countries had been half-submerged ever since that conflict. The United States, which for a time had ridden on the top of the surge, fell at the beginning of the year deeper into the trough than any other. In its extremity it turned, like Europe, to new experiments. Certainly in no other year since 1919 has the world seen so many radically new ideas and principles broached.

There has been what seemed to many a great change in ideas of government. Fascism has been striding onward; the United States has entrusted unprecedented peacetime authority to Mr. Roosevelt. There has been a radical revision of men's ideas upon international relationships. World organization has suffered heavily, and theories of "autarchy" or self-containment have made many converts.

In the field of economics also there has been a momentous shifting of ideas—in the United States in particular, which has turned to reduction of production, to restriction of competition and to government intervention for the raising of commodity prices. Bold new financial theories are accepted in high places; most of the world is off the gold standard; the validity of that standard in its old form is being questioned, and in the two most powerful nations attempts are being made to manage the currency.

These new ideas, however varied, have one common quality. They are fundamentally the products of a time of unexampled crisis. A number of them bear plain evidence of exaggeration or distortion and one or two even of hysteria. During great tempests there are moments when the earth itself seems to heave and tremble. After they have passed men realize that this was a delusion, that through all the rush and shock of wind and wave the earth stood solid as ever—its quivers were imagined.

Of late, Americans have had a tendency to pass from one exaggeration to another. Six years ago they talked of a new economic era of unprecedented possibilities, of prosperity that nothing could check and stocks that "will go to a thousand." Bank presidents said that we had but started on our way, and economists of repute wrote that the soaring stock prices registered a permanent revolution in national well-being. It is possible that at the nadir of the depression many ideas are as warped as were those expressed at the crest of the wave. When we get back to a fairly calm sea we may perceive that both were askew, and that "If hopes [1928] were dupes, fears [in 1933] may be liars."

At any rate, the year 1934 is certain to offer a severe test for many of the ideas and principles propounded in 1933. There is evidence that it will be a year of slowly returning prosperity. The best reason for thinking this is that the recent upward tendency seems to be world-wide. It is the same in England, America, Scandinavia and Australia, which are off the gold basis, and in France, Belgium and Switzerland, which are still on it; the same in nations with managed currencies and in nations without them; the same in high-tariff countries and in moderate-tariff countries. A general trend, whose origins economists trace back to midsummer of 1932, seems to be at work.

Theories formed to fit a depression will soon, we may hope,

be working in a period of growing normality. Laws and governmental agencies devised for populations badly frightened, and hence ductile and obedient, will have to be applied to populations which are resuming their individualistic habits. And there are other factors as well. Men's whole attitude toward great public questions may change rapidly, as our recent dramatic verdict upon Prohibition has just indicated. Altogether, the next twelve-month will undoubtedly sift much which the last year has produced.

Without violating Lowell's wise maxim, "Don't prophesy onless ye know," it is possible to make one flat statement: The recent assertions that ideas of government have undergone a radical change will not be sustained by future events. These assertions rest upon a misreading of the facts. The assumption in certain quarters that in the United States something has befallen democracy, that the concentration of power in the President's hands has meant a "revolution," already begins to appear absurd. No country, for evident reasons, is less inclined to revolution than the United States. What actually happened in this nation in 1933 was just the opposite, a magnificent vindication of democracy. We proved anew the flexibility of our government, its capacity for meeting unexpected tensions.

The sudden expansion of Presidential authority to overcome a great emergency conformed entirely with the intent of the founders of the Republic. They meant that in war, in periods of internal strife and in great economic crises the President should be endowed with sufficient power to conquer all difficulties. Again and again Presidents have assumed such power. Jefferson did so when he stretched the Constitution till it cracked, Jackson when he met nullification, Lincoln during the Civil War, Wilson during the World War. When the present crisis subsides, Mr. Roosevelt's powers will subside also.

In fact, it is in times like the present and under such bold and resourceful leaders as Mr. Roosevelt that our democratic institutions are at their best. There is some reason to feel discouraged about them when weak Presidents fail to exercise their authority in due degree—and we do not need to go back to Pierce and

Buchanan to name such Presidents. There is no reason to feel anything but optimism when we see Congress and President co-operating as they did last spring, the Chief Executive showing sustained leadership and the people responding loyally to the demands of the government. This is representative government as Locke and Montesquieu outlined it two centuries ago and as James Bryce and Woodrow Wilson expounded it more recently.

We have plenty of balance in reserve. The legislative branch will be playing its usual rôle in a few days, and the judiciary is still to be heard from. But the best defenders of democracy have always contended that balance has to give way at times to stern executive leadership.

What has happened abroad in 1933 is similarly misread if it is construed to the disadvantage of democracy in general. It is true that in Germany the cause of popular government has suffered one of its severest setbacks since Napoleon III overthrew the Second Republic. But two facts should mitigate our disappointment.

It is now obvious that democracy had a poor chance in Germany. Some parts of the Versailles treaty were a leaden weight about the neck of the new régime. The harsh way in which those clauses were executed, the repeated blundering over reparations, the lamentable march into the Ruhr, Poincaré's efforts to detach the Rhineland were in effect a succession of blows to the Weimar Constitution. Even so, there was hope for German democracy as led by Stresemann and others. If the Lausanne agreement on reparations and the last-minute concessions on disarmament had come two years, or even one year, earlier a different story might have been told. Democracy failed only under severe handicaps.

The second consideration is that the Reich has only reverted to its earlier status. It is true that in Italy, Russia, Germany and Austria there is no democracy today. But in most of these lands there never was. Before 1918 they were all autocracies. It is not to be supposed that the traditions, habits and outlook which make democracy possible can be created by the wave of a wand. Nor is there any reason to feel that the temporary success of autocracy anywhere proves any facts detrimental to democracy. Autoc-racy has often scored successes like those of Mussolini today and those which Hitler may achieve tomorrow. But they have always been temporary, while those of democracy have usually been permanent.

The year 1933, in short, left democracy unscathed, and the coming year is likely only to confirm the verdict that we need not revise any of our ideas of government.

In the economic sphere there is much that is still confused and bewildering. In many respects the American people are still at a half-way point. Yet, again a few statements may be ventured without treading on the dangerous ground of prophecy. For one, the year 1933 seemed to show that the United States is at last accepting a long-contested principle: the principle that no prosperity is a true prosperity unless it embraces substantially the entire population.

This may sound axiomatic. Yet we can now see that during the decade of the Twenties it was disregarded by most Easterners and by a number of those in the highest governmental places. The prosperity which we boasted from 1921 to 1929, and which many recklessly misused, left large sections of the country untouched. The great mass of the American farmers, the great majority of bituminous miners, a large part of our textile workers, to name only three groups, were shut out in the cold.

The first of these groups was all-important. Mr. Peek said a few pungent words in Chicago the other day about the folly of trying to make a profit system work while depriving 6,000,000 farmers, who are at the foundation of our whole national life, of any hope of profits. It has been generally acknowledged during 1933 that if the administrations which scolded the farmer so vigorously for demanding just such aid as had been granted to industry in the post-war tariffs had spent a little more energy in devising rational assistance to agriculture, we might have been far better off today. A dollar spent six or eight years ago under some substitute for the McNary-Haugen Bill would have saved many dollars this last year. Instead, the farmer was rebuffed with a lecture on political economy—the lecturers themselves forgetting some of the most elementary tenets of national economy in the larger sense.

Of all the new ideas put into effect by the Roosevelt administration, the idea that the prosperity of the farmers is worth just as much governmental thought and effort as that of the industrialists ought to be surest of continued approval. The administration has turned to a series of frankly experimental devices to help agriculture.

The policy that men should be paid not to grow wheat, cotton, corn and hogs would have astounded an earlier generation. It may not win indefinite acceptance; the coming year may bring it under heavy fire. The farmer himself, still a stanch individualist, who would far rather grow all he could for a large foreign market than grow half of what he could for a restricted domestic market, may insist on changes. Some of them have already been hinted at by Secretary Wallace in his utterances on foreign trade as it affects the farmer. But the general principle that the country can never again afford to let the prairies and the plantations drop lower and lower in poverty and discouragement just because its factories and brokerage houses are still flourishing may be taken as fairly established for 1934 and all future years.

The fate during the coming year of the various ideas bound up in the NRA will likewise be interesting to watch. That system of government advisership and assistance to industry, as Mr. Roosevelt calls it—repudiating the word "control"—has hitherto been under the guidance and surveillance of the Executive alone. It will now pass under that of Congress as well, while the legislation creating it remains to be tested in the highest court.

Unquestionably, if and as the economic crisis passes, the tendency to regard this as purely emergency legislation will gain strength. With much of it certain to lapse, the really interesting question is what permanent residuum will remain. That it will at least leave some permanent benefits of a social nature in higher minimum-wage standards, in shorter hours and in the reduction of child labor may be devoutly hoped.

Some of these benefits will have to be embodied in entirely new legislation. To make sure of the one last named, the abolition of child labor, another constitutional amendment will be required, and already there is evidence that Mr. Roosevelt's bold measures have given impetus to the movement in the States for ratifying it. We may hope that 1934 will prove that much in the NRA standards which has been hailed by social meliorists most jubilantly will remain as a permanent legacy.

Doubtless the fundamental question in the economic sphere, however, is whether the country will long support the new principle that prosperity may be attained and kept by cutting down production, restricting competition and thus raising price levels. This principle, if carried to its logical conclusion, really comes near being "revolutionary" in a minor sense of the word. It is certainly in direct conflict with some of the convictions most deeply ingrained in the American breast.

Most plain citizens of this country still regard the anti-trust laws and all other legislation against collusion, combination, interlocking directorates and the like with the deepest jealousy. Many people have a keen remembrance of some of the evils of monopoly in the days when trusts were most lawless; many have an unshakable faith in the value of competition. The West in particular looks upon this legislation as one of the bulwarks of economic and political liberty.

In general, again, most Americans, however illogically, hold that there is a direct connection between unfettered production and a rising standard of comfort. Various writers, like Walter Lippmann have lately pointed out that the outcry against overproduction is always raised when depressions occur, that we have often heard it in the past when production was but a fraction of what it now is, and that it has always been forgotten when good times recur.

As for prices, the American public is capable of coming very quickly and sharply to the conclusion that prices and living costs are too high. In this whole field it is clear that the Roosevelt administration has raised many questions which are far from settled. The coming year must go a long way toward providing the answers.

Questions of finance may well be left to the experts who are now quarreling so acrimoniously upon the subject. Obviously this debate has as yet come nowhere near its conclusion. Its vehemence has so far perhaps succeeded in impressing upon the general public just one truth. There is no fiat from Heaven which has ordained that the gold dollar of 23.22 grains shall be immutably indispensable to American well-being.

That dollar was fixed, not by supernatural decree, but by act of Congress in 1834. This legislation superseded an earlier law of Congress, which in 1792 fixed a decidedly different gold content (to wit, 24.75 grains) for the dollar. It is possible to conceive of the government fixing a third gold content in 1934 without bringing the nation to utter ruin. The most important characteristic that money can have is stability, and gold has been far from stable.

When, once before, in the years preceding 1896, declining prices called the gold standard into sharp question, the problem was solved by a greatly enlarged production of gold. Bryan was able to remark, with complete justice, that the Republicans wanted the gold standard and got it, and that the Democrats wanted more money and got it. Today the solution may have to be very different. It is clearly evident that it will have to be a compromise solution and that it will have to take into account the arguments for higher commodity prices and for a scaling down of debts.

Moreover, most people are now convinced that we need not expect an ideal solution, for in the very nature of the question that is impossible. We did not have an ideal currency before the crash and we should not expect or demand to have it afterward.

As we look back over the year 1933, viewing the world as a whole, it is impossible to avoid the conclusion that the most disturbing development has been the weakening of international ties. So far as the hope of world cooperation and unity goes, the past twelve-month has recorded several heavy defeats. The World Economic Conference in London, while not completely fruitless, did in general prove empty and abortive. The Disarmament Conference came to nothing. Moreover, Germany's rupture with it led to a still more deplorable event. The League of Nations has now been weakened by the withdrawal of the Reich, following hard on that of Japan. Of the world's seven greatest powers, four— United States, Germany, Russia and Japan—are left on New Year's Day of 1934 outside its portals.

The year closes with a more strident and aggressive nationalism evident all over the world than at any time since 1919. Even in South America, despite the Pan-American Conference and the undoubted gains it has achieved—particularly in the evidences of a greater Latin-American cordiality for the United States—there are gloomy facts to be faced. The war between Bolivia and Paraguay continued until one combatant suffered a decisive and bloody defeat.

Moreover, all over the globe the sentiment of nationalism has been heightened by the comparatively new doctrine of "autarchy" or self-containment. The doctrine, like so much else, belongs to the ideology of the emergency. In one nation after another "autarchy" has grown out of or been correlated with plans for far-reaching internal readjustments to restore prosperity. These readjustments, according to the prevailing doctrine, can be made more easily if the national life is largely isolated from the world economy. Collective control, so the theory runs, is possible only in an insulated or semi-insulated State.

The United States was unfortunately one of the first nations to take a long step along this path. The Smoot-Hawley tariff, so universally condemned by economists, provoked in 1930 a long series of retaliatory enactments or decrees by other nations. As the crisis grew worse, the tendency progressed further; the British Imperial Conference at Ottawa gave it fresh impetus. Today "autarchy," despite the verdict of such economists as Sir Arthur Salter that it is as foolish economically as it is dangerous politically, is being discussed and all too forcibly urged in most of the great capitals.

It is to be hoped that the year 1934, if it does little else, will subject this and all other tendencies or theories making for greater national isolation to a severe and destructive test. Unless the conclusions of virtually all careful students of the subject are wrong, "autarchy" is indeed economic folly.

The largest single source of the world's present ills, economic as well as political, is to be found in nationalistic conflicts and barriers. The world depression has descended directly from the World War, its effects accentuated by nationalistic jealousies and disputes over reparations, debts and tariffs. If the coming year is to bring us a permanent hope of better times it must do something to reverse these unfortunate tendencies of 1933—to strengthen the League, to reduce the burden of armaments, to lessen the constant danger of an explosion in Europe, to lower trade barriers and to bring the nations of the world into closer relations and greater friendliness.

Five Years, and the New Deal Ponders

by Delbert Clark

WASHINGTON

AS HE APPROACHES the end of his fifth year in the White House President Roosevelt, facing the possibility of another general depression, is feeling his way toward the accomplishment of two apparently contradictory objectives—the completion of his program of economic reform and the conciliation of business. Threats, not too heavily veiled, of drastic action against monopolies (which is taken to mean "against big business") are followed by a swift series of amicable conferences with those same big business men on ways and means to meet the recession and devise a better system for the future.

Yet the contradiction is more apparent than real. The abrupt business decline, and the harsh talk that went with it, have provided the needed stimuli for putting to work the best thought of government and business on a long-range program of intelligent cooperation. The slump is immediate and must be met, although economists are virtually unanimous in the belief that it is abnormal and temporary.

Beyond the slump, beyond urgent measures to reverse it, is what the New Dealers indicate as the final objective—a permanent rearrangement of our national economy to prevent or mitigate such violent fluctuations in the future.

Just a little over a year ago Mr. Roosevelt stood in a pelting rain in front of the Capitol and rededicated himself to "the fulfillment of a vision—to speed the time when there would be for all the people that security and peace essential to the pursuit of happiness." Up to now, despite the vast amount of reform and experimentation that has been written into law, only the groundwork has been laid for the fulfillment of that vision. Many of the most controversial of the New Deal laws have been distinctly for the emergency—the rest have been for the most part preparatory or collateral.

What remains is the far more difficult problem of effecting a consumer-producer-distributor balance such as no country in the modern world has yet achieved by democratic methods. For all its broad social implications, it is a strictly economic matter, this evolution of a new order for business, and economics is a highly experimental and inexact science. Whether it can be evolved depends on the wisdom not of government alone but of industry, agriculture, labor and those engaged in the ramified field of distribution.

Mr. Roosevelt's philosophy in regard to these reforms has been a baffling and curiously evolving thing. He began as an ardent experimentalist, wedded to the theorist rather than to the practitioner. This phase continued for several years, its ups and downs conforming roughly to those of the general business indices. Then, for about a year, business improved at a fairly steady pace, and the reform movement appeared to concentrate principally on the subject of efficiency in government.

With the sudden drop in business beginning last August the opportunity again presented itself for a completion of the program of economic alteration, but with this difference: the President seems now to believe that little additional legislation is needed, that what is essential is the working out of a cooperative system whereby business, agriculture and labor may sit down with government and consider their common problems. Ideally, it represents the diffusion, rather than the concentration, of government.

What Mr. Roosevelt now desires is the expansion of the

national income (by which he means consumption capacity) to a point where unemployment will virtually disappear and relief become a bagatelle. He wants a balance in industrial and agricultural production to level off the ups and downs of the business cycle. Correlatively, he seeks a balanced income for labor with a net increase in the lower brackets.

None of these things can be accomplished, he appears to believe, by the passing of Federal laws; the only laws sought are one to modernize the anti-trust statutes for the benefit of both industry and the consumer, another to set moderate standards of maximum hours and minimum wages and a third to fix some equitable measure of public responsibility for the growing labor unions.

Two major obstacles stand in the way of these new objectives: the innate distrust of both industry and labor of any measure of regulation and the temperament of Mr. Roosevelt himself.

It may be stated calmly and without passion that Mr. Roosevelt instinctively prefers to dominate, to lead, to drive, rather than to sit around the council table with men not his immediate subordinates or trusted friends. It is perhaps a heritage from his aristocratic lineage and early environment. He is a Democrat by choice and conviction, not by inheritance.

The rush and tumult of a changing world may have at times led the President off on strange tangents and into strange pitfalls, but the general direction of his impulses has not changed. That direction, as he has repeatedly said, is toward a happier, more prosperous America, its happiness and prosperity measured by the well-being of the lowest stratum.

In this attitude he is confronted by the cold fact that certain segments of our population have yet to realize that America is no longer in the pioneer stage. Our life as an independent nation has been fairly brief, and we have had at our disposal a vast country of seemingly limitless resources. To many of Mr. Roosevelt's critics it seemed that suddenly, in 1933, a line was drawn between individualist pioneering and a new and alarming era of large-scale planning. Actually, that line was not drawn then, but emphasized. The transition had been steadily in progress, yet no previous national administration had publicly recognized it. It remained for the Roosevelt Administration to effect what seemed to be a needlessly abrupt shift in direction.

Businessmen in any field do not like regulation, and they do not like abrupt changes. They have become accustomed through many prosperous decades to think in terms of steady expansion and a limitless market. And, even when realizing that this is no longer the case, they profoundly distrust experimentation.

In their own fields of activity the automobile manufacturers, the steel fabricators, the textile weavers introduce innovations only after exhaustive laboratory tests, and apparently they do not understand why they must be subjected to the effects of laws which have not undergone such a test. But where is the laboratory in which to test legislation? That was the problem of Mr. Roosevelt and his New Deal, a problem not of test tubes and reagents but of human beings.

While the business index sinks and the nation waits, Mr. Roosevelt is not visibly dismayed. He has not recanted but he has opened the door to cooperation between government and the governed in a realization, apparently, that in a republic such as ours the government cannot be an entity set apart but is a composite of all the diverse and disparate elements that make up the nation.

Subordinates think that matters will turn out all right. Oddly enough, at this juncture when depression threatens and the Roosevelt laws are widely attacked, New Dealers close to the President are full of verve and enthusiasm. They have no fear for the future, believing that the process of "streamlining" democracy has gone much too far to be stopped by conservative criticism or a business recession.

They look into the future—ten years ahead—to the time when the cooperative commonwealth will have been realized, and they are not impatient at the fact that it has not been realized in five. Their attitude, properly weighed and adjusted for the factor of subordinate enthusiasm and hero worship, can be taken as that of "the Boss" himself.

In the light of this appraisal, it is appropriate to estimate the achievements of the New Deal to date. How far has it gone?

How effective have been its reforms? Can it survive relatively intact? Can it—which is more important—prove the efficacy of its reforms in combating this new depression?

Passing over the purely emergency acts at the outset of the Roosevelt Administration, acts calculated to meet a present crisis and liquidate it, these salient objectives appear in the New Deal program:

(1) Conservation and scientific utilization of our natural resources.

(2) Reorganization of agriculture along the lines of a well-ordered basic industry, to insure plenty at all times and burdensome surplus never.

(3) Reconstitution of the industrial ethic, with equal stress on ownership, management and labor, to make "enlightened self-interest" a fixed principle.

(4) Rehabilitation of the "consumer" by means of cheap job-lot capital, lower interest rates, emergency credit where needed, and more nearly equitable charges for necessities.

(5) Rehabilitation of the great cities through slum-clearance and decent housing for minimum incomes.

(6) Gradual removal of the control of capital from the hands of selfish interests and unproductive organisms.

(7) Future security for the working classes by means of a permanent program of social insurance, based on the theory that the casual ties of a highly competitive industrial system are the responsibility of the central government.

(8) Thoroughgoing governmental reorganization, executive and judicial, to "modernize" the machinery for administering all the foregoing as well as the old, routine Federal functions.

(9) Cultivation of international amity.

How well has the New Deal succeeded in its nine major objectives?

Conservation and scientific utilization of our natural resources has proceeded steadily, with only temporary setbacks. The public power policy remains the subject of violent controversy, but to date it has overcome virtually all obstacles, and the Supreme Court has unanimously sustained the government's authority to assist municipalities in constructing their own plants. The TVA is conducting a gigantic experiment in soil-and-water conservation, flood control, power production and regional social planning, and the Administration is proceeding with legislative plans to district the entire country along similar lines. The Civilian Conservation Corps is cleaning up and replanting our ravaged forest areas, and the Soil Conservation Service is engaged in a great cooperative venture to salvage depleted farm land.

Agricultural reorganization is still in a state of flux, with the Administration now attempting to accomplish the difficult transition from emergency subsidies to permanent crop control and an ever-normal granary. The farmer's purchasing power has been restored, but through makeshift measures, and it cannot be said for a long time to come whether the permanent plans for control of this highly individualistic, highly decentralized industry will be successful.

In attempts to reconstitute the industrial ethic, the very speed of the operation has created problems of organization that are now plaguing both industry and labor. The NRA, designed to balance one factor in industry against another for the general good, was outlawed by the courts and no substitute has been devised. Organized labor has greatly expanded its sphere, under government protection, but is having difficulty digesting its enriched diet, and has split into two bitterly hostile factions.

Consumer rehabilitation has proved a difficult task. While emergency credit has been made available at lower cost, while real estate mortgages have been refinanced and new mortgages insured, living costs have risen; an economy only partially planned, interacting with uncontrolled natural forces, has threatened time and time again to upset the attempt to raise prices, control them at a "reasonable" level, and assure normal profits to all classes of industry and labor.

Along the same line, the New Deal has run into difficulties in diffusing the control of capital. Progress has been made under the Securities and Exchange Commission and the Federal Reserve System. Presumably it never expected to alter the national financial picture overnight.

Social security has made a modest and admittedly imperfect beginning, and slum clearance, plus low-cost housing, has been authorized and is about to start, preceded by considerable experimentation by the government itself, and a large amount of middle-class housing through the Federal Housing Administration.

Governmental reorganization—executive—is still pending in Congress; the judicial problem raised by the Administration has solved itself through retirements and changes of heart, following the disastrous defeat of the New Deal on the fundamental issue of packing the Supreme Court.

International amity—so far as the relations of this country with others are concerned—is in far better condition than five years ago. We have greatly enhanced the respect felt for us by the world at large; we have largely eliminated the historic distrust entertained by Latin America. The economic approach of Secretary Hull has gone far toward removing causes of international distrust generally. The current tense situation in the world is not of our making.

The New Deal has attempted a colossal task and, if it has failed in many particulars, it has admittedly made progress along an unblazed trail.

Where Is the Nation Heading?

by Harold L. Ickes

THE ANSWER to the question, "Where are we headed?" is a simple one, although it must necessarily be expressed in general terms. We are headed toward the goal of the greatest happiness for the greatest number of our people. And that is where we ought to be headed if we have any decent regard for the welfare of others or any intelligent concern for our own best interests.

After all, the human race has always been headed toward this same goal. There have been times when, in our quest for the greatest good of the greatest number, we have found ourselves standing still, mistakenly believing that at last we have reached the end of the long trail. At other times we have strayed into the wrong path through listening to false shibboleths or following ignorant or selfish leadership, only to bring ourselves up on the brink of an abyss.

On such occasions the progress back to the right path which, whether we consciously will it or not, we shall follow to the end, has been slow and painful and beset with dangers. But we have never lost hope, we have never been ready to call quits. Always the human race has gone forward, and always it will go forward. That persistent, unconquerable urge to make it possible for our

From the *New York Times Magazine,* May 27, 1934, copyright © 1934, 1962 by The New York Times Company.

children to lead fuller and richer lives than we ourselves have been able to live is a spiritual quality that distinguishes man from the rest of the animal kingdom.

In our attempt to say where we, as a nation, are now headed, it may be well to consider briefly where we were headed before we changed our direction on March 4, 1933. For almost four years before that day we had been drifting, going nowhere at all. Caught in the worst economic jam the country had ever known, we were milling around in a confusion that grew steadily worse. And throughout the eight years before that, ending in the fatal autumn of 1929, we had been wandering in a fool's paradise of false prosperity and hastening directly for the jam.

In 1929 we had strayed far from the path which the nation at the start had marked out for itself. We were spiritually drunk. We were living, so we assured ourselves, in a new economic era, an era that was the ultimate goal of human aspiration. The old simple virtues seemed outworn; they seemed quaint relics of a naive earlier generation. To the accompaniment of blaring jazz we refused any longer to take thought for the morrow. Brought up under a strict injunction to live within our incomes and save for a rainy day, we were encouraged even by bankers to withdraw our savings and invest them in insecurities.

It is not without significance that the latest Pulitzer prize for editorial writing went to the country editor who took for his subject the question, "Where Is Our Money?" and answered by saying, "We Spent It." Precisely so; and, as individuals and communities, we dissipated our credit also. Did we need extra funds to pay for our joy ride that was to stretch beyond the far horizon? Any stock broker would open a trading account on a slender margin, permitting us to buy stocks and commodities that we never proposed to take title to, or to sell what we never expected to own. The way to keep the frenzied dance going was to buy what we neither wanted nor could afford.

In order to stimulate the purchase of the excess products of our industrial system our financial wizards invented the plan of installment buying, thus enticing people to pyramid purchases of unnecessary goods just as they were pyramiding speculative purchases of securities and commodities. The waitress in the restaurant took advantage of any lull to rush for a look at the stock ticker. The elevator boy on his way to becoming a capitalist passed along market tips to the janitor, who eagerly placed a second mortgage on his home in order to play them.

We dwelt in air-castles and spent our days nervously clutching, like monkeys, at the narrow white ribbons on which the busy ticker was imprinting symbols indicating prices of stocks on the New York Exchange. Everyone might become rich without effort. In our haste to get our share we took no heed for the future nor felt any concern for our neighbor. We boasted, and honestly believed, that a miraculous new kind of era had come, an era of physical comforts and material luxuries; an era, we were told, of chicken dinners and two-car garages for all.

In those wild days we lost sight of spiritual values or deliberately ignored them. Racketeers flourished, and we read of their deeds with half-amused tolerance. We made heroes and prophets of clever crooks who were able to build up fortunes outside the law. We condoned the misdoings of men in high public office. "Why shouldn't they get theirs, too?" We were vexed at honest men who insisted upon exposing such outrages as the Teapot Dome steal. Provided we were acquiring wealth, either actually or on paper, we did not care what others, like-minded, were doing. There was enough to go around, and the chief end of man was to glorify gold and get all he could of it.

After the World War, when our country was spiritually deflated and emotionally exhausted, our leaders had proceeded to take us back to "normalcy." An inspiring slogan that, to appeal to the spiritual quality in man! Our statesmen were perfect for their decade. It is only fair to say that had they attempted to lift their voices in deprecation of the materialism of the age no one would have heeded them. They and their public thoroughly understood one another.

"Get while the getting is good" became the national motto. Laissez-faire was on the throne. National leaders seemed great to the crowd if they simply let the crowd alone, and greatest of all seemed those who cheered on the orgy of speculation from the sidelines and issued encouraging statements whenever the stock market showed signs of fatigue.

At a time when we desperately needed the right kind of leadership to restore us to some degree of sanity, we had no leadership except the materialistic sort. If statesmanship implies an ability to peer even a little way into the future, we had no statesmanship. We had Presidents merely because, under our form of government, we are required to have Presidents.

During that materialistic decade few people thought of asking "Where are we headed?" It is a hopeful sign that the question is asked so often today. Many people ask it sincerely, in profound concern for their country. They are still shaken by the crash of 1929; they are still appalled at what they saw when the awakening from the crazy dream of the Nineteen Twenties came at last. It is a question that every citizen with any patriotism in his soul ought to be asking. For not all of us have repented of those days or will admit that they were evil. Not all of us have forgotten the fleshpots.

Significantly, those who most sharply and even threateningly demand "Where are we going?" are men who were political leaders of that era of folly. They are newspapers that sang paeans of praise of that era while it lasted. They are bankers and brokers and captains of industry who led that mad-dervish dance. The implication in the question, as they ask it, is that we were dwelling in peace and happiness; that all was right with the world until March 4, 1933.

Yet the question is a proper one, even though it is most frequently asked for the ulterior purpose of covering up the defects and the crimes of an economic period that constitutes a blot on our national history—a blot that will take more than one generation to wipe out. All of us are rightly, if anxiously, concerned over what lies ahead for us.

Just where, then, are we headed? First, and unmistakably, we are headed back from that make-believe land of mirages and will-o'-the-wisps where, ten years ago, we hoped to establish ourselves permanently. We are retracing our erring footsteps, and it is hard going. At the same time, in my firm belief, we are entering a period of sound and genuine well-being: a period illuminated by our recent discovery that we cannot safely disclaim social responsibility for our acts in the economic world and that we cannot truthfully assume that we are not our brother's keeper.

We have learned much about economics since we went on that twelve-year detour of ours. Theodore Roosevelt and Woodrow Wilson had tried to teach us, and we promptly forgot. We had to go down into the depression to learn our lesson. And now, as we struggle back to the highroad where we should have been traveling all the while, we humbly and thoughtfully take up again our traditional task of making our country a good place to live in for every man, woman and child.

To itemize some of our major objectives: We want to make sure, by adopting the pending constitutional amendment, that child labor in this land will be abolished forever. We must do away with sweatshops. We must protect women workers from unreasonably long hours of toil at tasks beyond their strength.

We would see to it that every man or woman who works does so in wholesome surroundings and for wages that will provide the necessities of life and leave something over for modest pleasures and luxuries. We say that workers should have a share of leisure to enjoy the American civilization they help to build; that it is not enough any more that any worker in a land of plenty should derive from a life of toil only the bare privilege of staying alive to toil. We would require employers to recognize the legitimate demands of labor, and we would require labor, on its part, to be reasonable and just.

Generally, we are headed toward a day of social consciousness in our business dealings with one another. Whether that goal can be reached by our people voluntarily, or whether some measure of social control will be necessary remains to be seen. We declare, however, that our economic system shall no longer run wild periodically, ruining itself and throwing millions of us out of work. The day will come, I hope, when that system will be so enlightened as to see that it can best serve self-interest by serving the common welfare and when it can be trusted to regulate itself.

We have given it every opportunity in the last year to effect reforms of its own volition; we have even lifted old and vital laws to help it meet the emergency. If that experiment, conceived and conducted in good-will, has erred, it has erred, I believe, on the side of lenity. It may be found that large monopolistic business has seized unfair advantages over little business. It may be that management today lacks the ability to organize itself to cooperate for the common good. In that case there is only one agency strong enough to undertake the task, and that is the government. Through harsh experience we have come to see that it is the right and the duty of the community to intervene in whatever may be harmful to the good of the people.

As a nation alert at last to dangers long ignored, we would strengthen our banking system so that never again will innocent depositors lose their savings as the result of incompetent or dishonest banking methods. While permitting the stock and commodity markets to perform the rightful functions which only they can perform, we would put laws on the statute books to prevent another such delirium of irresponsible gambling as that which contributed so heavily to the crash of 1929. Through legislation we would save honest business from the old lethal operations of financial pirates and the securities exchanges.

We would make it impossible for a handful of ruthless, predatory men to accumulate immense fortunes through exploiting less fortunate people in no position to protect themselves. We believe the day is over in America when men who are extravagantly rewarded for their skill in serving their special group at the expense of all other groups can hope to escape social censure.

In taxation we are headed toward new laws that will discard the time-honored principle of "soak the poor." By a just and fair system we would, for the common welfare, assess taxes in proportion to ability to pay. In the public realm we would conserve our natural resources and prevent waste and reckless exploitation, at the same time drawing upon those resources for legitimate needs.

We look forward to cleaning up slum areas in cities and countryside; to bringing farm prices into fair relation with factory prices and otherwise aiding our greatest and worst-stricken industry to rehabilitate itself. We propose to inaugurate a system of old-age and unemployment insurance, realizing that this is the most economical and self-respecting method of meeting an obligation which society must somehow meet in the end. We want to provide schooling facilities ample to educate every child to his capacity to absorb and use an education. And our aim in foreign affairs is to play a generous and honorable role as a means of maintaining peace throughout the world.

To attempt to forecast the future of the public works program is not for one so closely identified with that program as I am. Some of the severest criticism today is directed at the government's large-scale effort to create jobs for the millions of workers who were left idle by the collapse of the old economic order, and at the same time to produce permanent social gains, under the most careful supervision possible for us to establish in housing and other construction, in water power, flood control, land reclamation, re-forestation and like projects.

I would only say that it is unthinkable to me that before business has absorbed a greater part of the unemployed this nation will abandon its policy of standing by those of its citizens who are still without means of sustenance through no fault of their own. I regard the continuance of this work, even the increase of it, if necessary, as the nation's first duty. To be parsimonious in this respect at this time will be at the cost of human suffering and will, in my judgment, gravely retard recovery.

It is asked whether industry, with its increasing use of labor-saving inventions and its new economical methods of distribution, can ever again absorb all of our unemployed. Possibly, as the years go on, the nation will have to create and support new and useful public services, such as some of those under the CWA and the CCC, in order to provide honorable work for all. That is a question for the future.

These are some of the goals toward which we are headed. Utopian goals? Yes, utopian indeed, but I do not apologize for suggesting that Utopia is a proper goal for us to strive for and that we are worthy of such a realm if we can achieve it. We are a spiritual people, and life for us would not be worth living if we did not have this urge to reach for what will always seem beyond our reach. If we cannot have it for ourselves, we want it for our children, those projections of ourselves into immortality.

As a people, on election day of 1932, we willed that the

advances listed here should come to pass. Despairing of the sordid policies that had led us to the verge of ruin, we turned our eyes for salvation to the long-neglected fundamental ideal of our nation —the ideal of the greatest good for the greatest number; the ideal of government of, by and for the people.

Thousands of us, self-seekers of every kind—and that includes most of us—wondered that we had forgotten it so long. We wondered that never before had it been so clear to us that the welfare of each of us depends on the welfare of all of us, and that the forceful, the shrewd, the successful and the fortunate among us are safe only when all of the people are safe.

For a year and more that ideal has lighted our national course. It has inspired every step taken by the government in the huge labor of repairing the wreckage left by the blind and selfish forces that brought us to the catastrophe of 1929 and the desolation of 1932. But now that further ruin is stopped and recovery begins to come, those same forces are pulling themselves together, viewing with alarm and uttering cries calculated to frighten the faint-hearted.

According to them, we are headed for paternalism, regimentation, socialism, communism and a dictatorship; we are moving toward bureaucracy, the authoritarian State, the iron hand of government in business, the abrogation of the sacred right of individual initiative, rule by people with brains, the scrapping of the Constitution and the scuttling of our free democratic order —to mention but a few of the bogies they raise to startle us.

These advocates of the economic anarchy of the Nineteen Twenties, asking us to forget what their system did to us, would have us think that we are headed for dreadful goals indeed and that we had better put ourselves quickly under their beneficent guidance again. Resorting to a mossy stratagem that worked well for them in the gilded past, they would pin the badge of bolshevism on the New Deal.

But they offer no substitute for the New Deal except an invitation to us to return to the Old Deal, and this they do in the name of patriotism. They offer themselves as saviors of our cherished democracy from its foes. They do not seem to know that this democracy has never been more alive and hearty and able to defend itself than in this year of 1934. Criticism is expected and welcomed in a republic, and one does not like to accuse critics of sinister motives. But surely there is more in the minds of these particular critics than mere Bourbon inability to learn.

Paternalism? I wonder how much of it the American people would stand if an attempt were made to force it upon them. Regimentation imposed by authority would have as small a chance with us. As a people, we regiment ourselves cheerfully in times of national emergency. We did so in the World War. In the present crisis the policies we are following were willed by a free people glad to practice self-restraint and cooperation for the national welfare.

President Roosevelt said: "Here is the situation. There may be a way out if we all work together. Will you help?" The affirmative response was fairly unanimous. The administration has imposed nothing that the people did not ask for. It is but carrying out their mandate.

Oddly, a considerable part of the alarm sounded today against "regimentation" comes from the group of industrialists who have done more to regiment us and constrict individuality than any other influence among us. I think of their vast factories and the men and women at work there at the machines performing monotonous sets of operations day after day through their working lives. Men who have made robots of so many of our people might well think twice before they accuse others of regimentation.

If you call it voluntary self-restraint for the common good, I should say that we are headed for that. The opposition to such a move is bitter, of course. The cry about the loss of our individual initiative and the curtailment of our proud democratic freedom is particularly agitated and anguished. But a democracy that resolves to abolish piracy and other uneconomic practices of its anti-social members does not thereby impair any respectable right of any individual. It only increases the chance of the multitude of individuals to find their due share of happiness.

We have learned in these hard years that laissez-faire, the system of letting the strong alone to do as they will, in the hope that somehow good will come from it to all of us, is a pernicious doctrine in an age when the individual's potentialities for doing social harm are immensely multiplied, as they are in the machine age. We have learned that "the pursuit of self-interest is not an assurance of national prosperity."

As we try to apply this new discovery to our shattered economic life there arises an outcry about a dictator in the White House. It is hard for some to grasp the very clear fact that the voice "dictating" is the voice of democracy itself, speaking through its chosen leader and servant. There are those who, affecting a deep concern for democracy, would have democracy silent, submissive, grateful for such crumbs and crusts as may fall from oligarchy's table. Some of us have a better opinion of democracy than that.

I should like to believe that our system of self-government is eminently capable, when it has learned such a lesson as that of the last five years, of finding ways to strengthen and preserve itself. I should like to believe that we are heading toward a better and finer flowering of democracy than we have ever known. Certainly we have been an inspired democracy, and a resolute one, since March, 1933. At the end of fifteen months we are still headed toward our humane goals. I should like to believe that we can continue in that direction until our purposes are attained.

But we shall have to be vigilant. In the long run, the chances always favor the Tories, and these gentry among us are now, after a period of highly appropriate silence, becoming clamorous. We need to bear in mind that the most impatient of those who today attack the nation's recovery program are the very people and the very interests who mainly made that program necessary.

For twelve long years they led us wandering in the wilderness after gross, false gods. They brought us to the verge of bankruptcy. They turned the country over to President Roosevelt on a day when every bank in the country was closed as the result of their lack of vision, in the first instance, and of their inability to cope with the consequences, in the second.

Here was statesmanship for you! Yet these same "statesmen" are now demanding: "Where are we headed?" After all, it is a rare tribute to the ability of the President that they should expect him, within the space of little more than a year, to repair the wreck of their twelve years of misrule.

They go so far, some of them, as to say that the status quo of the Hoover administration should have been left undisturbed, thus assuring a quicker and more substantial recovery than has been brought about under the leadership of President Roosevelt. They are particularly displeased with the "brain trust." Even men on the floor of Congress who proudly display Phi Beta Kappa keys on their expanding waistlines seem not to want ripe judgment or expert advice in the conduct of our national affairs.

Certainly, for some years before March 4, 1933, there was little, if any, evidence of the use of brains in the national administration. As certainly, too, we are not headed back toward the catch-as-catch-can, unscientific system that prevailed then.

One of the specific criticisms of some of the steps we take in our new direction of march is that they are violative of the Constitution. This criticism is expressed so vigorously and so frequently that it will not be inappropriate to consider it here; for, after all, it is a grave criticism. It is directed, as a matter of fact, at the Supreme Court of the United States and not against the legislative or the administrative branches of the government.

The duty of the Supreme Court is to pass upon the constitutionality of legislative acts, and that court is alert to protect the Constitution in its essential integrity. It is absurd to argue that this country is in the slightest danger of having imposed upon it a series of unconstitutional laws so long as the Supreme Court continues to function. To argue thus is to question the wisdom or impugn the motives of the distinguished men who constitute that tribunal.

Of course, no one would be cynical enough to suggest, even in passing, that there may be an ulterior motive underlying the clamor about the violation, present or prospective, of the Constitution. No one would assume for a moment that the gentlemen who are in the forefront of this attack upon the Supreme Court are proceeding in the hope that their talk may penetrate the sanctity of the court itself and affect the judgments of the men who compose it. No such improper motive, I am sure, could possibly motivate the actions of these gentlemen, many of them outstanding members of the bar, in their assault upon the administration.

It should not be forgotten that while the legislative and executive branches of the government were swept by the overwhelming votes of the people into new hands in November, 1932, there has been no change in the personnel of the Supreme Court. That body as it stands consists of the nine men who composed it before the coming into power of this administration. Six of the nine were, and presumably still are, members of the Republican party. One, and perhaps two others, are Democrats.

Regardless of the party affiliations of these nine jurists, it is a matter of record that seven of them were appointed by Republican Presidents and the two who were nominated by a Democratic President had that honor conferred upon them by President Wilson. A mere statement of these facts is sufficient to meet the charge that we are in the slightest danger of breaking away from the Constitution.

A knowledge of history helps the American people to remain perfectly calm amid such uproars as the reactionaries in our midst are now beginning to raise. We remember, for example, the furor that raged around President Lincoln. In 1863 The New York World was saying: "The administration shines, like the moon, by reflected light. It borrows its ideas and its policies, so far as it has any, from these crazy radicals. By surrendering itself to their wild and reckless guidance, it is ruining the country."

Not a single word of this invective against Abraham Lincoln and his policies need be changed to serve the purpose of those who berate President Roosevelt's leadership today.

These attacks upon our courageous, experimenting progress toward a new and hopeful order of things in the United States would be amusing if they were not so ominous. A democracy contains all sorts of minds and philosophies. There is no certainty that the Tories may not prevail and take charge of our destinies once more. What will happen in this country after another of their periods of materialistic rule, with possibly another 1929 at the end of it, is not even a guess.

Meanwhile, we are headed on the course which the founders of the nation charted. We are "on our way" to raise the standard of living of the great mass of the people, to equalize opportunities and to redistribute wealth fairly and equitably. And I have faith that the great majority of the American people wish this to be our course.

The New Deal's "Revolution" Defended

by Donald R. Richberg

IN A BURST of NRA enthusiasm, in July, 1933, I committed the impiety of asserting, in a speech which was widely broadcast, that "the long discussed revolution is actually under way in the United States." If this comment had been made in a tone of horror and coupled with a fierce denunciation of the New Deal, it would have been approved by most of those who were shocked by such candor. But, on the contrary, I observed that the American people were "enlisting joyously in a revolutionary program of cooperation" and "undertaking a revolutionary experiment in self-government."

It did not mitigate this offense, apparently, when I went on to say that this was a revolution "not in purpose but in method"; and that the freedom and security of the individual were its objective; and that the NRA was not seeking the control of industry "but industrial freedom from control, either by a few dictators, or by the irresponsible movement of economic forces."

Looking backward, it is now plain that the word "revolution" commonly creates a fear complex in the minds of most people who have a large stake in the existing order. It brings to them the vision of grimy mobs with reckless leaders, of secret tribunals, arbitrary orders and tumbrils rolling over cobblestones on the way to the guillotine. Economists may write dull books about the "industrial revolution" or the "economic revolution," but for anyone holding conspicuous public office to assert with any seeming satisfaction that a social or political revolution is actually in progress is to court misunderstanding and abuse. Hostile critics thereafter feel justified in denouncing such an opponent as an "avowed revolutionary," and cartoonists portray him as a wild-eyed, unshaven creature trampling down women and children as he attacks the American home with a firebrand in one hand and a bomb in the other.

In the last few years countless articles, editorials and cartoons have warned the American people against "revolution" and against particular "revolutionists." The general theme is that politicians of the New Deal stripe, starry-eyed intellectuals, labor leaders, miscellaneous reformers and welfare workers compose a "popular front" movement behind which genuine Communists foment discord, plot revolt and prepare to seize power in the inevitable day of the next and worst collapse of private business.

Having no respect for communistic theories or methods, I have no associations which would qualify me to appraise either the shrewdness of Communist plans or the strength of actual Communist organization. Perhaps, therefore, I underestimate their capacity for troublemaking, particularly because I am convinced that the American people are so deeply individualistic, so imbued with ideals of personal liberty, and so conscious of the values of private property ownership, that they have little interest in any program designed to submerge individual ambition and success in service to the general welfare. Americans do not easily thrill to an exhortation to sacrifice their opportunities for self-service in order to advance the abstract ideal of a Good Society.

If we are going through a revolution in the United States, we should assume that it is not communistic in leadership, methods or objectives. Of course we must expect political opponents to denounce each other in unmeasured terms. My candidate must be as pure as driven snow and yours a black-hearted self-seeker. The conservative is attacked as a hidebound reactionary. The progressive is proclaimed the agent or dupe of communism.

But the most conservative banker does not cling to "horse and buggy" ways. He rides in an automobile. He uses adding machines, telephones and other modern conveniences. He watches charts and trends. Despite even an avowed conservatism in politics and religion he probably scratches his ballot and plays golf on Sunday. He is not leading the way back to oil lamps and the Puritan Sabbath.

On the other hand, the most ardent New Dealer will be found to have a lot of "old-fashioned" ideas about clothes and social conduct, education of children, private initiative, individual liberty and the proper compensation to be paid for brains and executive ability. Despite his devotion to social justice he wants to see his children enjoy more than average comfort and security. He is not leading the way to communism or anything like it.

Looking back to the hot summer of 1933, should I now repent of my rashness in proclaiming that the long-discussed revolution was under way; or should I first define the "revolution" of which I spoke, and then proceed to demonstrate that the progress of this revolution is more clearly evident today than it was in 1933? Since the latter course is obviously more soothing to one's pride, perhaps I will be forgiven for choosing it. Also, I may be able to convince a few people that it is much easier to deal with the problems of a revolutionary era if one does not shut one's eyes to the fact that a revolution is under way.

In the first place, let us understand that the word "revolution" is not used in one of its less important meanings to describe merely a sudden change in form or control of government. There is far less historical significance in the violent overthrow of a particular ruling dynasty than in the gradually changing economy that transforms the life of a people and incidentally pushes up new popular leaders or a new ruling class.

Every competent economist or political scientist lays more importance on the industrial revolution than on the Wars of the Roses or the Puritan Revolution that deposed Charles I. The rise of modern capitalism, the general acceptance of laissez-faire doctrines of political economy and the rapid spread of democratic ideals of self-government and individual liberty all coincide by no accident with the industrial revolution brought about through scientific discoveries applied to the development and use of machine power. Our industrialized civilization was not the product of political action.

One hundred years of the industrial revolution developed a series of problems and evils definitely pointing to another revolutionary period. On the one side appeared a persistent concentration of wealth and the rise of a large, powerful class of property owners, secure in a comfortable or luxurious existence. On the other side appeared a larger and larger class of dependent wage-earners and a more and more insecure farming population.

The popular refrain that the rich were growing richer and the poor growing poorer gave warning of a new struggle for power, which in a democracy must mean that governmental force would be eventually brought over to the masses by their superior voting strength.

Socialistic theories and programs were the early natural response to a call for political action. Professor Carver of Harvard (certainly to be classified as a conservative) pointed out in 1925, in his book on "The Present Economic Revolution in the United States," that it appeared for a time as though "the modern world was between the devil of plutocracy and the deep sea of socialism."

But the Socialist program made slow headway in America. Private property is an institution rooted deeply in the homes of millions of farmers and city dwellers. Independent living is the pride of all—including millions of wage-earners. So, instead of embracing socialism, farmers united politically and economically to protect their independence by legislation and cooperation. Skilled labor formed its unions and entered upon a long struggle to establish some personal control over wages and working conditions. Small businessmen called upon politicians to fight the trusts.

There was, on the other side, no class solidarity among the prosperous. "Wall Street," "the money trust," "the overlords of industry" were convenient epithets to describe powerful forces composed actually of men who fought each other with the same vigor with which they exploited labor and consumer.

As a result, the progressive movement arose in politics, supported by recruits from all classes. It developed strong factions in old parties; it created new national and local parties. And it met with such a response that at the turn of the century most of the conspicuous leaders in politics asserted stoutly their liberalism; and many outstanding figures in the business world responded to the demand for social justice with at least protestations of their earnest intention to conform business operations to requirements of the general welfare.

It is not necessary to question the good faith of many farsighted business men and politicians, who saw that an unbridled competition in money making, unlimited property rights and an absolute individual freedom would not answer all the problems of an interdependent society. But it must be conceded that little progress was made prior to the World War in reordering our national economy. A social revolution in habits and standards of living and in the relations of people was under way; but business and government were not accommodating their activities to the new demands.

Business was still helpless to prevent cycles of unemployment or even to stabilize its operations in good times. Government had neither accepted the obligation nor found the means to assure the continuity of essential business against interruptions by destructive competition, cyclical disturbances or conflicts between employers and employees. Nor had government accepted the obligation or found the means to assure to farmers the security of their homes and a fair reward for their labor, although they were relied upon to supply the necessities of life to millions of people absolutely dependent upon their continuing service.

Here then we might have observed prior to 1914 a great variety of evils, injustices and dangers which were generating a revolution in our political economy.

Then came the World War, bringing with it a deceitful, borrowed prosperity and, after our entry, a spurious, temporary sense of solid, selfless devotion to the common good. Of course, we did not actually improve our economic condition by borrowing billions and spending them for destructive, non-productive purposes. Yet after the war we added private borrowing to our previous load of public debt and went to work to build ourselves homes and workshops for the future loaded down with debts which the workers of the future would be unwilling and indeed unable to pay.

Thus we made inevitable a revolutionary period in which debtor and creditor relations must be hastily adjusted, in which landlords and tenants, and employers and employees, would engage in a desperate struggle for the economic and political power which apparently gave security and freedom to some by imposing insecurity and dependency upon others.

The first phase of the foreordained revolution was the first three years of the depression when we relied almost entirely and vainly on the "natural" operation of economic laws to solve our perplexities. Debtors defaulted because they could not pay. Creditors took over profitless properties or left debtors in possession, according to individual judgment of the lesser evil. Unemployment was left as an individual problem; and relief of acute distress remained a local issue.

A fundamental error of the period lay in the failure to recognize that revolutionary forces were actually at work, that the economic system would not continue to function without establishing somewhere some effective controls, and that the choice lay between devising controls within the system of private enterprise or creating a system of exterior political control which in the end would mean the destruction of private capitalism.

The New Deal philosophy which captured the public imagination in 1932 and 1933 was not a scientific analysis of this political economic issue. It was simply a realistic appeal to people in distress to cooperate with a government determined to relieve them temporarily and then to work out reforms that would protect them against a recurrence of the same evil conditions.

The New Deal did not ask its followers to adopt a simple final solution for a thousand different problems. It definitely rejected the use of any cure-all, socialistic formula. It did not threaten to make revolution. But its fundamental soundness and its great popular appeal lay in its acceptance of the fact that an economic and social revolution was under way, and of the campaign fact that only revolutionary extensions of political power would be adequate to preserve the economic and political fabric of national life.

But it should be immediately pointed out that there is a vast difference between a revolutionary extension of power—as in the establishment of Federal relief for unemployment distress—and a revolutionary assumption of power such as would be found in the taking over of private business in order to provide employment.

The New Deal has been predominantly an effort to carry out the first type of program. That is why it has obtained the support of a majority of the American people who, rightly or wrongly, are convinced that the powers of government must be extended to bring about a better functioning of our economic system. But our people also believe that the competition of private property owners and managers and free labor offers a better assurance of industrial justice, of fair prices and wages, than any political control; and they believe that the incentive of private gain will carry us ahead further and more rapidly than any incentives or compulsions of service to the general welfare.

The New Deal has suffered from the absence of clearly defined objectives or clearly defined limitations. To the scientific analyst it has neither blueprints nor specifications, and not even an architect's sketch of the house of government that is being built. Accordingly, some assume that the announced purpose to preserve and strengthen the fundamental institutions of American life is a sham and that a new economic and political system is being built behind a screen of falsework and temporary structures. Others simply assume that superficial repairs and emergency supports are being utilized from day to day because the present tenants have no sound plan for the permanent improvement of our governmental structure.

But the true objectives of the New Deal should be judged not by the scheming of its extremists, or by the errors, the wastes and failures of well-meaning but inadequate subordinate figures, or by political compromises with ill-informed or selfish pressure groups which are a price that must be paid for the ultimate values of democratic government.

And so, realizing that economic and social changes are the

real causes of political change, we should inquire into the underlying economic and social forces that produced the New Deal. If they are "revolutionary," then a government, to be responsive to the needs of the time, must adopt new objectives and seek to attain them by new exertions and extensions of its delegated powers. A responsive government does not make revolution. It is only as revolutionary as it has to be.

The industrial revolution and the development of mass production and distribution have transformed a nation of independent self-reliant people into a nation of interdependent people relying for the most part on the continuous flow of goods and services from thousands of scattered producers into every separate home. Freedom and security for every household depend not on letting each breadwinner work out his own salvation but on assuring each breadwinner that somewhere there is work for him to do and that other breadwinners will be able to continue producing the things that he needs and that he can purchase with the money paid for his labor.

The major objective of modern government is no longer the mere maintenance of law and order. It is the maintenance of an economic system that will keep in continuous operation, and in which the rewards of work will be so fairly distributed that the masses of the people will support the government in its sanction and support of the economic system.

If government is to achieve this objective without actually dominating and directing the machinery of production and distribution, it must manage in some way to make a system of private enterprise self-regulating and responsive to its public obligations. It must make sure that private management does not exploit investor, worker or consumer, but promotes and safeguards the interests of all who sustain private enterprise.

Today we find as a fact that collective competition—not individual competition—dominates our economy. This "gradual collectivism" (recently deplored by Mr. Hoover) is not the product of political action but a direct product of the freedom of private business. Captains of industry and finance have welded together hordes of stockholders, investors and consumers in the support of huge collective enterprises that, although separately operated, are only dependent parts of a collectively organized system of production and distribution.

There is the appearance of a surviving individualism in the small retail store and the family-size farm, and in the fast-disappearing independent owners and operators of small business and professional enterprises of great variety. But how little influence these individualistic ventures have upon social and economic conditions when compared with great manufacturing, transporting and distributing corporations, such as steel, automotive, oil, lumber, coal, textile and food-processing corporations, public utilities, banking and credit institutions and labor organizations!

These privately developed organizations have created a collective economy, privately controlled in separate units, but without any definitely planned control as a whole, except so far as government by Federal and State laws attempts to lay down and enforce the rules of what is described as "fair competition"—not a competition between man and man but between these collective activities of large groups of owners, managers and workers.

Thus the former automatic controls of supply and demand, effective through individual competition, no longer provide reliable and safe regulators of industry—as assumed by laissez-faire economists. Instead, the difficult and hazardous decisions of collective managers regulate supply and demand by schedules of production and sales campaigns which determine temporarily not only the supply of goods but also the effective demand for them by increasing or decreasing employment and purchasing power. As a result, waves of optimism and pessimism among industrialists and financiers accentuate, if they do not actually create, hopeful upswings and tragic downswings in the general welfare.

The central problem which is demanding a solution is to establish somewhere, somehow, some measures of control sufficient at least to assure a reasonable continuity of operation in the intricate machinery of production and exchange. But in order to assure continuity there must also be assurance of an approximate economic justice in the distribution of rewards for human effort, so that by a fair exchange of products and services a satisfactory living will be assured to the masses of people who are expected to maintain willingly the economic system and to uphold the government which must be relied upon to maintain law and order in economic operations and social relations.

It may be conceded that if private enterprise had been left entirely free from governmental interference it would have tried to establish far-reaching private controls designed to assure the stability of industry and trade. The obvious trend of private initiative has been, first, to enlarge the business unit so as to do more and more business under one management, and then to urge these large units into a mammoth corporation and to work out a concert of action between the few remaining powerful competitors so that an entire industry or trade can be "stabilized" and a profitable, continuous operation assured.

But there have always been strong forces opposed to such concentrations of economic power. Small business facing extermination, wage-earners facing servitude, consumers fearing exploitation have united to swing political power against the creation of private monopolies. It has been an accepted principle of political and economic policy in our democracy that monopoly power under private control would certainly be abused.

It might be argued that a centralized control over oil or steel or meat packing would make possible lower prices, better distribution and stable operations. But even if this debatable proposition were accepted, people generally would not be willing to trust to the good intentions of any commercial autocracy. With a sound instinct fortified by centuries of experience, the American people adhere to the fundamental theory of our constitutional form of government, which is that absolute power over the lives and fortunes of others cannot be safely entrusted to human beings, and the only enduring safeguard against tyranny and oppression is to maintain balance of power and automatic checks upon unbalancing extensions and enlargements of power.

Thus the problem of establishing controls over the collective operations of modern big business could not be solved by leaving private managers free to establish them. That solution has never been possible. But the alternative of State socialism is likewise offensive to the American philosophy and tradition of individual liberty. No plausible argument can disguise the fact that State control of industry and trade means the concentration in a political oligarchy of absolute power over the daily lives of all.

What, then, can we do to bring better order and direction and discipline into the competition of collective organizations which are so large that their uncoordinated movements and conflicts leave the general welfare at the mercy of destructive recessions of employment and trade, without ever assuring an adequate utilization of the human and natural resources available for the advance of civilization?

It seems that the simplest example of wise and necessary governmental action, harmonious with our traditions and appropriate to needs of the day, is to be found in the regulation of automobile traffic—a typical development of the present century.

The right of private ownership and operation of a new method of individual transportation has been preserved. Government has built new highways for motor cars, encouraging and aiding their use. Government has also licensed the operators of dangerous mechanisms and subjected them to laws regulating the speed and manner of operation. Government has established traffic lights and one-way roads. In times of congestion, traffic is rerouted; and when road repairs are under way detours are required. Despite all restrictions, however, individual control of when and where and how to travel is sustained.

The analogy to governmental activity in the field of modern business is logical. But let it be emphasized that a combination of governmental aid and supervision is needed; and that one reason for widespread opposition to recent extensions of political power over commerce is that there has been such an evident enthusiasm for restrictive supervision and so little visible interest in extending aid.

It is very much as though the dirt roads of the nineteenth century had been left unimproved, but, when the rutted highways became jammed with automobiles, the size and number of cars permitted to travel had been drastically restricted, truck and bus traffic had been ordered back on the railroads, and political power had been exerted to stop industrial change from creating a political problem, instead of being exerted to aid industrial change by solving the problem.

It is easy to persuade every collective organization of modern business that its freedom should be protected by curbing the power of any competing organization. Large enterprises should be prevented from exercising monopoly power, in the view of all small business men. Large employers should be prevented from dictating terms to wage-earners, in the view of all labor organizations. Labor unions should be prevented from coercing employers or workers, in the view of all employers. Government action is sought and obtained for some of these negative purposes. But, having thus assured such a freedom of collective action that the field of industry may become a battleground of powerful collective organizations, are there not two further needs for government action which are being largely ignored?

First, is it not necessary that the government should impose obligations on all concerned to cooperate with one another and with government in settling their conflicts within the industrial field without a resort to the arbitrary use of economic or physical power?

We do not permit the individual to redress his wrongs by resorting to force. Although individuals and groups still attempt to "take the law into their own hands," the stability of our society rests on reserving the lawful use of force to public officials acting under prescribed and limited authority. We have established principles of law and tribunals for the settlement of rights of contract and to prevent or compensate for injuries to persons or property.

It is not possible to apply exactly the same machinery of administering justice to economic conflicts between groups of collective power. But the same principles are appropriate to guide government action. And when we observe the successful operation of workmen's compensation laws, the Railway Labor Act and some of the best phases of the NRA, it is plain that government can go a long way toward the elimination of commercial and labor conflicts and a long way toward establishing industrial justice, if it is once generally recognized that there is an imperative obligation upon government to preserve peace and to insure fair dealing in industry as an essential of economic well-being. Freedom to coerce or to oppress others is not that "liberty" which our government has been established to preserve.

Second, is it not necessary that the government should give positive aid to all collective groups of industrial enterprise by charting, improving and protecting the safety of the roads over which they must travel?

When laws are drafted to lay restraints on individual freedom, to create rules of competition, and to impose obligations to the public, to workers and to consumers, it is obvious that the application of the broad requirements of such general laws to an infinite variety of specific cases will create an infinite number of difficult problems. If obligations are rigidly defined, the need for volumes of exemptions and exceptions will develop rapidly. If obligations are broadly stated, the need for countless detailed interpretations will be evident from the start.

The need for political action to protect and aid business, to encourage enterprise, to promote employment and to stabilize industrial operations is not satisfied with merely prohibitory, restrictive legislation. The roads of lawful conduct need to be broadened and paved, and then clearly marked with reliable danger signs and traffic lights.

This calls for positive administrative aid. When laws must be written in general terms, of uncertain application in specific cases, which is the difficulty with most business regulation, then a citizen certainly should be entitled to an administrative ruling on the legality of his conduct before he should be treated as a criminal.

Civil remedies can be provided to compensate for private injury, or to establish the validity of an administrative rule. But the threat and employment of criminal prosecution, against men who are willing and anxious to obey the law but compelled to guess at what is the law, do not make sense as a governmental method of encouraging and promoting the business of the country upon which employment, wages, taxes and the daily comfort and prosperity of all depend.

We come—at long last—to the answer to the question: Is it revolution? Yes, an economic and social revolution is what we are passing through, abundantly shown by material changes in working and living conditions. This compels revolutionary changes in the activities and immediate objectives of government, amply indicated by the new responsibilities imposed by general consent on Federal and State governments in conserving and advancing the general welfare.

But the issue as to whether this political revolution shall be a violent, painful and undesirable transformation of the purpose and form of government or a moderate, gradual adaptation of government activities to the requirements of a new economic and social order depends on the answer to a final question: Is public policy to be directed by class-conscious extremists?

On the left, fanatics strive to hasten radical reforms. On the right, fanatics seek to block any forward movement. Will such leaders be able to take command of opposing forces and make war in the industrial field, as they seem to desire; or will the great masses of moderates turn away from the bitter tongues and clenched fists of all the extremists and find unity in a common preference for working together instead of fighting each other— even though that may be a revolutionary program in which government must lend a helping hand?

To avoid any eventual choice between communism and fascism, into which extremists would drive us, we need the alert interest of millions of men and women, who will steadfastly decline to make such a choice, who will remain equally intolerant of both creeds, but who can look at the facts of a current world-wide economic revolution without a shuddering recoil and can plan calmly to play a worthy part in adjusting their economic life and their government to the conditions of a revolutionary era—even as their forefathers did in 1776.

Suggested Reading

THE LITERATURE on the New Deal is large and fast-growing. Undoubtedly the best scholarly study in short compass is William E. Leuchtenburg, *Franklin D. Roosevelt and the New Deal* (New York, 1963), also available in paperback. Arthur Schlesinger's three volumes in his *Age of Roosevelt* (Boston, 1957–1960) carries the story down to the election of 1936. It is partisan but highly readable. On Roosevelt himself the major work is Frank Freidel's multi-volume biography, *Franklin D. Roosevelt* (Boston, 1952–1956), which has now reached the election of 1932; despite its detail, it is a treat to read. The best single-volume life is the critical but highly informative James McGregor Burns, *F.D.R.: The Lion and the Fox* (New York, 1956), also available in paperback. Rexford Tugwell, *The Democratic Roosevelt* (Garden City, 1957) is a penetrating study of the President by one of his admiring, if disappointed advisers, and is now also in paperback. Still the best memoir about Roosevelt is Frances Perkins' sympathetic *The Roosevelt I Knew* (New York, 1946), also in paperback. Raymond Moley, *After Seven Years* (New York, 1939) is a valuable critique of the New Deal and FDR by a member of the Brain Trust. The most highly unfavorable scholarly study of Roosevelt and the New Deal is Edgar E. Robinson, *The Roosevelt Leadership, 1933–45* (Chicago, 1957). The best short, critical appraisal of the New Deal is Paul K. Conkin, *The New Deal* (New York, 1967). Also worth examining for their more radical critiques are the introduction to Howard Zinn, ed., *New Deal Thought* (Indianapolis, 1966) (paper) and the chapter on the New Deal by Barton Bernstein in B. J. Bernstein, ed., *Towards a New Past* (New York, 1968) (paper).

Although the volumes by Schlesinger provide some details on the social history of the period, to understand the New Deal it is necessary to look into the social impact of the Great Depression. For the early years a good account is contained in the last chapters of Irving Bernstein, *The Lean Years* (Boston, 1960) (paper). The fullest treatment of social history, though now rather old, is Dixon Wecter, *The Age of the Great Depression, 1929–41* (New York, 1948). David Shannon, ed., *The Great Depression* (New York, 1960) (paper) is an excellent collection of contemporary writings delineating the impact of the depression. Caroline Bird, *The Invisible Scar* (New York, 1966) (paper) is a popular interpretation of the depression from the perspective of the post-1945 prosperity. Robert and Helen Lynd, *Middletown in Transition* (New York, 1937) expertly dissects Muncie, Indiana, in the middle of the Roosevelt years.

On the question of the relationship between the New Deal and the Progressives, Chapter VII of Richard Hofstadter, *The Age of Reform* (New York, 1956) stresses the discontinuity; Andrew M. Scott, "The Progressive Era in Perspective," *Journal of Politics,* XXI (November 1959), takes the most extreme position in defense of continuity. Richard S. Kirkendall, "New Deal as Watershed: The Recent Literature," *Journal of American History,* LIV (March 1968), surveys the debate but comes down finally on the side of continuity. Otis L. Graham, Jr., *An Encore for Reform* (New York, 1967) (paper) shows that the Progressive leaders did not find much continuity. A strong argument against continuity in outlook is made by Edgar Kemler, *The Deflation of American Ideals* (Washington, 1941). A case for a different kind of continuity is well developed in William E. Leuchtenburg, "The New Deal and the Analogue of War," in John Braeman, ed., *Change and Continuity in Twentieth-Century America* (Columbus, Ohio, 1964) (paper).

Specialized studies abound, but among those I have found interesting and important are the following. Ellis W. Hawley,

The New Deal and the Problem of Monopoly (Princeton, 1966) is broader and more provocative than its title suggests. No member of Congress is more important in the New Deal era than Senator Wagner of New York, so that J. Joseph Huthmacher, *Senator Robert F. Wagner and the Rise of Urban Liberalism* (New York, 1968) meets a real need. A fine study of a neglected aspect of the New Deal revolution is Jane DeHart Mathews, *The Federal Theater, 1935–39: Plays, Relief, and Politics* (Princeton, 1967). Paul Conkin, *Tomorrow a New World: The New Deal Community Program* (Ithaca, N.Y., 1959) delineates a little-known but symbolically important part of the New Deal outlook on poverty and rural life. For a thorough study of the important Rexford Tugwell, see Bernard Sternsher, *Rexford Tugwell and the New Deal* (New Brunswick, N.J., 1964). There is still, surprisingly enough, no full economic history of the New Deal years other than the now dated, though full, Broadus Mitchell, *Depression Decade* (New York, 1947). The revolution in organized labor can be followed with sympathy in Edward Levinson, *Labor on the March* (New York, 1938) and more objectively in the scholarly Milton Derber and Edwin Young, eds., *Labor and the New Deal* (Madison, Wisc., 1957). There is no full-length published study of the Negro under the New Deal, but a good introduction to the subject is Leslie Fishel, "The Negro in the New Deal Era," *Wisconsin Magazine of History*, XLVIII (Winter 1964–1965).

Index

AAA. *See* Agricultural Adjustment Act.

Abolition, 27

Agricultural Adjustment Act, 8, 16, 17, 19, 81

Allotment Act, 97

American Civil Liberties Union, 50

American Federation of Labor, 165

Armed Forces, 13

Baldwin, Roger, 25, 26

Banking Bill, 87, 180, 182

Banks, 29, 180–183, 212

Battle for Democracy, The (Tugwell), 20

Bendoff, Patrick, 137, 141, 142

Bentham, Jeremy, 188

Berle, Adolf, Jr., 16

Bernstein, Barton J., 21, 22

Blum, Léon, 24

Brain Trust, 79–80, 85, 217

Brandeis, Louis, 17, 89

British Imperial Conference, 198

Brookhart, Senator, 35

Bryan, William Jennings, 3, 197

Bryce, James, 193

Budget, national, 20

Business. *See* Industry.

CCC. *See* Civilian Conservation Corps.

Chase, Stuart, 186

Civil Works Administration, 156, 213

Civilian Conservation Corps, 13, 14, 74–75, 98, 120–127, 152, 205, 213

Clark, Delbert, 187, 188

Clayton Act, 14

Cold War, 188

Collier, John, 95–102 *passim*

Commonwealth Club, FDR's address to, 16

Communism, 51–52, 54, 221

Congress. *See* U.S. Congress.

Coolidge, Calvin, 181

Coughlin, Father, 30, 31, 64, 65, 66–67, 70

CWA. *See* Civil Works Administration.

Debs, Eugene, 50

Deflation of American Ideals, The (Kemler), 20

Democracy, 33–34, 36, 46, 51, 192, 193, 194, 215, 216, 218

Depression, 11, 12, 29, 65, 146, 184, 196, 211, 225

De Valera, Eamon, 78
Dewey, John, 30, 41–47
Disarmament Conference, 197
Dollfuss, Engelbert, 78

Eccles, David, 185
Eccles, Marriner, 147–148, 180–186
Economic Security Bill, 164
Economic system, 211–212, 224–225, 227–229
Eisenhower administration, 27
Electricity. *See* Tennessee Valley Authority.
Emergency Administration of Public Works, 152
Employment Act, 26, 148
Education, 42–43, 45, 159–160

Fair Labor Standards Act, 15
Farley, James A., 87, 91
Farm relief, 62, 171–179
Farmers, 30, 81, 82, 147, 152, 154, 171–179, 194–195. *See also* Tennessee Valley Authority.
Fechner, Robert, 120
Federal Art Projects, 11
Federal Committee for Apprentice Training, 118
Federal Deposit Insurance Corporation, 8–9
Federal Emergency Relief Administration, 130, 152, 156–163
Federal Home Owners Loan Corporation, 132
Federal Housing Administration, 132, 133, 206
Federal Reserve Board, 180–181, 182, 184
Federal Reserve System, 181, 182–183, 205
Federal Theater, 11–12
Federal Writers' Project, 11
FERA. *See* Federal Emergency Relief Administration.

FHA. *See* Federal Housing Administration.
Fishel, Leslie, 13
Ford, Henry, 61, 81

Gee, Charles and Sterling, 138
Gold standard, 197
Government controls, 230–232
Graham, Otis, 9
Greenbelt towns, 131–132
Green, William, 165, 166
Guffey bill, 87

Hague, Frank, 21
Hanna, Mark, 4
Harding, Warren G., 49
Hastie, William H., 13
Hitler, Adolf, 78, 194
Holding Company Act, 18, 87
Hoover, Herbert, 4, 20, 92, 227; administration of, 217
Hopkins, Harry, 20, 21, 145, 156, 165–166, 167
Housing, 75, 128–135, 162–163, 205–206. *See also* Wagner-Steagall bill.
Howe, Louis, 79, 92
Hudgens, R. W., 140, 143
Hull, Cordell, 206
Hundred Days, 8, 16, 85

Ickes, Harold, 13, 19, 187, 188–189
Income tax, 184–185, 212
Indian Office, 98, 99–101
Indians, 12, 74, 94–102
Industry, 81–82, 84, 132, 153–154, 166, 167–168, 200, 203, 213, 227–228, 231
Insecurity, 44–45, 65
Insurgents, 45–46

Jackson, Andrew, 192
Jefferson, Thomas, 192
Johnson, Hugh, 67

Johnson administration, 4, 27
Jones, Jesse, 7

Kemler, Edgar, 20
Kennedy, John F., 20; administration of, 4, 27
Kennedy, Renwock C., 144
Keynes, John Maynard, 24

Labor, 14–15, 205. *See also* Green, William.
Labor Disputes Act, 164
Labor Relations Bill, 87
Land conservation, 154–155
Laski, Harold, 23–24
League of Nations, 197
Leuchtenburg, William E., 30
Lilienthal, David E., 104
Lincoln, Abraham, 192, 218
Lippmann, Walter, 196
Long, Huey, 30–31, 64, 65, 67–68, 70
Lowell, James Russell, 192

McCarthy, Joseph, 21
McCormick, Anne O'Hare, 5, 19, 29
McKinley, William, 4
McNary-Haugen bill, 194
Mellon, Andrew, 6
Miller, John Henry, 141
Mills, Ogden, 92
Moley, Raymond, 18, 79
Morgan, Arthur E., 104
Morgan, Harcourt A., 104
Morgenthau, Henry, 186
Morrison, Herbert, 128
Mussolini, Benito, 78, 193

National Industrial Recovery Act, 17
National Labor Relations Act, 8, 14–18 *passim*, 26

National Recovery Act, 14–18 *passim*, 80, 81, 86, 166, 188, 195, 196, 205, 220, 231
National Youth Administration, 117
Negroes, 12–14, 75, 136–144
Nevins, Allan, 187–188
New Deal, 3–4, 7–28, 76–77, 79–93 *passim*, 145, 147, 187–189, 203–206, 214, 220–222, 225–227. *See also* individual programs.
New York State Housing Board, 129
Nineteen Twenties, 208–210
Norris-La Guardia anti-injunction act, 14–15
NRA. *See* National Recovery Act.

Pan-American Conference, 198
Party system, 39–40, 45
Peace Corps, 74
Perkins, Frances, 6, 8, 18
Pettway, John, 138
Pettway, Little, 136, 141
Pettway, Mark, 138
Pickett, Clarence E., 81
Pied Pipers, 86, 87. *See also* Coughlin, Father; Long, Huey; Townsend, Dr. Frank E.
Planning, 19–21
Poverty, abolishment of, 65–66
Present Economic Revolution in the United States, The (Carver), 223
President's Council of Economic Advisers, 26
Price, A. Grenfell, 12
Progressivism, 9–12, 20, 223–224
Public Works Act, 129–133 *passim*

Railway Labor Act, 231
Recovery Agreement, 157
Relief, 149–163
Resettlement Administration, 130, 172, 173, 175
Richberg, Donald, 187, 189
Roosevelt, Eleanor, 13, 58

Roosevelt, Franklin D., 4–9, 12–18 *passim,* 30, 76–93, 123, 181, 190, 192, 193, 195, 215, 216, 217, 218; admiration for T.R., 58; conservatism, 4–7, 9, 73, 74, 92–93; economic and social philosophy, 88–90, 200–203; First Inaugural, 145; Governor of New York, 55–63, 81–82; liberalism, 60–61, 63; political philosophy, 90–91; on the presidency, 59–60; radicalism, 92

Roosevelt, James (father of Theodore), 58

Roosevelt, Theodore, 9, 58, 59, 88, 188, 211

Rosenman, Samuel, 79

Russia, 51–52, 54

Salter, Sir Arthur, 198

Schlesinger, Arthur M., Jr., 17

Securities and Exchange Commission, 205

Security program, three-point, 82

Smith, Al, 56

Smoot-Hawley tariff, 198

Social Security Act, 7, 8, 17, 26, 31, 205

Socialism, 50–54, 223

Soil Conservation Service, 205

Stalin, Joseph, 79

Subsistence Homesteads, 152

Swope, Gerard, 92

Taft-Hartley Act, 26

Tariff, 62–63, 198

Technocrats, 66

Tenancy. *See* Farmers.

Tennessee Valley Authority, 5, 10, 11, 16–22 *passim,* 74, 103–111, 130, 204–205

Thomas, Norman, 26, 30, 48–54, 92

Townsend, Dr. Frank E., 30, 31, 64, 65, 69–70

Truman, Harry S., 12; administration of, 27

Tugwell, Rexford G., 7, 16, 19, 20, 22, 79, 137, 147, 186

Unemployment, 21–22, 44–45, 52, 62, 146–147, 164–170, 184, 213

U.S. Congress, 8, 13, 15, 23, 29, 34–38 *passim,* 87, 180, 206

U.S. Supreme Court, 86, 206, 217–218

Utilities, public, 82

VISTA, 74

Wages and Hours Act, 27

Wagner, Robert F., 9, 18, 21, 164–170 *passim*

Wagner-Steagall bill, 9, 21, 128, 134–135. *See also* Housing.

Wallace, Henry, 22, 195

Wheeler-Howard Act, 74, 94, 97, 98, 101

Wilson, Woodrow, 58, 59, 181, 192, 193, 211

Works Progress Administration, 14, 145

World Economic Conference, 197

World War I, 198, 209, 224

World War II, 188

WPA. *See* Works Progress Administration.

Wyckoff, Walter, 49

Young, Owen D., 92

Young, Roy A., 181

Youth, 12, 74, 112–119. *See also* Civilian Conservation Corps.

Youth Administration. *See* National Youth Administration.

van Zeeland, Paul, 24

Zinn, Howard, 21, 22

A Note on the Editor

Carl N. Degler's book *Out of Our Past* established him as one of our most important American historians. Mr. Degler grew up in Newark, New Jersey, and studied at Upsala College and Columbia University. For many years he taught at Vassar College; he is now Professor of History at Stanford University. His other books include *Pivotal Interpretations of American History, Affluence and Anxiety,* and *Age of the Economic Revolution.*

New York Times Books
published by Quadrangle Books

American Foreign Policy Since 1945
edited by Robert A. Divine

American Politics Since 1945
edited by Richard M. Dalfiume

American Society Since 1945
edited by William L. O'Neill

Cities in Trouble
edited by Nathan Glazer

The Meaning of the American Revolution
edited by Lawrence H. Leder

Modern American Cities
edited by Ray Ginger

Nazis and Fascists in Europe, 1918-1945
edited by John Weiss

Available in Paperback and Cloth Editions
Current Catalog On Request